Pilgrims and Pilgrimage in the Medieval West

Titles in the Series

Pilgrims and Pilgrimage in the Medieval West

DIANA WEBB

I.B.Tauris *Publishers*
LONDON · NEW YORK

Paperback edition published in 2001 by I.B. Tauris & Co Ltd
6 Salem Road, London W2 4BU
175 Fifth Avenue, New York NY 10010
www.ibtauris.com

In the United States of America and in Canada distributed by
St Martin's Press, 175 Fifth Avenue, New York NY 10010

First published in 1999 by I.B. Tauris & Co Ltd

ISBN 1 86064 649 2

A full CIP record for this book is available from the British Library
A full CIP record for this book is available from the Library of Congress

Library of Congress catalog card: available

Set in Monotype Dante by Ewan Smith, London
Printed and bound in Great Britain

Contents

Abbreviations

AB	*Analecta Bollandiana*
Alberigo	J. Alberigo, G. Dossetti, P.-P. Joannou, C. Leonardi and P. Prodi, *Conciliorum Oecumenicorum Decreta*, 3rd edn (Bologna 1973)
AS	*Acta Sanctorum*
ASI	*Archivio Storico Italiano*
CCR	*Calendars of Close Rolls*
Cenci	Cenci, C. OFM, *Documentazione di Vita Assisana 1300–1530* (3 vols, Grottaferrata 1974-76)
CEPR	*Calendars of Entries in the Papal Registers relating to Great Britain and Ireland*
CEPR, Petitions	*CEPR, Calendar of Petitions, I, 1342–1419*
CIPM	*Calendars of Inquisitions Post Mortem*
Clement VI, *Lettres*	*Lettres Closes, Patentes et Curiales intéressant les pays autres que la France*, ed. E. Déprez and G. Mollat
Clement VI, *France*	*Lettres se rapportant à la France*, ed. E. Déprez and G. Mollat
Councils & Synods	*Councils & Synods with other Documents relating to the English Church, planned under the General Editorship of F.M. Powicke* (Oxford 1964–81)
CPR	*Calendars of Patent Rolls*
CYS	*Canterbury & York Society*
EETS	*Early English Text Society*
Foedera	Thomas Rymer, *Foedera, Conventiones, Literae et cujuscunque generis Acta Publica* (17 vols, London 1704–17)
FSI	*Fonti per la Storia d'Italia*
Glaber	*Rodulfi Glabri Historiarum Libri Quinque*, ed. and trans. J. France (Oxford 1989)
Grandisson	*The Register of John de Grandisson, bishop of Exeter (1327–1369)*, ed. F.C. Hingeston-Randolph (3 vols, London 1894)

Hamo de Hethe	*Registrum Hamonis Hethe Diocesis Roffensis, AD 1319–1352*, ed. C. Johnson (2 vols, *CYS* 48, 91)
Innocent IV	*Les Registres d'Innocent IV*, ed. E. Berger (3 vols + index, Paris 1884)
JMH	*Journal of Medieval History*
John XXII	*Lettres Communes de Jean XXII*, ed. G. Mollat (16 vols, Paris 1904–47)
LC	*Literae Cantuarienses* ed. J.B. Sheppard (3 vols, *RS* 75)
Mansi	J.D. Mansi, *Sacrorum Conciliorum nova et amplissima collectio* (31 vols, Florence 1759–98)
Margery	*The Book of Margery Kempe*, ed. Meech and Allen
Materials	*Materials for the History of Thomas Becket, Archbishop of Canterbury*, ed. J.C. Robertson (7 vols, *RS* 67) 1
Meaux	*Chronica Monasterii de Melsa, auctore Thoma de Burton abate*, ed. E.A. Bond (2 vols, *RS* 42)
MGH	*Monumenta Germaniae Historiae*
MGH SS	*Monumenta Germaniae Historiae, Scriptores*
Paston Letters	*The Paston Letters*, ed. J. Gairdner (6 vols, London 1904; one volume reprint, London 1983),
Peregrinaciones	Vasquéz de Parga, L., Lacarra, J.M. and Riu, J.U., *Las Peregrinaciones a Santiago de Compostela* (3 vols, Madrid 1948–49)
PL	*Patrologiae cursus completus: Series Latina*, ed. J.P. Migne (221 vols, Paris 1879–90)
RIS	*Rerum Italicarum Scriptores*, new edn
Rot. Scot.	*Rotuli Scotiae in Turri Londoniensis et in Domo Capitulari Westmonasteriensi Asservati* (2 vols, London 1814–19)
RS	*Rolls Series*
Tulle & Rocamadour	J.B. Champeval, ed., *Cartulaire des Abbayes de Tulle et de Roc-Amadour* (Brive 1903)
Urban V, *Communes*	*Lettres Communes*, ed. M.H. Laurent and M. and A.M. Hayez (11 vols, Rome 1954–86)
Urban V, *Secrètes*	*Lettres secrètes & curiales du Pape Urbain V se rapportant à la France*, ed. P. Lecacheux and G. Mollat (Paris 1902–55)
Vendôme	C. Metais, ed., *Cartulaire de l'Abbaye cardinale de La Trinité de Vendôme* (5 vols, Paris 1893)

Introduction

When I first planned this book, I thought of it as a 'source-book'. Since, I have come to think of it more as an anthology. It would be quite possible to compile another one, drawing on a rather different range of texts, or emphasising certain types of text to a greater extent than they have been emphasised here. I have used miracle stories, for example, more selectively than might be expected, given that they can be seen (with some cautions) as the record of pilgrim experience. What follows is a brief explanation of what will and will not be found here.

The processes of preparing for and going on pilgrimage formed multiple strands in the life of medieval European societies, as they have done and continue to do in other societies. Pilgrimage generated some more or less specific types of source material: miracle collections, as mentioned, and also narratives of actual journeys, a category which overlaps with the 'guide-book' for pilgrims, of which the twelfth-century Compostela *Pilgrim's Guide* is perhaps the most celebrated. Pilgrimage aroused relatively little theological or theoretical concern, although there was a persistent current of low-key criticism which sometimes became more vocal, as with the Lollards in fifteenth-century England. Broadly, it was accepted as a meritorious, though not obligatory, Christian practice; the *bona fide* pilgrim was entitled to the protection of the law and the support of the faithful. These rights were articulated by popes, councils and secular rulers alike, and as secular law-courts developed, they incorporated into their practice provisions such as the right to stays of action while absent on pilgrimage. Many of these legal and quasi-legal rights, however, were not peculiar to the pilgrim, but shared by him with the merchant and other legitimate and peaceful travellers.

The pilgrim fitted into the surrounding social and institutional landscape, and left traces of himself in a wide variety of records. There are the incidental mentions of chroniclers, especially when the great and good (and not so good) ventured on pilgrimage; the records of court proceedings; the interventions of popes, bishops and secular rulers to extend assistance to prospective pilgrims. The pilgrim was sent on his way at a ceremony of blessing in his local church and perhaps also with the good wishes and modest contributions of his fellows in a guild; he needed food and accommodation and sometimes, unfortunately, burial along the way; if he survived, he took souvenirs home with him, and these began to be manufactured and marketed in the west in the twelfth century. It is on the very miscellaneous sources for all these and other activities that this book concentrates, in the hope of illustrating how a religious practice implicated a wide range of supporting services and institutions. For all my good intentions, I know that not every conceivable aspect of pilgrimage, still less every possible type of source, is represented in the book that has resulted. As already intimated, types of text which are, so to speak, specific to pilgrimage, such as guide-books and the personal narratives of pilgrims, have been used only sparingly. Many are accessible in English translation, and are best, if possible, read as a whole.

Time, space and my own competence have restricted the book's scope in a number of other ways. I hope that the reader is aware that pilgrimage did not originate with Christianity and that it has never been, nor is it now, an exclusively or peculiarly Christian phenomenon, but I have not attempted to treat the comparative dimension. I do not trace the history of Christian pilgrimage from its late antique beginnings, and pilgrimage in Orthodox Christendom is also missing. My chronological focus is on the period after *c.* 700, more especially after *c.* 1100, and my geographical focus is on western Europe. This was a period in which a common Christian culture, born in the Mediterranean, which included among other practices journeys to sacred sites and the tombs of the venerated dead, had taken root in northern and western Europe and produced local offshoots. In the sixteenth century that culture resolved itself into something rather different, still to a large extent united by the possession of a distinctively European and Christian heritage, but displaying regional variants, some of which dispensed with pilgrimage along with other old beliefs and practices.

The book is divided into four parts, of which the first two are devoted to pilgrimage in western Europe generally. The first treats the period from the eighth century down to the twelfth as formative. There are difficulties with any choice of dividing line, and to separate the twelfth century from the thirteenth would be as problematic as separating it from the eleventh. For the purposes of this subject, the First Crusade is as much a link in a chain as it is a boundary marker. It can be regarded as the culmination of a century of intensified western pilgrimage to the Holy Land, while for many years after 1100 the 'crusader' (as we would now call him) remained terminologically indistinguishable from (what we would call) the 'pilgrim'. A generalised belief in the salvific value of pilgrimage was probably as old as the custom itself, and grants of indulgences which gave it a more exact quantitative value are found before 1100. The clustering of commercial interests around shrines had certainly begun earlier. The pace quickened thereafter, as in virtually every aspect of European life. The purpose of Part One is to show how western pilgrimage took shape in the period down to the twelfth century; an introduction tries to identify some salient themes. Part Two is internally subdivided into broad topics each with its own introduction, and covers the period from the twelfth century down to approximately 1500. Both include some English as well as European material.

Part Three is devoted to the practice of pilgrimage as reflected primarily, though not solely, in the published records of English royal government from the thirteenth to the early sixteenth century. These riches have perhaps best been exploited to date by Constance Storrs, in her study of English medieval pilgrims to Compostela. She made extensive use of the published Calendars of *Patent Rolls, Close Rolls, Inquisitions Post Mortem* and *Entries in the Papal Registers concerning Great Britain and Ireland*, which so conveniently make available (even if usually only in summary form) a vast quantity of material from the later medieval period. Storrs also drew on the monumental volumes of Thomas Rymer's *Foedera*, an eighteenth-century compilation from governmental records which focused primarily on what might be termed public policy, especially the external relations of the English kings. Rymer gave extended texts, in Latin or less frequently French, where the modern *Calendars* usually give only English summaries, and drew on classes of record which have not yet been calendared in print. Precisely because of his major concerns, the student turning his pages cannot but be made aware of the frequently fraught context, of war or at least tension between the kings of England and the French and the Scots, in which pilgrimage by natives of the British Isles took place for much of the fourteenth and fifteenth centuries.[1]

The *Patent Rolls, Close Rolls, Rolls of Parliament* and *Statutes of the Realm* reveal royal preoccupations with 'public order' and 'public interest' issues, such as the regulation of the movements of subjects and exports of valuables and horses, especially in wartime and the generally troubled days of the later fourteenth century. For their part, the higher-ranking inhabitants of this much-governed country utilised the machinery of state to protect their interests, obtaining licences to travel abroad and safe-conducts and registering the appointment of attorneys for the expected term of their absence. Most such entries are brief and stereotyped, but more picturesque detail is by no means absent. Even the most routine entries convey information, such as (usually) the destinations of pilgrims and the duration of the protection extended by the king, which, it is to be presumed, is related, even if only loosely, to the expected length of the journey. It is also possible to identify individuals who went on pilgrimage more than once (or, at least, made repeated preparations to go on pilgrimage). The influence of ties of friendship and lordship, or the existence of a family tradition of pilgrimage, can sometimes be detected.

The records of the royal courts sometimes take us nearer to the lives and voices of the pilgrims. The *Inquisitions Post Mortem*, which begin in the later thirteenth century, have a special value. These enquiries were held for a number of purposes, notably to establish whether the heir of a deceased person was now of full age and able to enter into possession of his or her inheritance. This involved receiving testimony from local men who claimed to remember the year, and most often also the day, of the heir's birth and baptism. Abundant detail often accompanies these testimonies. The witnesses sometimes claimed to remember that the birth occurred in the year of a pilgrimage undertaken either by themselves or by a kinsman or by other folk known to them. Sometimes they said they had departed on the very day of the birth, that they had been informed of it while on pilgrimage, indeed, in a few instances, that they had been on pilgrimage with the father when news of the birth reached him (does this suggest that one motive for going on pilgrimage was to pray for a safe delivery?). The entries often enable us to glimpse parties of neighbours setting out together to Compostela or to Canterbury; one man setting out to Santiago and another from the same village to the Holy Land in the same year; returning pilgrims being welcomed by their neighbours. Reference was occasionally made to death abroad on pilgrimage, in which case the testimony of witnesses to the death and burial might also be recorded. As their approximate ages are recorded, we also get an impression of the average age at which pilgrimages were undertaken: respondents, typically in their fifties and early sixties, but sometimes younger, remember going on their travels twenty-one or more years previously.

The English official material which forms the substance of this section is supplemented by some material of other kinds, including relevant entries in the papal registers. These become more abundant after 1300, mostly having to do (as elsewhere in Christendom) with the commutation of pilgrimage vows, but occasionally shedding light on unusual personal predicaments. The emphasis, though not the sole emphasis, of Part Three is therefore on pilgrimage seen as it were from the top down, by people in authority. As already noted, English material is to be found elsewhere in the book, some of it (such as wills, or extracts from *The Book of Margery Kempe*) affording a different, less 'official' perspective, some of it (like episcopal sentences of penitential pilgrimage) illustrating general themes. There would be no justification for subtracting England from a comparative view of medieval pilgrimage; but the concentrated richness of the archival material makes it possible to scrutinise the ways in which one relatively powerful and well-recorded medieval government accommodated the practice of pilgrimage by its subjects in times of peace, war and domestic discontent, and how those subjects participated in a common Christian culture. It cannot be too strongly stressed that this is only a selection from a much larger potential range.

Obviously the same has to be said with even greater emphasis of Parts One and Two. It would be beyond my capacity, or that of any one scholar, to convey the remotest notion of the enormous quantity of material, archival and non-archival, much of it surely not yet brought to light, which exists all over Europe for the study of this subject. My own Italian interests and especially my recent work on a unique source in the Archivio di Stato of Pistoia have led me to include in Part Two a section devoted to that city; this is, as it were, a sampler, an indicator of possibilities.

Part Four deals briefly with the theme of 'Criticism and Evaluation' of pilgrimage from the twelfth century to the eve of the Reformation. The story of European pilgrimage does not, of course, end in the sixteenth century. If it suffered a dramatic and prolonged interruption in Protestant Europe, it flourished, with some regional and chronological variation, where Catholicism proved both resistant and resurgent, and of course where it was effectively undisturbed.[2] No attempt has been made here to follow these varied fortunes, in England or elsewhere. The limited purpose of Part Four is to indicate that criticism of pilgrimage, or at least the expression of reservations about its religious value, were ancient, and displayed some remarkable elements of consistency over the centuries.

The over-riding purpose of this book, then, is to give some impression of the rich variety of the sources available and to invite the reader to look further, both into the texts translated or summarised here and into others like them. The vast majority are in print. Pressures of space have inevitably meant that summary and abbreviation have often been necessary, but every effort has been made to ensure that the result is not misleading. Where calendared records have been used, the sources have already been translated and summarised; sometimes further abbreviation has taken place here.

Each of the introductions to the various sections of the book attempts to survey major themes, and includes some numerical cross-references drawing attention to relevant items in the following selection of sources. Not every one of the documents is thus signposted. To attempt to do this, especially in Part Three, would have risked being fussy and visually intrusive. The introductions, it is hoped, will provide a background against which the sources can be understood.

There are several levels of resource available here to the reader. There are the translated sources themselves, with all the limitations and caveats that have been uttered; there are others quoted or referred to in the sectional introductions; and there are the works cited in the bibliography (and *their* bibliographies). A comprehensive bibliography of pilgrimage, even of medieval European pilgrimage, would be a book-length enterprise in itself. My list of sources is particularly selective, concentrating chiefly on those which have been used or referred to in the book itself. Obviously the entire area covered by sanctity and hagiogaphy, relic and miracle, is related to the subject of pilgrimage; a few recent and accessible works in those fields have been included, but this cannot be a bibliography of sanctity. It aims simply to be useful to the student and to furnish possibilities of onward progress. Where a work that is included in the bibliography is cited in the notes, it is referred to there only by the author's surname and (if necessary) date of publication.

I have of course several debts to acknowledge. Perhaps the most profound is to all those writers whose references and footnotes have helped me to identify the sources I have used. Having identified them, I had to find them, and here my thanks have to go to the never-failing sources of supply of the London-based historian: the British Library, the Institute of Historical Research, the Warburg Institute, and once again the London Library, that treasure-house of the un-expected. I must not forget also to mention the staff at the Archivio di Stato of Pistoia, who patiently brought me, day after day, the rather large volumes of the registers of the Opera di San Jacopo. The book was completed during a period of sabbatical leave kindly granted to me by my employers, King's College London. I have to thank Dr Lester Crook of I.B.Tauris for enthusiastically taking up the idea for the book and Ewan Smith for all his work on its production; Professor David d'Avray for commenting on the project at several stages, with his usual mixture of penetrating criticism and kindly encouragement; and my husband Tony for what can only be described, in a hackneyed but indisputably accurate phrase, as his never-failing support.

A Note on Terminology

The majority of the sources included here have been translated from Latin, and it was from classical Latin that the terminology used to describe pilgrimages and pilgrims derived. The word *peregrinus* was familiar to Cicero and other Roman writers as an adjective meaning foreign or alien. The same word as a noun and its derivatives *peregrinatio* (denoting the activity or behaviour of wandering around away from one's place of origin), and *peregrinari* (the corresponding verb) were also used. The adverb *peregre*, also known to classical authors, was much used in medieval sources, almost invariably to denote pilgrimage; the very common phrase *peregre iter arripuit* or *peregre profectus est* effectively means 'he set out on pilgrimage'.

For a contemporary of Cicero, a *peregrinus* was in an uncomfort-able and legally disadvantaged position; the medieval *peregrinus* was expected to experience privation and even danger, but he also hoped to acquire merit. It took time, however, for *peregrinus* and its deriv-atives to shed completely their original, more general, connotations of simple 'foreignness' , which lingered for centuries not only in Latin but in the Latinate vernaculars. In the earlier medieval period especially, careful attention to context is necessary before one can be sure that one's *peregrinus* is a 'pilgrim' and not just a stranger or a foreigner. Even if he is, the journey he is engaged on is not necessarily described as a *peregrinatio*, which continued often to mean 'wandering about' or simply 'travelling'. What we would call pilgrimages may well be described as journeys undertaken 'with the purpose of prayer' (*orationis causa* or *studio*) or 'to the shrines of the apostles/saints' (*ad limina apostolorum/sanctorum*) or 'to holy places' (*ad loca sancta*). A journey *ad Sanctum Jacobum* or *ad Sanctum Sepulcrum* similarly did not have to be labelled a *peregrinatio* to be identifiable.

The expedition to the Holy Land which took place in response to Urban II's call to arms at Clermont in 1095 was called by contemporaries a *peregrinatio* (or sometimes simply a 'journey', *iter*) and the participants (who after all included non-military personnel) were *peregrini*. From the beginning, however, the cross, affixed to the pilgrim's garments, was the distinctive emblem of the Holy Land journey, and the term *crucesignatus* ('one signed with the cross') was by the later twelfth century being more commonly used to describe what we would call a 'crusader'.[3] The word took on additional usefulness with the launching of 'crusades' against enemies other than the Muslims in the Holy Land: for example the 'crusaders' against the Cathar heretics of southern France were so described (in Latin and French) early in the thirteenth century. The differentiation of vocabulary continued through the thirteenth century, and the phrase 'a general passage' (*generale passagium*) came into use to describe a full 'crusading' expedition.

For well after a century after 1100, therefore, a *peregrinus* to Jerusalem might be going with or without a sword in his hand, and only the context will inform us. A *peregrinus* elsewhere is increasingly likely to be a pilgrim rather than just a foreigner, although the adjective was still sometimes used just to mean 'strange' or 'foreign'. Similarly, a *peregrinatio* is increasingly likely to be a pilgrimage. In addition, terms deriving from the names of particularly celebrated shrines came into being: a *Jacobipeta* was going to Compostela, a *Thomipeta* to Canterbury. A *Romipeta* might well be going to Rome, but the word was occasionally used generically to mean 'pilgrim', as the similar *romeus* frequently was. A 'palmer' was originally one who had been to the Holy Land and brought back with him a branch of palm. Raimondo 'Palmario' of Piacenza bore this name already in the late twelfth century, and the *Oxford English Dictionary* records its occurrence in the English language by about 1300. 'Palmer' became a not uncommon surname, and like *romeus* tended sometimes to be used generically.

· ·

PART ONE

Pilgrimage down to the Twelfth Century

CHAPTER I

. . . .

The Development of Medieval European Pilgrimage

At several points in his *History of the English Church and People*[1] Bede stresses the growing lure of Rome for the great men of the English kingdoms in the late sixth century. King Oswiu of Northumbria, stricken by sickness in 670, 'was so greatly attached to the Roman and apostolic customs that he had intended, if he recovered from his illness, to go to Rome and end his life there among the holy places' (IV.5). Caedwalla of Wessex actually did so, in 688, with the intention of 'being washed in the fountain of baptism within the threshold of the apostles', and Bede devotes considerable space to the edifying circumstances of his death. His successor Ine (688–726) followed in his footsteps after a reign of thirty-seven years, 'so that he might be thought worthy to receive a greater welcome from the saints in heaven'. Roman pilgrimage was by now an increasingly common undertaking: 'At this time, many Englishmen, nobles and commons, layfolk and clergy, men and women were eager to do the same thing' (V.7). Bede hints that with increasing familiarity there was a decline in the value attached to pilgrimage, and that not everyone benefited equally from it, observing, apropos of the pilgrimage of Oftfor, later (*c.* 691) bishop of the Hwicce, that 'in those days [it] was considered to be an act of great merit' (IV.23). Commenting on the many Roman pilgrimages of Benedict Biscop (d. 689), Bede contrasted the benefits that he had derived from his journeys to Rome with the futility of the journeys undertaken by certain (unnamed) others [1].

It was a major part of Bede's purpose to advertise and celebrate the links that bound the English church and kingdoms to Rome; now they were becoming more of a reality than they had been in the early, hesitant and often disrupted years of the conversion. Bede's younger contemporary, Boniface of Wessex, spent much of his life in that purposeful kind of *peregrinatio* which combined self-exile from home and kin with the evangelisation of lands not yet won for Christ. He remained in contact with friends and family in England, with whom he exchanged gifts and advice, as well as with the Frankish rulers and with the bishops of Rome, to whom he looked for his authority. Among the kinsmen who eventually joined him in the mission field, St Willibald is of particular interest because he was one of the few English pilgrims to the Holy Land of whom we know anything in this period.[2] Willibald and his brother and future fellow-missionary Winnebald persuaded their father to join their original pilgrimage to Rome, in about 720; he died *en route*, at Lucca, already a stopping-place on an increasingly well-worn road.

There was a flurry of hospital foundations by lay and ecclesiastical notables at Lucca in the eighth century; only a few can be mentioned here. In 720, a group including Teutpald and his brother appointed a priest in the church of San Silvestro who was to 'receive pilgrims and console the poor, widows and orphans'; the church evidently possessed both a hostel and a bath.[3] In 721 Pertuald, father of a future bishop, recorded in execrable Latin some additional gifts to his existing foundation of San Michele, made on his own return from pilgrimage to Rome [2]. It was a not infrequent stipulation, made for example by Pertuald's son Peredeo when he bequeathed half the residue of his estate to San Michele in 778, that the priest in charge of such a foundation should every week feed a number of *peregrini*, or *pauperes et peregrini*.[4]

There is also evidence for hospital foundation and other provision for pilgrims at Rome itself. The biographies collected in the *Liber Pontificalis* laid great stress on the popes' charitable activity in such areas as the foundation and endowment of *xenodochia*, although it is impossible to know how many of the beneficiaries were pilgrims in our sense, how many the indigenous sick and poor of Rome. Zacharias (741–52) ordered the distribution of provisions to 'the poor and the pilgrims who doss at St Peter's'. Both Adrian I (772–95) and Leo III (795–816) improved access to St Peter's: Adrian 'realized many people's safety was at risk since the road was narrow and jammed on the riverbank in the portico leading to St Peter the apostle's, and there was a crush when they crossed to St Peter's'; Leo restored the steps leading to the basilica and also improved the accommodation nearby, including a bath-house, for 'God's poor and pilgrims'.[5] By 800 there were four *scholae* of foreigners in Rome, Frankish, Frisian, English and Lombard, who joined in the welcome given to Charles the Great. These organisations provided facilities, including worship, for visitors to the city; in 817 the English *schola* burnt down.[6]

In the course of the eighth century the Frankish people too had entered into a special relationship with Rome under Carolingian rulership. Carolingian capitularies and ecclesiastical councils pronounced sanctions against those who harmed and preyed upon pilgrims, but also upheld efforts to impose some discipline upon pilgrims themselves [3]. As pilgrimage grew in popularity, criticism began to focus on particular abuses. There was special concern about the propriety of pilgrimage for women, especially those who had vowed themselves to the cloister. In one sense this was merely a corollary of the belief that the professed religious had 'chosen the better part' and should seek Christ in the life of prayer and contemplation rather than on the road. The monastic ideal, in the form which became known as Benedictine, laid great stress on 'stability', as the English abbess Eanfryth, who sought Boniface's advice about a Roman pilgrimage, somewhere around 720, was well aware. Feeling herself advanced in years, she wanted to seek forgiveness of her sins, but 'We are aware that there are many who disapprove of this ambition and disparage this form of devotion. They support their opinion by the argument that the canons of councils prescribe that everyone shall remain where he has been placed, and where he has taken his vows, there he shall fulfil them before God.'[7] These sentiments had a long future: St Bernard and many others, in the twelfth century and after, would endorse them.[8] In vowing herself to God, a woman was making what many regarded as an especially superhuman effort to overcome the specific frailties of her nature. That she was, if let loose, a danger both to herself and to others was axiomatic. Devout women had participated enthusiastically in pilgrimage since the fourth century, and criticism had begun instantly.[9]

Boniface was, however, cautiously encouraging when, perhaps in the 730s, he responded to a request from Eadburga, abbess of Minster in Thanet in Kent, for advice about a projected pilgrimage. He said that he would not presume to advise her for or against the project, but he did report that 'our sister Wiethburga' had found great peace of mind at the shrine of the apostles. A letter written to Boniface by Aethelberht II of Kent, who came to the throne in 748, is evidence that Eadburga did in fact go to Rome and met Boniface there, perhaps in 745 when he attended a synod with Pope Zacharias. If so, this was not all that long before, in about 750, he urged Archbishop Cuthbert of Canterbury to take steps to stem the tide of Englishwomen who were taking the road to Rome, for the result was that 'A great part of them perish, and few keep their virtue. There are very few towns in Lombardy or Frankland or Gaul where there is not a courtesan or harlot of English stock ...' Boniface may simply have found himself forced to this conclusion; or he may have been neither the first man nor the last to have more confidence in individual women whom he knew and admired than he had in women in general.

Before the end of the eighth century, the Synod of Friuli legislated against pilgrimage by nuns [3,e]; many similar enactments would follow down the centuries. There is little to indicate that ordinary laywomen met any real obstacles to setting out on pilgrimages, but their presence could be disconcerting, especially for the custodians of monastic shrines. When a collection of new relics arrived at Fleury early in the ninth century, the crowds which came to venerate them included a number of women, who could not be admitted to the church. The brethren found a pragmatic solution to the difficulty [4], but managing access for women would remain a problem for monastic communities in later centuries, which in fact underlines the point that, whatever restrictions were placed on the movements of female religious, the laywoman was an integral part of the general public for pilgrimage.[10]

Women were certainly not the only pilgrims who caused problems. The Council of Châlons in 813 uttered a comprehensive critique of the malpractices of pilgrims both lay and ecclesiastical [3,h]. These included the misbehaviour of the rich and powerful (who might extort money from their dependants on the pretext that they were going on pilgrimage) and of the poor (who might use pilgrimage as an excuse for vagabondage and mendicancy). The use of pilgrimage as penance, and perhaps just as important, the vague perception that pilgrimage was meritorious and led quasi-automatically to the forgiveness of sin, generated serious problems of understanding. Especially in the Celtic church, pilgrimages, which were sometimes scarcely distinguishable from sentences of exile, had been prescribed for a variety of offences. An early eighth-century Irish collection of canons prescribed pilgrimage as one possible penalty for the violation of relics. If the sacrilege was accompanied by murder, the pilgrimage was to last seven years; if only by theft, for three. The *Penitential of Columban* envisaged seven years' pilgrimage for a clerk who begot a child.[11] Such long-term vagrancy, to the would-be architects of an orderly Christian society, was not necessarily desirable. Rabanus Maurus, albeit conceding that exile was the appropriate biblical penalty for parricide, painted a nightmare picture of parricides wandering around the land-scape practising a variety of vices, and thought it better that they should stay in one place, doing penance in case, through God's mercy, they might be able to obtain forgiveness.[12] Instilling into the sinner a proper understanding of his need for contrition, confession and the performance of his penance under the eye of his own priest, was a necessary part of the extension of pastoral discipline to the laity, as the closing words of the Châlons canon indicate. Over two hundred years later, c. 18 of the Council of Seligenstadt (1023) attacked the foolish misapprehension that a person guilty of a 'capital crime' could purge himself of his guilt by going to Rome and seeking forgiveness of the pope, without having fulfilled the penance laid upon him by his confessor [6,c]. A more satisfactory solution, which preserved the respect due to the pope as the supreme source of ecclesiastical authority, was to send the penitent to Rome to receive his penance [6,a]. This practice can be seen at the root of the reserved jurisdiction later exercised by the pope over certain offences.

The word 'indulgence' is used by Rabanus Maurus in the passage quoted above, and also in the Seligenstadt canon, meaning more or less 'forgiveness'. Before 1100, the concept seems to have been some-what generalised and inclusive. Indulgences, as they became familiar after the eleventh century, remitted a stated quantity of penance. They rested on a distinction, later much refined by theologians, between the sinner's guilt before God (*culpa*) and the punishment due for the sin (*pena*). The former was addressed by contrition and confession, followed by absolution, the latter by the performance of penance. Indulgences remitted penance either in terms of time or of a certain proportion of the total due. With the crystallising con-ception of Purgatory as an intermediate state, still existing in time, in which penance which for whatever reason had not been worked off in life could be performed, indulgences came more and more to be regarded as alleviating the burden of posthumous suffering feared by the sinner. Down to the early twelfth century the amount granted was sometimes expressed in imprecise terms of 'remission' or even of 'blessing'.[13] William of Malmesbury claimed that Pope Calixtus II (1107–19) encouraged English penitents to go twice to St David's in order to obtain the amount of 'blessing' that they would have derived from one journey to Rome [11].

Pilgrimage as penance imposed by ecclesiastical (or other) authority, and pilgrimage either as self-imposed penance undertaken voluntarily or as a pure act of devotion, co-existed throughout the medieval period. In the eleventh century, such a pilgrimage might be imposed on a high-ranking sinner, or such a person might ostentatiously take that burden upon himself. In about 1060 Peter Damian was supervising the correction of the simoniacal clergy of Milan: the archbishop announced that he was sending his clerks to Rome or Tours, but that he himself would go to Compostela.[14] It is not always possible to be sure whether a pilgrimage which was clearly penitential in character was voluntarily undertaken or imposed. The conspicuous pilgrimages of a conspicuous sinner such as Fulk Nerra, count of Anjou, are a case in point. Fulk went three times in all to Jerusalem, in 1003, 1010 and at the end of his life, in 1038 or 1039. He went first out of fear of hell, because he had shed a great deal of human blood in various battles. He came back in high spirits and for a while abated his natural ferocity, founding the abbey of Loches as a further precautionary measure. In 1010 he went to Jerusalem via Rome, where Pope Sergius IV, presumably on the principle of setting a thief to catch a thief, complained to him of the depredations of the robber-baron Crescentius on pilgrims and merchants coming to Rome. In 1040 he died at Metz on his way back from his last pilgrimage. Robert of Normandy, another great lord with something to repent, went 'barefoot' to Jerusalem in 1035 in expiation of the murder of his brother; he died at Nicaea on his way back.[15] In 1066 henchmen of Count Theodoric of Trier were responsible for the murder of the bishop-elect of the city, Conrad; a few years later Theodoric set off 'with burning faith' to Jerusalem in remorse for his crime. According to one chronicler, his ship foundered in a sudden storm and he and companions 'cleansed by the waves of the sea from the filth of sin ... passed over to the Lord'.[16]

Long-distance pilgrimage, voluntary or penitential, was not an everyday experience. The norm, for both landholding aristocracy and peasant cultivators, was a much more regionalised, even localised, ritual of veneration paid to the relics possessed by local monasteries and other churches. This could be a regular event, based on family and personal ties with the shrine and with the saint, and formed an element in the ongoing relationships between monks, frequently the custodians of celebrated relics, and their neighbours both powerful and less powerful. The peace councils which began in the tenth century tried to mobilise the reverence with which local populations viewed the relics which were paraded on these occasions, and to induce the more thuggish elements in the military aristocracy at least to act as if they shared it.[17]

The model pious nobleman of the late ninth century, Gerald of Aurillac (d. 909), included frequent (and clearly voluntary) pilgrimage to Rome among his religious exercises; his biographer Odo of Cluny believed that he had been there seven times. He made over his property to St Peter, and 'every second year' visited the tombs of the apostles, hanging ten *soldi* around his neck, 'like a serf bearing a cense payment to his lord'. The conspicuous generosity with which he accompanied his pilgrimages became notorious, so that those who had benefited from it on previous occasions asked anxiously when he was next coming, and the 'savage Saracens' who infested the Alps hastened to carry his baggage across *Mons Iovis* (later called the Great St Bernard) for him. The narrative shows him performing miracles on his travels: recovering two pack-horses which a thief stole near Asti but could not force to cross a certain stream; healing a blind boy at Lucca, a blind man in a reedy field beyond Sutri 'near the settlement which is called San Martino, where the Roman pilgrims are accustomed to camp', and another, when he was returning from Rome, as the party approached the place called Le Briccole; turning water into wine when he was returning from Italy and was on the road 'which leads to Lyon from Turin', in a region which had been devastated by the Saracens. The miracles were exceptional, but the description of Gerald's conduct, as a lay pilgrim, was intended to be exemplary.[18] He had companions on his journeys, for example Amaugier, who restored the church of Palazinges, ravaged by the Northmen earlier in the ninth century, 'for love of the blessed apostle Peter', and 'used very often to go with his kinsman Gerald of Aurillac to Rome'.[19]

The Council of Châlons in 813 had mentioned only Rome and Tours by name as likely pilgrim destinations, and the only shrines apart from Rome mentioned in Gerald's *Life* are St Martin at Tours and St Martial at Limoges. The legend that the apostle James was buried in the far north-west of Spain gained currency from the ninth century on and began to attract pilgrimage to Compostela,[20] which in time nourished incidental pilgrimage to a host of places along the major routes leading to it. Among them were Limoges, Conques, Le Puy and Noblat (the shrine of the hermit St Leonard). The first pilgrim known to have gone to Compostela from France was bishop Gottschalk of Le Puy, in 951.[21] The first known pilgrim from Italy, the Armenian hermit Simeon, made his journey later in the tenth century. He also visited, among other unnamed shrines, 'the oratory of the great and incomparable Martin' at Tours.[22] The itinerary followed by

Robert the Pious of France on the remarkable pilgrimage tour he undertook in 1019–20 gives an idea of some at least of the prestigious shrines in southern France a little later. 'Wishing to die to the world', Robert began with St Stephen at Bourges, and proceeded to visit the shrines of St Maiolus (formerly abbot of Cluny) at Souvigny, St Mary (of Le Puy), Julian of Brioude, St Gilles in Provence, St Saturninus of Toulouse, St Vincent of Castres, St Antoninus at Saint-Antonin, Ste Foy at Conques and Gerald of Aurillac. He returned via Bourges to Orleans in time to receive Easter communion.[23]

Pilgrims shared the roads (and the protection of the law) with travellers of other types. Along with merchants, envoys and ecclesiastics travelling on business, they sought out the easiest and safest passages, often corresponding with ancient trackways and Roman roads, where the going had already been identified as relatively easy and along which such support services as existed were available. Much has been written about the *Via Francigena*, the route, or complex of routes, which led the traveller from north-western Europe to Rome.[24] It was usual to use either the Mont Cenis or the pass of Mont Joux (*Mons Iovis*). At the head of the Mont Cenis stood the great abbey of Novalesa, dedicated to St Peter, where Louis the Pious endowed a hospice early in the ninth century.[25] Once down into the north Italian plain, the traveller usually made for Piacenza on the old Roman Via Emilia, otherwise known as Strata Claudia, where there was a manned crossing of the river Po. In 850 Donatus, an Irishman who had become bishop of Fiesole near Florence, gave a church in Piacenza, dedicated to the Irish saint Brigid, to the monastery of Bobbio, requesting that 'if any *peregrinus* of my race should arrive, two or three of them should be received and looked after there'.[26] From Piacenza the Rome-bound traveller followed the line of the Emilia/Claudia, which, dotted with major cities such as Parma and Bologna, still marks the major artery of road and rail communication as far as the Adriatic coast at Rimini. At some point along this road he would branch off along one of a number of known tracks across the Apennines. Willebald and Winnebald were obviously following the best-known of these when their father died at Lucca.

The earliest 'description' of the Francigena dates from 993, when archbishop Sigeric of Canterbury returned from a visit to Rome. By chance, his itinerary survives, including both the details of his tour of the churches of Rome and his overnight stops on the way back to England [5]. He passed through Siena, San Gimignano and Lucca, and evidently crossed the Apennines by the pass known as *Mons Bardonis*, for the itinerary mentions the monastery of San Moderanno at Berceto on that route. He proceeded via Piacenza and Vercelli and crossed the Alps by Aosta and the *Mons Iovis*, striking north via Lausanne, Besançon, Reims and Arras. A total of eighty overnight stops between Rome and the Channel means a journey of about twelve weeks in total, depending how quickly the archbishop found a ship and whether wind and water permitted a speedy passage. Odo's account of Gerald of Aurillac's various journeys to Rome, a century earlier, includes incidents at Piacenza, Lucca, Le Briccole and Sutri, all places mentioned on Sigeric's itinerary, and he too went by the *Mons Iovis*. The hermit Simeon, going from Italy to Compostela just a few years before Sigeric's journey, crossed the Apennines by *Mons Bardonis* and followed the same basic route to the Alps via Piacenza and Vercelli, but he then went by the Mont Cenis, for he rested for three days at Novalesa. His biographer, unfortunately, is extremely vague about the itinerary he followed after leaving Italy, saying only that he traversed 'Aquitaine' and 'Gascony'. We may surmise that like later Italian pilgrims who went overland to Compostela he descended into France via Grenoble and the Rhone Valley, picking up what would later be called the *Via Tolosana*.[27] Around 1100 a document recording agreement between the bishop and count of Grenoble about the boundaries between certain of their properties mentioned the 'public road which goes towards Rome or to St James'.[28] Some of the traffic between Italy and Spain, however, went by sea. The Icelandic abbot Niklas of Munkathvera, heading south for Rome across the Apennines in the middle of the twelfth century, was the first to comment that there was a junction at Luni, on the coast of Tuscany a day's journey from Lucca, with 'the roads coming from Spain and the land of St James'.[29]

The road created its own saints. Of these, pride of place must surely be given to Bernard of Aosta, whose charitable and evangelising work in the alpine region has been immortalised by the names subsequently given to the Great and Little St Bernard passes, not to mention the dog.[30] A tenth-century *miles* of Provence called Bobo or Bovo, while engaged in active service against the Saracens who terrorised the Alpine passes, made a vow that he would 'lay down his arms, succour orphans and widows henceforth and visit the shrines of the Apostles Peter and Paul once a year, and more if he could, for the rest of his life'. Strengthened in his endeavours by a vision of St Peter, he carried out his vow, taking with him a mule which he almost never rode, putting it rather at the disposal of the blind, the lame or the poor, whom he also fed. His biographer emphasises the point that as an *eques*, unused to travelling on foot, he was worn down by 'pedestrian exertion'.[31] Bobo thus (like Gerald of Aurillac) chose humility and austerity when his rank entitled him to something different, and exemplified the life of active service and practical charity which was open to the layman who sought holiness while not entering the cloister. Pilgrimage fitted the mode of life he chose both as a form of penance and devotion and as an opportunity to display charity to those he encountered along the way. He died on his way to Rome, reputedly around the year 986, at Voghera, on the road between the Mont Cenis and Piacenza, and was venerated there.

Pilgrimage was a devotional exercise which the fighting man could carry out without entirely changing his way of life. That there was an ideological tension between the monastic ideal, viewed as the one secure path to salvation, and society's observed need for men who wielded the sword, emerges clearly from the long letter which Peter Damian wrote in 1067 to the marquis Raniero, who was trying to get out of the Jerusalem pilgrimage Damian had enjoined on him [7]. Raniero was left in no doubt that he belonged to an inferior order, of those who did not (and could not, because of their secular entanglements) keep the Lord's commands; but precisely because he was not vowed to the life of perfection, pilgrimage was appropriate for him. On the one hand, Damian upheld the idea that the monk had chosen the better part and should stay where he was placed; on the other, in order to persuade Raniero to undertake the pilgrimage imposed upon him, he drew on the treasury of folklore which he shared with his fellow-monks, a store of anecdote about their experience of God's miraculous assistance when they themselves, in the world, had confronted the hazards of pilgrimage. Bobo and Gerald of Aurillac turned to God in a moderated style, never abandoning the *vita activa* even while they took on certain monastic austerities.

It was also open to the man and woman who remained in the world to earn merit by charity, to pilgrims among others. If, as the church continued to affirm, those who preyed upon pilgrims and other legitimate travellers were anathema, those who endowed hospitals or contributed to the upkeep of roads and bridges were correspondingly entitled to praise. They included a number of saints, such as Margaret of Scotland, whose provision of free ferry services across the Firth of Forth for pilgrims to St Andrews [10] has won her an enduring name (Queensferry on the south side of the estuary and

North Queensferry on the other). At Lucca there was another wave of benefaction to hospitals in the late eleventh century, again involving both clergy and laity.[32] The wording of these grants was variable. Benefactors might speak in terms simply of the 'poor', of 'poor pilgrims', or more inclusively of orphans, widows, the poor and pilgrims, either permanently resident or transient. By the mid-twelfth century the hospital of Altopascio on the *Via Francigena*, not far from Lucca, was receiving bequests. One prospective Jerusalem pilgrim, in 1130, left his bed and bedding to his daughter with the proviso that if she died before she had found a husband, the bed was to go to Altopascio.[33]

It was one thing to provide charity for pilgrims, another to be sure that your pilgrim was genuine. A story of St Trudo, written before the end of the eighth century, tells how a robber assumed the *habitus peregrini* (which is not further described) in order to spy out how he might force an entry into the saint's church. The monks were deceived by appearances into offering him the usual services, including foot-washing.[34] The somewhat later story of the conversion of the knight Otgar relates that, as he toured monasteries in search of a suitable place to make his vocation, he carried a staff (*baculus*) to which little pieces of iron were attached by thongs. By thumping it firmly on the floor he could make a distracting noise, with which he tested the seriousness of the monks: would they come running when they heard it?[35]

By the eleventh century at the latest, liturgical provision was being made for the departing pilgrim, which centred on the benediction of the staff and purse or satchel [12]. That some sort of public ceremony had marked the departure of pilgrims, perhaps for centuries, seems almost to be implied by the penitential uses made of pilgrimage and the attempts of lay and ecclesiastical authorities to impose a degree of control on the practice; the penitential pilgrim should surely not have been allowed to slip out of his neighbourhood unnoticed.[36] In the middle of the eleventh century the blessing of the departing pilgrim's insignia could be reckoned among the prerequisites of a parish priest, and in the early twelfth it was listed among his routine duties.[37] Among the witnesses to a grant of tithes made to the bishop of Grenoble, some time before 1132, was the *conversus* Guigo, 'on the day when he received his satchel (*sportam*) for his journey to St James'.[38] The prayers and blessings attested for this period contain elements which continued in use down the centuries.[39]

With the passage of time variant rituals specifically for Jerusalem pilgrims and 'crusaders' came into being. Ekkehard of Aura wrote of the excited response to the call to crusade:

> Many showed the sign of the cross miraculously imprinted on their foreheads or their clothes or on some part of their body, and believed that by this mark they had been enrolled in the army of the Lord. Others again, prompted by a sudden change of mind or enlightened by nocturnal visions, resolved to put off familiar things and sew the sign of mortification on their vestments, while larger numbers of the people than you would think possible ran headlong to the churches, and in a new rite priestly benediction was bestowed on their swords along with their staffs and satchels (*novo ritu gladios cum fustibus et capsellis sacerdotalis benedictio dispertivit*).[40]

It was presumably the blessing of the sword which looked new to the chronicler.

The promotion of a variety of cult-centres by the production and dissemination of miracle stories, which gathered momentum in and after the eleventh century, immeasurably enriched the literature of pilgrimage and makes it possible for us at least to indulge in some speculations about the sociology and psychology of its clientele. The saints in action served the interests both of the monks and clergy who venerated them and of the public which sought their help and made offerings to them in hope and gratitude. It is a very marked feature of miracle-collections throughout the middle ages that saints and shrines seem to be in competition. It became a *topos* to allege that the saint one happened to be celebrating had cured a sufferer who had come away empty-handed from every other shrine he or she had visited, even from St Peter at Rome. Related among the miracles of St Benedict at Fleury is the cure of a girl who was taken to St Denis and St Martial before it was realised that Benedict, who was near at hand, would be more effective.[41] The compilers of miracle-stories naturally had a strong interest in impressing the local population with the power of their saint, and one way of doing this was to emphasise his or her efficacy on behalf of suppliants from far away. Sometimes a saint would even (allegedly) appear in a vision and instruct a pilgrim to go elsewhere. The mid-eleventh-century compiler of the miracles of San Prospero at Reggio, on the *Via Emilia* in northern Italy, refers to a native of Benevento in southern Italy who was on his way to Tours when he was cured at Reggio. *E contrario* a 'Frenchman' who, on his way to Rome, was abandoned by his servant at Reggio, was cured there (after three years!), as was a native of Tours on his way back from Rome. A blind 'mountain-dweller' was told while he was begging with others in the atrium of St Peter's in Rome that he should go to Reggio to obtain his cure. Here, the picture of the competition, and of the trajectory along which pilgrims were travelling, is simple and clear-cut.[42] However we may judge the literal truth of such stories, they do help to sketch the mental catchment-area of the writers, the shrines they were aware of, the places they imagined that their audience had heard of.

The miracles of Ste Foy of Conques were collected, mostly in the first half of the eleventh century, by a number of authors. The author of the first two books, Bernard of Angers, has things to say about the popular appeal of pilgrimage which are important and interesting not only in themselves, but because they articulate anxieties which would remain alive in some people's minds and return in force with the reformist agitation of a much later age.[43] His lengthy treatment of the celebrated image of Ste Foy, which is preliminary to a number of miracles in which people are punished for their irreverent attitude towards it, takes the reader from his own hostile initial reactions to cult statues of this type, which he describes as a regional speciality of the Auvergne, Rouergue and Toulousain, to his better understanding of their functions and their justification.

Bernard first saw a resplendent image of Gerald of Aurillac, made of the finest materials and placed on an altar, so modelled that it seemed to the peasants praying before it to see and hearken to them. Speaking in Latin to his companion, Bernard sarcastically likened this 'idol' to an image of Jupiter or Mars. In his theoretical attitude he stood at a point of juncture between old and new. He could accept a three-dimensional image of the crucifixion (athough not all Christians did), because of its unique memorial function; in Pamela Sheingorn's recent translation, 'it arouses our affective piety in the commemoration of Our Lord's passion'. The saints, however, should be commemorated only in words or on painted walls, in 'insubstantial', two-dimensional form. Custom, however, and not just recent custom, was against Bernard: '... we allow the statues of saints for no reason other than very old, incorrect practice and the ineradicable and innate custom of simple people.' He recognised, furthermore, that had he spoken out against the veneration of Gerald's image he would have risked 'punishment' from the bystanders.

His initial reaction to Ste Foy's statue, when he beheld it a few days later, was similar; it was 'a mute, insensate thing' and it was irrational to address prayers to it. He changed his mind when he was told the story of the priggish clerk Odalric who had openly dissuaded the people from making offerings to the image. This clearly could not be tolerated, by Foy or by her custodians, and Odalric, whose character is further blackened by the suggestion that he retired to bed drunk, was soundly beaten in his sleep by the indignant saint. Bernard was impressed by the fact that 'he who criticised the statute was punished as if he had shown disrespect for the holy martyr herself', but he was still feeling for a proper explanation of its underlying rationale. Either it could be accepted (despite his previous reservations) as a *memoria* of the saint which excited devotion, or its form was to be taken neutrally: 'it is a repository of holy relics, fashioned into a specific form only because the artist wished it.' Bernard concludes with a string of negatives: 'Therefore Sainte Foy's image ought not to be destroyed or criticised, for it seems that no one lapses into pagan errors because of it, nor does it seem that the powers of the saints are lessened by it, nor indeed does it seem that any aspect of religion suffers because of it.'[44]

In the second book of the collection, Bernard again reveals himself taking a conservative and high-minded line about popular practices and being corrected by those of a better understanding. It was customary to leave the doors of the church open so that pilgrims 'with candles and lights' could attend the vigils. Unfortunately, the illiterate peasants, unable to follow the psalms and chants, whiled away the time 'with little peasant songs and other frivolities'. Bernard expressed the view that a stop should be put to this, only to be met with the argument that, once again, the practice was ineradicable and anyway not evil. In time past, the senior monks had in fact tried to exclude 'the swarms of peasants' from vigils, only to find that the doors sprang open of their own accord. Once more, Bernard had to work this out. He concluded that 'an innocent little song, even a peasant song' could be tolerated, not because it was intrinsically desirable as far as God was concerned, but because He was prepared to look into the inner person 'and shows good will toward human ignorance and simpleness'. Furthermore, if the closure of the doors were to be effectively enforced, perhaps 'the crowds that frequent the sanctuary would also disappear'.[45]

The crowds that frequented the sanctuary meant business opportunities, and the gathering momentum of pilgrimage, along with other forms of travel, created opportunities for money-making by the suppliers of all sorts of goods and services along the road. Gerald of Aurillac's Alpine baggage-handlers doubtless did not work just for him. At Piacenza, where there was a regular ferry service across the Po, the clerk who was in charge of the port and 'as usual, was expecting a profitable toll from the *romei*', was one day in an exceedingly bad temper, but, mollified by Gerald's peaceable words and a gift, he remitted the toll due from the whole party and filled up their wine-bottles. At the end of the tenth century, the hermit Simeon made this crossing by miraculous means, because the usual boat was not there.⁴⁶

Among the stories of Ste Foy there are some vivid word-pictures of the commercial interests that were already beginning to cluster around such shrines. Bernard of Angers related how a merchant from the Auvergne noted the demand for wax at Conques and thought that the price being exacted from the pilgrims who wanted to offer candles was far too low. His plans to enrich himself literally misfired when a particularly beautiful taper which he had concealed in his clothing because he could not fit it into his bags spontaneously combusted. The saint would not tolerate outright avarice, but in a story told by a mid-eleventh-century continuator she was prepared to help a Gascon recover a piece of cloth which he had brought with him to the shrine 'to sell at a profit', presumably at a market near the church. We are assured first that he did not initiate this practice, and secondly that because of his love for the saints he did not himself make a fuss when the cloth was stolen from him.⁴⁷

We do not hear of souvenir-sellers as yet. This did not mean that no one thought of bringing back mementoes of their holy travels. Decorated ampullae containing holy oil or water had been available in Palestine in the sixth century and examples found their way west.⁴⁸ Clerical pilgrims to Rome brought back quantities of relics, some of which they distributed as gifts: St Wilfrid for example collected and carefully labelled relics from the churches of Rome,⁴⁹ and Benedict Biscop came back far from empty-handed, with relics and other still more substantial mementoes of his travels [1]. In the early eleventh century, pilgrims to Mont St Michel in Normandy liked to take away stones from the mount, but this could be hazardous if done without authorisation.⁵⁰ Richard of St Vannes, abbot of Grace-Dieu in Normandy, who led a large-scale pilgrimage to the Holy Land in 1026–27, was given a bag full of relics by the patriarch of Jerusalem and came back 'laden with relics gathered at Jerusalem and everywhere round about'. The term 'relics' is less likely to signify human remains than any object or objects which had formed part of, or been in contact with, a shrine, from dust and chips of masonry to fragments of cloth. This is vividly illustrated by the eagerness with which Richard collected a stone, thrown by an impious Saracen, which happened to fall into the Holy Sepulchre.[51] Such objects were more than mere mementoes. They were, in the first place, talismans for the return journey, and, distributed among friends and benefactors on returning home, they conveyed something of the blessings that the pilgrim himself had derived from his experience [8,d].

It was presumably only the prospect of a moderately long journey which prompted men and women to make testamentary disposition of their property before their departure, or to enter into other property deals with local monasteries, sometimes to raise money for the trip. Records of these begin to survive in monastic cartularies in modest numbers in the tenth century [9]. Aimon's life of Abbo of Fleury, who died in 1004, relates how the father of Bernard, abbot of Beaulieu, who had selected him for the monastic life from his 'horde' (*caterva*) of sons, had made the journey to Jerusalem *poenitentiae voto*, almost the first of the inhabitants of Gaul in that age, so Aimon said, to do so.[52] Among clerical and monastic pilgrims to Jerusalem, Bernard of Angers refers to a monk of Conques who later became its abbot. At Ephesus he encountered a clerk called Peter of Le Puy who had settled in the east specifically to make money as a guide and interpreter: 'He knew the land and sea routes, the public roads, the ports of call, the side roads and the customs of the peoples and their languages just as well as business people who travel around the various parts of the world.'[53] It is not stated specifically that Peter expected to make his money out of western pilgrims, but these were certainly on the increase. The chronicler Ralph Glaber referred to a 'usual route' for French and Italian pilgrims, by sea, which changed when the conversion of Hungary opened a land route. The traffic experienced fluctuations, for example when the caliph Al-Hakim ordered the destruction of the Holy Sepulchre in 1009. Glaber, who records this event, thought that westerners began to go to Jerusalem in increasing numbers after the Sepulchre was restored, beginning with persons of humble rank and progressing to include, for the first time, 'women, noble and poor'.[54]

Glaber apart, there are several eleventh-century chronicle accounts of large-scale Holy Land pilgrimages. Richard of St Vannes led over seven hundred people to Jerusalem, subsidised by the duke of Normandy [8,a]. This expedition went overland via Hungary, as did the one headed in 1057 by abbot Thierry of St Evroul; Orderic Vitalis relates that there was by this time 'a fine hospital' on the borders of

Bavaria and Hungary where the pilgrims were welcomed. The members of this party made differing choices of onward route when they came to Antioch, the abbot opting for a sea passage from there to Jerusalem, the monk Herbert pressing on overland. Neither was fated to progress: the abbot died peacefully in Cyprus, and Herbert fell ill at Lattakieh and went straight home as soon as he could get out of bed.[55] In 1064–65 a group of German bishops headed an expedition which thoughtlessly made such a display of its resources as to arouse the hostile interest of the people whose lands they passed through [8,c].[56] These were pilgrims neither poor nor (as the event showed) unprepared to fight; but however willing the laymen at least were to defend themselves, it is clear that they were not adequately equipped to do so. There is a strong suggestion in another account of the same events that the Muslim authorities in the vicinity of Jerusalem did not approve of depredations on Christian pilgrims, if only because it threatened a profitable traffic. The governor of Ramleh underlined the point by detaining the pilgrims in his city for two weeks, during which time they presumably had to purchase goods and services from the natives.

Willibald, in the early eighth century, had experienced some problems in the Holy Land. When he and his companions were arrested on suspicion of spying, an old Arab who spoke with them (and somewhat misunderstood the place of pilgrimage in Christian culture) testified that like other westerners he had seen they merely wished to 'fulfil their law' by visiting the Holy Places.[57] In the eleventh century, however, descriptions of stone-throwing mobs of Saracens, wishing not merely to rob but specifically to disrupt the pilgrims' devotions, served to give the sufferings of the Christians the character at least of threatened martyrdom, and to set off their heroic virtue, especially when (as in the case of Richard of St Vannes or Ulrich prior of Celle [8,b]) the account had a hagiographical or quasi-hagiographical intent. Crusading propaganda tended to make the most of local difficulties experienced by Holy Land pilgrims, and William of Malmesbury, describing a penitential pilgrimage undertaken in the mid-eleventh century, may have exaggerated the difficulty of getting to Jerusalem before it had been 'liberated' [6,d].

These accounts testify to an accumulation of belief and superstition about the nature and value of the Jerusalem pilgrimage, and also illustrate the growth of a strain of affective piety, centred on Christ's passion, which would have a large part to play in the future. Richard of St Vannes and Ulrich of Celle both saw themselves in their mind's eye re-enacting the events of the Gospel story, while it was *de rigueur* to weep tumultuously at the contemplation of the Holy Places, a reminder that Margery Kempe's effusions over four hundred years later belonged in a respectable tradition. Ulrich seems to have ascribed a different sort of significance to the Roman pilgrimage which he undertook with a companion on his return from Jerusalem, before they both became monks of Cluny. The Holy Land inflamed interior devotion; at Rome, because of the binding and loosing power conferred upon the apostles, one could find absolution from one's sins. This emphasis on the apostolic power as a magnet drawing men to Rome is as significant in the eleventh-century context as the Christocentric focus of the Holy Land experience. Peter Damian gives a vivid picture of the Empress Adelaide forcibly sitting him down under the *confessio* of St Peter and confessing to him every last detail of her trivial sins from infancy upwards, as minutely as if the apostle himself were bodily present. While Damian (understandably) could not think what penance to impose on her, he wished that other pilgrims could be inspired by her example.[58]

With the twelfth century we approach what can, for convenience, be regarded as a new phase in the history of western pilgrimage. The ancient belief that pilgrimage carried with it the promise of forgiveness of sin took on greater precision in the form of the indulgence, and the history of western pilgrimage down to the sixteenth century is deeply coloured by this development, but this does not mean that everything about it was transformed. Much would simply continue to develop (and to become better documented) within the framework of a changing society: economically more diversified, more urbanised, more literate.

DOCUMENTS

1. The pilgrimages of Benedict Biscop (d. 689)

As often as he crossed the seas, he never returned, as some people do, empty-handed and without profit. Now he brought back with him a wealth of holy books, now a venerable gift of relics of the blessed martyrs of Christ, now architects for the building of the church, now glassmakers both to build and decorate its windows, now masters of the chant to serve with him in the church throughout the year, now a letter of privilege sent from the Lord Pope to secure our liberties from every external threat; he brought pictures of sacred history, which were intended not only for the adornment of the church, but so that those who could not learn of the works of Our Lord and Saviour by reading letters, could do so by examining these images. In these and similar ways he laboured so that we should not have the necessity of doing so. If he crossed the sea so often, it was so that we, abounding in the riches of the knowledge of salvation, could stay quietly within the monastic cloister and serve Christ with confident freedom. Even when he was overcome with bodily weakness and suffered severely, he always, among his other duties of thanksgiving to God, took pleasure in talking over and over again of the monastic observances which he had learned and taught, of the ecclesiastical customs which he had seen in all cities and especially at Rome, and of the holy places which he remembered having visited as a young man. [Bede, *Homilia* I, 13, in *Bedae Venerabilis Opera*, 3 (*Corpus Christianorum Series Latina* 122), pp. 93–4.]

2. Pertuald of Lucca makes gifts to his foundation of San Michele, 720

Christ Himself, the founder of all churches, gives us hope and certainty that what [sins] we do from our youth we can wash away by good and holy works. Wherefore, I the devout Pertuald, considering my soul, while, drawn not by my necessities but by the compulsion of God, I went far away from the city on pilgrimage, embraced the desire to protect the widow, child and orphan, and having returned home according to the will of God from the shrine of the blessed Peter, prince of the apostles, in the city of Rome, I have carried out to the best of my ability, with His assistance, the work which I there vowed to him. Wherefore I the devout Pertuald offer to God and to you, the church of the blessed Michael the Archangel, which I have established from its foundations near the house where I live [the properties now described]. ... These houses aforesaid, with the land both cultivated and uncultivated, and all the property moveable and immoveable, which pertains to them, I give to you, the aforesaid church of the Holy Archangel, together with other property of mine above-mentioned, as a gift for the saving of my soul, from this day forth to possess in their entirety, so that the priest who is established there or who shall be, may pray the Lord for my sins, perform the divine office, comfort the widow, the orphan and the poor, receive the needy and the pilgrim according to the precept of the Lord, and not cease to perform all these tasks. [*Codice Diplomatico Langobardo* 2, *FSI* 62, n. 28, pp. 101–5.]

3. Carolingian legislation and church councils

(a) The Capitulary of Pepin, 754–55

c. 4 ... And similarly we decree concerning pilgrims who for God's sake go to Rome or elsewhere that on no pretext do you detain them, at bridges, mountain passes or on shipboard, nor make any claim from any pilgrim on account of their portable property, nor exact any toll from them. [*Capitularia Regum Francorum* 1 (*MGH Legum*, 2), p. 32.]

(b) Council of Ver, July 755

c. 10 That monks, who truly live under a rule, shall not be permitted to wander off to Rome or elsewhere, unless in obedience to their abbot ...

c. 22 That tolls be not exacted from pilgrims who travel for God's sake ... [Ibid, p. 35.]

(c) Capitulary of Pepin of Italy, 782/6

c. 10 Concerning strangers and pilgrims who in the service of God are hastening to Rome or to [visit] other relics of the saints, that they may go and return safely under our protection: and should anyone dare to kill [one] of these pilgrims, let him pay sixty *solidi* in our palace. The composition for the homicide shall be paid in addition to whomsoever it pertains to by law. [Ibid., p. 193.]

(d) Admonitio Generalis, March 789

c. 75 To all. This too seems appropriate and praiseworthy to us, that strangers, pilgrims and the poor should have regular and canonical places of reception[59] in various places: because the Lord himself will say, on the great day of recompense, 'I was a stranger and you received me', and the apostle, praising hospitality, said 'In this too they pleased God, receiving angels as guests.'

c. 79 Partly to priests, partly to all. That those rascals and good-for-nothings who lawlessly wander about this land be not permitted to wander and practise deceptions on people, nor those who say that a penance has been laid upon them to go about naked with iron [chains]. It seems preferable, if they have committed some unusual and capital crime, that they should remain in one place labouring and serving and doing penance according to what has been canonically imposed on them. [Ibid., p. 60.]

(e) Synod of Friuli, ? c.795

c. 12 ... And at no time whatsoever shall it be permitted to any abbess or nun to go to Rome or to tour other holy places, if Satan should transform himself into an angel of light and suggest it to them as if for the purpose of prayer. No one is so obtuse or stupid as to be unaware how irreligious and reprehensible it is [for them] to have dealings with men on account of the necessities of travel ... [Mansi, XIII, cols 850–1.]

(f) The General Capitulary of the Missi, early 802

c. 5 That no one presume to commit any fraud, rapine or injury against the holy churches of God, widows, orphans or pilgrims; for the Lord Emperor himself, after God and His saints, is appointed their protector and defender.

c. 27 We command that throughout our realms no one dare to deny hospitality to rich or poor or pilgrim, that is, that no one shall refuse shelter, fire and water either to strangers perambulating the land for God's sake or to anyone travelling for the love of God and the salvation of his soul. If however he should wish to do more good to them, let him know [that he will have] a splendid reward from God, as He himself said, 'Whoever has received one little child for my sake, has received me' and elsewhere, 'I was a stranger and you received me'. [*Capitularia Regum Francorum* 1 (*MGH Legum*, 2), pp. 93, 96.]

(g) The Capitula Ecclesiastica of Haito, bishop of Basel, between 807 and 823

c. 18 ... That no one who is ordained or is to be ordained shall leave his parish for another, nor leave the care of his church to go to the shrines of the apostles by reason of prayer, nor shall anyone who has been suspended from communion receive communion from another, without the knowledge and permission of his bishop; and if he does so, that communion, ordination or move shall be of no validity. And this is proclaimed to all the faithful, that anyone who wishes to go to the shrines of the blessed apostles by reason of prayer shall confess his sins at home and thus set out; because the power of binding and loosing belongs to his own bishop and priest, not to another. [Ibid., pp. 304–5.]

(h) Council of Châlons, 813

c. 45 Grave error is committed by some who go thoughtlessly to Rome or Tours and to certain other places on the pretext of prayer. There are priests and deacons and other clergy who, living carelessly, think that they are purged of their sins thereby and may perform their ministry, if they go to these places. There are laity no less, who think they can sin, or have sinned, with impunity because they are going to pray at these places. There are some powerful men, who acquire a great deal by levying taxes on the pretext of a journey to Rome or Tours and who do it solely out of cupidity, pretending that they are doing so by reason of a visit to a church or holy places. There are poor people who do the same in order to have a better pretext for begging. Of this number are those who, wandering around falsely, claim that they are on pilgrimage, or who are so stupid that they think that they are purged of their sins simply by the sight of holy places, paying no attention to the saying of blessed Jerome, 'It is not having seen Jerusalem, but having lived well at Jerusalem, that is worthy of praise.' The judgement of the Lord Emperor is awaited as to how these [abuses] are to be corrected. Those people, however, who have confessed their sins to the priests in whose parishes they lived, and from them have received counsel as to the penance they are to do, if, intent on prayer, giving alms, amending their lives and reforming their conduct, they wish to visit the shrines of the apostles or of any other saints, their devotion is by all means to be commended. [*MGH Legum* III, *Concilia* 2.i, pp. 282–3.]

(i) Louis II, Capitulary of Pavia, 850

c. 1 It has come to our notice that gangs of robbers are plundering and sometimes wounding or killing those who go to Rome by reason of prayer, or who travel about our kingdom on business, and are plundering their goods. Therefore we desire that our counts and their *sculdassi*, in co-operation with episcopal vassals if need be, whenever they hear of such people, diligently investigate and seize and try them. And if they are found guilty of this crime, the penalties provided in the laws shall be exacted without negligence, so that our kingdom may be purged of such malefactors and those who come hither trusting in us, whether by reason of prayer or business, may be safe. [*MGH Legum* II, *Capitularia* 2, p. 86.]

4. Early ninth century: women pilgrims at Fleury

The relics of the saints were followed however by a large crowd of men and women, with great devotion, because of the miracles granted by God through the blessed martyrs. However since, according to ancient custom, women were entirely forbidden to penetrate beyond the outer gates into the interior of the monastery, these people, who had come a long way in pursuit of the relics, begged that they should be permitted, in answer to their prayers, to enter the church in which the relics of the saints had been deposited and fulfil their vows. By no means were they able to obtain consent, since this was against monastic observance. They persisted in their prayers, and certain persons of higher status (*quique nobiliores*), alerted by all this excitement, came from all around to see so holy a spectacle and added their prayers. With difficulty they prevailed on the abbot and monks to erect a pavilion outside the portal of the monastery, in a wooded area on the eastern side, and here the relics of the saints were brought at a certain time, that is on the vigil of the Lord's day, and remained there under the reverent guard of both monks and clerks, until the same hour on the Lord's day, when they were taken back to the sacred building. When this was done, multitudes of the common people, not only from the neighbourhood, but from faraway places, flocked there to seek remedy for body and soul. [de Certain, pp. 64–5.]

5. The itinerary of Archbishop Sigeric of Canterbury, c.993[60]

The arrival of our archbishop Sigeric at Rome: first to the shrine [*ad limitem*] of the blessed apostle Peter; then to Santa Maria, the *scola* of the English [now Santo Spirito in Sassia]; to St Laurence *in Craticula* [San Lorenzo *in Piscibus*, or San Lorenzino]; to San Valentino *in ponte Molui* [now disappeared]; to Sant' Agnese; to San Lorenzo fuori le Mura; to San Sebastiano; to Sant' Anastasio [Santi Vincenzo and Anastasio]; to St Paul [San Paolo alle Tre Fontane]; to San Bonifazio [Santi Bonifazio e Alessio]; to Santa Sabina; to Santa Maria *scola Graeca* [Santa Maria in Cosmedin]; to Santa Cecilia; to San Crisogono; to Santa Maria Trastevere; to San Pancrazio. Then they returned home.

In the morning to Santa Maria Rotonda [the Pantheon]; to Sant Apostoli; to St John Lateran. Then we ate with the lord pope John; then to Jerusalem [Santa Croce in Gerusalemme]; to Santa Maria

Maggiore; to San Pietro in Vincoli; to San Lorenzo [in Panisperna] where his body is.

These are the overnight stops [*submansiones*] from Rome to the sea.

1. The city of Rome 2. San Giovanni in Nono 3. Baccano 4. Sutri 5. Forcassi 6. 'Sancte Valentine' [near Viterbo] 7. Montefiascone [Sce Flaviane] 8. Bolsena [Sce Cristina] 9. Acquapendente 10. 'Sancte Peitr in Pail' [disappeared] 11. Le Briccole [Abricola] 12. San Quirico in Val d'Orcia 13. Torrenieri [Turreiner] 14. Ponte d' Arbia 15. Siena [Seocine] 16. Borgo Nuovo 17. Gracciano d' Elsa [Aelse] 18. S. Martino Fosci 19. San Gimignano 20. S. Maria a Chianni [Sce Maria Glan] 21. S. Pietro a Coiano [Sce Petre Currant] 22. S. Genesio [Sce Dionisii] 23. A bridging-point on the Upper Arno [Arne Blanca][61] 24. The river Usciana? [Aqua Nigra] 25. Porcari [Forcri] 26. Lucca 27. Camaiore 28. Luni 29. S. Stefano 30. Abbazia di S. Caprasio [Aguilla] 31. Pontremoli 32. Montelongo [Sce Benedicte] 33. Berceto [Sce Moderanne] 34. Fornovo sul Taro [Philemangenur] 35. Costa Mezzana [Metane] 36. Borgo San Donnino [now Fidenza; 'Sce Domnine'] 37. Firenzuola [Floricum] 38. Piacenza 39. Corte S. Andrea 40. S. Cristina 41. Pavia [Pamphica] 42. Tromello [Tremel] 43. Vercelli 44. Santhià [Sca Agatha] 45. Ivrea [Everi] 46. Poley [Publei] 47. Aosta 48. St Rhémy 49. Bourg-St-Pierre [Petrecastel] 50. Orsières [Ursiores] 51. St Maurice 52. Aigde [Burbulei] 53. Vevey [Vivaec] 54. Lausanne 55. Orbe 56. Yverdun [Antifern] 57. Pontarlier [Punterlin] 58. Nods 59. Besançon [Bysiceon] 60. Cussey-sur-l'Oignon [Cuscei] 61. Seveux [Sefui] 62. Grenant 63. Humes [Oisma] 64. Blessonville [Blaecuile] 65. Bar-sur-Aube 66. Brienne-la-Vieille [Breone] 67. Donnement [Domaniant] 68. Fontaine-sur-Coole [Funtaine] 69. Châlons-sur-Marne [Chateluns] 70. Reims 71. Corbeny 72. Laon [Mundothluin] 73. Sérancourt-le-Grand [Martinweath] 74. Doingt [Duin] 75. Arras [Atherats] 76. Bruay 77. Thérouanne [Teranburh] 78. ?? 79. Guînes [Gisne] 80. Sombre [Sumeran]. [*Memorials of St Dunstan, RS* 63, pp. 391–5.]

6. Penitential pilgrimage

(a) Penitential letters collected by Wulfstan, c.1000[62]

Lupus [i.e. Wulfstan] bishop of London to all his brothers and fellow-servants in God, greeting. We desire you to know that this man, deceived by diabolical fraud, has incurred the guilt of parricide.

Wherefore he has thrown himself at our feet tearfully seeking mercy, and admonished by us has gone in this grave necessity to holy places and many saints' relics and the pope of Rome, and returning to us has brought the text of a letter according to the terms of which and under our direction he is doing penance. Wherefore we pray that you pour forth the assistance of your prayers to omnipotent God so that Christ the Lord with his abundant clemency may deign to forgive him the guilt of such a great crime. [*Councils & Synods*, 1.i, pp. 233–4.]

John servant of the servants of God to the venerable archbishop Wulfstan the most affectionate greeting and apostolic benediction. This man came to the shrine of the apostles on account of a fratricide he had committed and for his other crimes, seeking from us the remedy of penance. We have enjoined on him the penance for the aforesaid fratricide for [all] the days of his life, to wit that on the second, fourth and sixth days [of the week] he shall fast on bread and water, he shall enter the church on the Nativity of the Lord and Easter, he shall eat flesh on Sundays and major feast-days. On the three days on which he abstains from flesh, he is to wear woollen clothing and go barefoot, he shall not give peace, he shall not cut his hair except three times in the year, he shall not communicate unless he comes to the point of death. If you choose to offer him any remedy, we give you leave. [Ibid., pp. 235–6.]

(b) From the Laws of Cnut, c.1020

c. 39 If anyone slays a minister of the altar, he is to be an outlaw before God and before men, unless he atone for it very deeply, by pilgrimage and also towards the kindred, or clear himself by an oath equal to the wergild.

c. 41 If a minister of the altar becomes a homicide or otherwise commits too grave a crime, he is then to forfeit both his ecclesiastical orders and his native land, and to go on pilgrimage as far as the pope may prescribe for him, and zealously to make atonement. [Ibid., pp. 491–2, 492–3.]

(c) The Council of Seligenstadt, 1023

c. 16 The holy synod also decreed that no one should go to Rome unless with the licence of his bishop or his vicar.

c. 18 Because many people are so deceived by the foolishness of their minds that they do not wish to accept the penance laid upon them by their priests for capital crimes, and believe firmly that the pope can absolve all their sins if they go to Rome: it seemed to the holy council that this indulgence is of no value, but first let them fulfil the penance laid upon them by their priests according to the nature of the crime and then go to Rome if they wish, having obtained licence from their own bishop and letters to the pope to take with them concerning these things.

c. 19 It was also decreed in the same council, that no penitent, while he is carrying out an imposed fast, should move from place to place, but stay where he has received his penance, so that his own priest can bear witness for him. If however because of hostile attacks he cannot fast, his priest may carefully entrust him to one of his fellows where he may fast in peace. [Mansi, XIX, cols 398–9.]

(d) William of Malmesbury recounts a penance imposed by Archbishop Atto of Cologne (1055–75) for accidental homicide, belatedly confessed

Splendidly, and according to the gospel precept, that one should first pour wine on to wounds so as to clean the infected recesses, and then add oil, so as to give the sinner hope of forgiveness, he imposed as a seven-year penance that he should tour the churches of the saints, his arms and belly bound with iron. The same breastplate was to bind his belly, the same lance his arms, with which he had with parricidal rashness spilt the blood of his kinsman, so that the cause of the guilt should also administer the punishment. He was to become accustomed to hunger and silence, and undergo heavy labour in the hope of good, by the wearing-down of his vices harvesting a heap of virtues. He was to endure in the hope of future glory what for the time being he undertook to obtain mercy, for future reward, what was now punishment. The penitent did what was commanded, and added many further torments besides, himself afflicting his body with hostile violence. He went to Rome, and got as far as Jerusalem – a marvellous achievement at that time, when the prowess of our Christians had not yet made those tracks passable. There, he had no sooner been admitted to pray before the Sepulchre, when by the power of God the breastplate fell apart into fragments. Returning, he toured the whole of Europe, undergoing many perils by land and sea. In the middle of his labours, he came to our monastery. There, while he was lying prostrate before the blessed mausoleum of the confessor [St Aldhelm] he received forgiveness. The force of his prayer was beating upon heaven; it penetrated the stars and drew down help from above. The chains were stripped from his arms, the iron was deeply cut and flew more than fifteen feet. The penitent, his spirit flagging, was burning with heat. But when he was sprinkled with cool liquid he recovered and paid his praises and thanks to God, in chorus with all the bystanders. [*Gesta Pontificum Anglorum*, V. 268 (*RS* 52), p. 425.]

7. Peter Damian to the Marquis Raniero, 1067

For the sins that you have confessed to me, great sir, I enjoined upon you that you should go to Jerusalem, and satisfy the divine justice with a lengthy pilgrimage. But although, as the scripture says, you know not what the morrow has in store, you put the matter off and, while you fear the uncertainties of the journey, you fail to provide for yourself a secure lodging-place. Thus in you is fulfilled the saying: He who watches the wind never sows, and he who is looking out for the rain never reaps.

We in fact exercise a certain judgement in the allocation of this penance. We do not restrain everyone who seeks counsel of us from this journey, nor do we give free rein to everyone who wants to go. Those who live the regular life and observe the rules of canonical or monastic religion, we urge to remain in the vocation in which they are placed and not to neglect those things which are essential in favour of those which are dependent on human judgement. Thus John saith, 'Let them who have hold, and let no one take their crown from them.' Those however who, sunk in the mire, serve the world, or those who claim the title of the spiritual militia but do not observe the rules of their calling,[63] we exhort to undertake the journey of spiritual exile, to satisfy with pilgrimage the fearful judge, whose laws and commands they do not uphold in the midst of their domestic preoccupations. And travelling in this manner, they may by making pilgrimage provide for themselves the tranquil lodging-place of the fatherland.

Therefore, dearly beloved, do not put up fanciful or imaginary objections, do not woman-like take fright at various dismal possibilities, but 'trust in the Lord and do what is good'. Often in fact, when one is most doubtful of human calculation, then it is that the heavenly clemency comes most readily to our aid, and when we despair of human comfort, we perceive that divine protection is at hand.

To speak of the journey which at present concerns us, we have learned from the report of a certain brother of devout life and honourable seriousness, a fellow-monk of ours, Richard, that only yesterday eight men, having fulfilled the vow of their pious desire, returning from Jerusalem, were sorely afflicted by four days of hunger while passing through uninhabitable territory. They began with one voice to call upon the divine mercy to come to their aid in their extremity, and 'he who gives to eat to all flesh' at once provided some nourishment for them in their dire necessity. They have scarcely ended their prayer when they perceive lying in their path a loaf of both great size and wondrous whiteness. They all marvel at the sight, certainly not unaware that a mass of such weight could not have fallen out of the load of an unknowing bearer. Then they acknowledge the gift of heavenly pity, and the bread of divine generosity, and as they were eight in number, they divide it into so many pieces. They were so sweetly and fully satisfied by it, that in all their lives no feast has ever so restored them.

This same brother Richard told me something else which I do not think it proper to pass over in silence. He says that our brother Agius, a man well on in years and notable in religion, while he was still living in the world, went on pilgrimage to the church of the blessed archangel Michael, which is built on Monte Gargano, near Sipontum. He and his brother, a secular man, had one horse between them, on which they took turns to ride to relieve the labour of the journey. But when he saw that their fellow-travellers needed help with carrying their bundles, he told his brother that they should both abstain from riding the beast, and out of charity for their companions make it available to carry their burdens. Later, while they were resting, worn out by the toil of the long road, and restoring their empty stomachs with food, brother Agius dipped a piece of bread in a cup of wine, but putting it down beside him put off eating while he rested. While they were thus taking their ease, behold, robbers suddenly attacked them, and got away with everything, including the horse. One of them stayed behind, and consumed brother Agius's food and drink. Immediately an intolerable pain seized him, and the fierce agony did not leave him until he had been forced to vomit everything up. Then, darting nimbly away, he ran swiftly ahead and persuaded his companions that unless they restored the beast to the servant of God as quickly as possible, they would not avoid the imminent peril of divine vengeance. Overcome by heavenly terror, they at once returned to the man of God and with groans sought forgiveness for their presumption, at the same time restoring the beast together with the things they had stolen. The divine mercy, therefore, is not far with its protection from those whom it considers to be devotedly labouring in its service.

Our brother Bonizo, also, an old and holy man, who has now lived for many years in a hermitage, and in whom the weakness of old age has not weakened the rigour of the life of continence, has himself told us how, when he was returning by ship from Jerusalem, he suffered shipwreck. The waves towered and the ship foundered, and all his companions perished in the stormy sea. He meanwhile seized hold of a package which was full of cotton cloth and sitting on it among the swelling waves for three days and two nights, fought with death like a fighting man, engaging with the sea. It happened then that some rowers, ploughing over the sea, saw him from afar and charitably drew him to them and restored him with food and looked after him kindly. So it was that he who preserved Paul unhurt day and night in the depths of the sea, sustained this brother too, in the very inundation of the raging storm, lest he be sucked into the watery maw. And by the command of him by whose virtue the gullet of the voracious beast spewed forth Jonah, the resilient wave spread out below this man not to swallow him up but to preserve him.

Consider within yourself, then, great sir, these and similar flowers of the divine mercy; doubt your own powers, as is proper, but put your trust in the infallible protection of him who is everywhere omnipotent. Corrupted flesh trembles, but the innocent fervour of the prompt spirit is emboldened. Go forth, get moving, contend, he will be the guide of your journey who is also author of the reward. It is your part to embark on the journey, God's to direct the footsteps of the seeker. He gives effect to good works who moves the affection of the pious heart. And he who prompts the spirit of man to well-doing, himself will beyond all doubt fulfil the vows of pious intention. [*Die Briefe des Petrus Damianus*, ed. K. Reindel (4 vols, *MGH*, 1983–93), n. 151, 4, pp. 1–5.]

8. Jerusalem pilgrimage in the eleventh century

(a) *The pilgrimage of Richard of St Vannes, 1026*

The burden of ruling [the monastery of] Grace Dieu now seemed heavy to this father, who desired to progress and more freely devote himself to divine contemplation, as the world had already died in his heart. It was well-known that certain people who had gone to Jerusalem had died a happy death there, among them a man from the region of Autun. Healthy and vigorous, and showing no sign of death, he had prayed in that place where the feet of the Lord last stood, and asked to be received in peace by the Lord; soon, feeling a little pain, he was taken home, and soon after that taken back to the place where he had prayed, where he yielded up his spirit to God, as well-attested stories made known.[64] [Richard] was also touched by a holy longing for a like good devotion, and planned to visit the Lord's sepulchre. He sought, and soon obtained, permission from the prince and bishops and leading men and vassals of the kingdom, first taking care to provide for his sons in every particular, so that he might, with the good will of all, undertake the sacred duties of pilgrimage. ... Richard count of Normandy provided him with all the expenses of the journey, for he was generous with alms, expansive in charity, notable in honour ...

... After many sorts of peril, he reached the longed-for places of Jerusalem. Entering the gate of the city, he sang with his companions in harmonious tones the responsory for Palm Sunday, 'When the Lord entered the Holy City', adoring Christ crucified, God blessed above all through the ages, and reverently embraced His burial place with the eyes of his faith. He faithfully toured all the places of the Nativity, Passion and Resurrection, and when he was not feasting on them with his eyes, he browsed upon them in his mind, for at the most delectable sight of the wonders of God, which he had so longed and prepared for in his desirous mind, he was filled with an unspeakable joy and gladness ...

Oh, what was his love towards God! What the exultation of his contrite and humbled spirit! What the jubilation of his heart, when he saw himself present where Christ was born, where he suffered, where he was buried, where his feet last stood when he ascended into heaven. Everywhere that he prayed, he soaked the ground with tears, the cry of his heart rose up to the Lord, his body sank down, his spirit rose aloft. He spent the night continually in vigils, he wore down his body with fasts, never without tears, never without prayers; his whole being exulted in the Lord, but he cloaked the gladness of his mind with serenity of countenance ... [Hugh of Flavigny, *Chronicon*, MGH SS 8, pp. 393–6.]

(b) Ulrich (later prior of Celle), 1062

Desiring therefore to unburden himself and to go untrammelled on pilgrimage for Christ, he restored his benefices and set out for Jerusalem with one servant and an almoner, making do with one horse. From the day of his departure from Freising right up to the day of his entry into Jerusalem he never mounted the horse until he had recited the entire psalter, ordering his servant to ride in the meantime, perhaps thinking of great Martin with his servant companion. When the holy man reached the holy places, it is impossible to tell with what emotions he beheld the monuments of the nativity, passion, resurrection and ascension of the Lord, with what genuflections he adored them, and with what rivers of tears he flooded them ... [*Vita Prior S. Udalrici Prioris Cellensis, MGH SS* 12, p. 252.]

He went to Bethlehem, which is dedicated to the Nativity of Christ. There, at the birthplace of the Lord, he opened the treasures of his most abundant breast, and offered the three mystic gifts of the Magi, symbolically though not in reality; confessing the son of God, king of Kings, true priest, made mortal through the assumption of the flesh, co-eternal with the supreme Father through the ineffable majesty of the Deity. Then he came to the River Jordan, in which the Saviour of the World washed away the guilt of our sins, and taking off his clothes descended into the water ... [*Vita Posterior*, ibid., pp. 255–6.]

[On his return home, Ulrich goes with the *scholasticus* Gerald to Rome]

Intending to emerge from the labyrinth of this world under the leadership of the holy scripture, they first went to the shrines of the holy apostles Peter and Paul; for the clemency of our Redeemer has conferred on them the power of binding and loosing, and by their merits and intercession they hoped to be granted absolution of their sins by the Lord. Most earnestly they commended their intention to them, praying that they might be enabled to complete the arduous course of the regular life, by which they longed to attain the celestial fatherland. [Ibid., p. 257.]

(c) The Great German Pilgrimage of 1064–65

(i) At that time, many nobles were going to Jerusalem to see the Lord's Sepulchre, deceived by a popular opinion that the day of Judgement was at hand, because Easter that year fell on the sixth day before the Kalends of April [27th March], when it is written Christ was resurrected. Stirred by this terror, not only the common people, but rulers, men distinguished by birth and rank, and the very bishops of various cities, resplendent in glory and honour, left their homeland, kin and riches, and by a narrow path, taking up the cross, followed Christ. The first leader and instigator was Gunther bishop of Bamberg, a man outstanding both for physical elegance and intellectual wisdom. In his company there were many men of reputation, both clergy and laity, from eastern France as well as from Bavaria. ... So they set out on the difficult path of pilgrimage, and many traps were set for them along the way by the pagans, and they lost many of their companions, with their possessions. For shame! the Enemies of Christ leapt on the back of the priests of Christ and pusued them across the plains on horseback, urging their steeds on with spurs. On this journey there was a memorable incident, which I will include by way of example, so that those who obstinately reject the counsels of the wiser may take fright at it. There was on this expedition a certain noble abbess, fair of form and devout of mind, who had abandoned the care of the sisters entrusted to her and against all the advice of wiser heads had subjected herself to the dangers of this pilgrimage. She was captured by the pagans, and in the sight of everybody, raped by the shameless ones for so long that at last, to the disgrace of all Christians, she breathed her last.

Afflicted by these and many other insults from the enemies of Christ, and everywhere a spectacle for angels and men, because they had chosen to enter the kingdom of heaven through many tribulations, they at last came to Jerusalem. There they fulfilled their vows and offering a sacrifice of praise to God returned rejoicing to their homeland. [*Vita Altmanni Epicopi Patavensis, MGH SS* 12, p. 230.]

(ii) [The expedition reaches Constantinople]. There they conducted themselves so honourably in all respects that even the 'Greek and imperial arrogance' wondered at it. Because of his great pomp, they suspected that Gunther was not a bishop, but the king of the Romans disguising himself as a bishop because he would not otherwise be able to go to the Holy Sepulchre. After a few days' further journey, they came to Lattakieh after various trials and tribulations. ... While they were staying for a few days in Lattakieh, many people returning from Jerusalem began to arrive every day, announcing innumerable deaths among their companions, recounting their recent misfortunes and showing still bleeding wounds; they declared publicly that no one could pass that way, because the savage Arab people, thirsting for human blood, had taken possession of that whole land. [*Annales Altahenses Maiores, MGH SS* 20, p. 815.]

(iii) Meanwhile the aforesaid bishops were making their way to Jerusalem. They displayed the magnitude of their wealth carelessly to the peoples through whose lands their journey lay, and would have suffered disaster if divine mercy had not restored a situation made dangerous by human temerity. For the barbarians, who flocked in hordes from the cities and the fields to look at these illustrious men, were seized first by great wonder at their foreign appearance and magnificent array, and then, as happens, by no less a hope and desire of plunder. They had crossed Lycia [in Asia Minor] and entered Saracen territory, and were little more than a day's journey from the city called Ramleh. Then, on the Friday before Easter, around the third hour of the day, they were attacked by Arabs, who learning of the approach of such notable people, flocked armed from all directions to snatch the spoils. Many of the Christians thought it a religious act to help themselves and to defend, with physical weapons, their own well-being which as pilgrims (*peregre proficiscentes*) they had devoted to God. At the first encounter they were overwhelmed, suffered many wounds and stripped of everything they possessed ... [Lambert of Hersfeld, *Annales, MGH SS* 5, pp. 168–9.]

[The pilgrims take refuge for three days in Chabarabba, still under threat from the 'Arabs']

On the following day, around the ninth hour, the general of the king of Babylon, who was governing the city of Ramleh, hearing what had happened, came with a great crowd to liberate our people, although he was a pagan. He thought that if they perished as a result of such wretched slaughter, nobody thereafter would cross that territory on pilgrimage (*causa orationis*) and he and his people would suffer considerable loss in consequence. Hearing of his approach, the Arabs fled in all directions, and he, taking those who had been seized and bound, opened the gates to allow our people to leave. They went to the city of Ramleh, and were there detained, against their will, for two weeks by the governor and townspeople. At last allowed to depart, they entered the Holy City on 12th April. [*Annales Altahenses Maiores, MGH SS* 20, pp. 816–17.]

(d) A returning pilgrim, Hervé, archdeacon of Ste Croix of Orléans, founds the priory of Notre Dame de la Ferté-Avrain, 1033–36

Since it is well-known that earthly life is fragile and doubtful and the end of every mortal existence is uncertain, also that all worldly possessions are swiftly coursing to their ruin, I, Hervé ... considering these things, and fearful of being overtaken by sudden death, first went to Jerusalem, desiring there to bewail my sins with tears. Returning then, I brought with me relics of the most Holy Sepulchre of Our Lord Jesus Christ, in veneration of which, inspired by God, I embarked on the construction of a worthy church for these relics, near the castle of my lord Landric, with his licence and permission, and with the consent and agreement of my brothers Alberic and

Theduin. I want to endow this church from my possessions, as best I can and with my brothers and friends, because I have built [the church] not only for the remission of my own sins, but for the salvation of the souls of my kin, that is of my father Havran and mother Adela, and also of my dead brother Peter and of the others still living, Alberic and Theduin above-mentioned ... [*Bibliothèque de l'Ecole de Chartes* 51 (1890), p. 205.]

9. Wills and other agreements made by departing pilgrims

(a) A gift to the abbey of Tulle, 986

As death remains certain, and spares no one, every man is obliged to make provision from his possessions so that he may have the Lord as the restorer of all goods, who says, 'Give alms, and behold, all things shall be clean to you.' Wherefore I, Gerald of Avelena, wanting to go to Jerusalem and to give my son Adhemar as a monk to blessed Martin, with the consent of my wife Garsenda give and concede to St Martin, some of my property in the place called Tulle ... [Tulle & Rocamadour, p. 50.]

(b) 1024, April 28th: 'Proof' of the will of Seniofredo Flavi

We [the executors] saw and were present in person when Senio-fredo Flavi, setting out to visit the shrine of the blessed apostle James, called us and others of his men together and in his own words stipulated his will and ordered us to hearken and to be witnesses to it. ... And after he had done all this he made the above-mentioned journey, and when he had returned in the year written below he set out on an expedition in Spain against the Saracens, and there in the service of Almighty God he was gravely wounded and departed this life in the month of March which has just passed. [*Cartulario del 'Sant Cugat' del Vallés*, ed. J. Rius Serra (3 vols, Barcelona 1945–47), 2, n. 377.]

(c) 1045, October 22nd

I, Remundo, priest, acknowledge that I am weak and a sinner and because of the horrible sins which I have committed, I fear the pains of eternal judgement; however, not despairing of the mercy of Christ, I desire to attain the joys of Paradise. I want therefore to go to the shrine of the blessed apostle James ... [Ibid., n. 582.]

(d) 1123, January 4th

In the name of the Lord, I, Maienna, a woman, and my son Berengar, want to go to the Lord's Sepulchre, and we are making a will of all that we possess, so that if we happen to die before we make another this shall have force. First, I Maienna leave my sheep in alms to San Cugat, so that if I do not return and my son does, he shall have half and the other half [will go] in alms, and if either of us does not return, those alms shall be given; and my own work, in wool or linen, may be sold to make cloths for the church of San Cugat. [Ibid., 3, n. 863.]

(e) 1070, September 28th

When the clerk Gislerius went away to Jerusalem on pilgrimage, he gave to the monks of Holy Trinity Vendôme two *arpents* of vines in the place which is called *Villa Domini*; which his brother Hubert who was called 'the rich man' (*Dives*) had already previously given to them, who himself had gone first to Jerusalem on pilgrimage. Aremburgis, wife of the aforesaid Hubert, consented. [Vendôme, n. 221, p. 354.]

(f) 1075

May our successors as inhabitants of this place know that the knight Guicherius, when he held the honour of Châteaurenard, imposed a custom on the land of Holy Trinity at Pruneto, by force and unjustly, that every year the villeins of that land, like it or not, should render him a measure of oats. When he had been committing this rapine for some while, it happened that he decided to go to Rome on pilgrimage (*causa orationis*) and asked the monks of Vendôme to give him some assistance with his journey. They raised the issue of the evil custom he was perpetrating. He fully acknowledged the injustice, but was unwilling to amend it altogether, as he should have done, and said that he would not abandon this abominable custom unless they gave him 20 *soldi*; although it was unjust, the monks preferred to do this, as there was no one to do them justice, rather than that their land should be subject to this evil custom for all time, protesting nonetheless at the injustice that was being done them. He renounced the injustice which he had done the monks' lands, for himself and for his successors, in perpetuity. [Ibid., n. 251.]

10. Help for pilgrims: Margaret of Scotland

And since out of religious devotion people come from many places to frequent the church of St Andrew's, she established lodgings on both sides of the sea which divides Lothian from Scotland, so that after the toils of the journey pilgrims and the poor could obtain rest and refreshment and find provided there everything for their bodily needs. She established servants there for that sole purpose, to furnish the necessities of the arrivals and carefully minister to them. To them she also entrusted ships so that they could ferry people across, both going and returning, nor were they ever to demand any charge for their crossing from those whom they had conveyed. [Turgot, *Life of St Margaret*, III (AS June 2, p. 333).][65]

11. The merits of Calixtus II, 1119–24

The praiseworthy magnificence of the pope in increasing good went further, to restrain the unbridled and congenital greed of the Romans. At this time there were no ambushes for travellers around Rome, no injuries done to those entering the city. The offerings at St Peter's, which the powerful had seized out of impudence and greed, abusing with disgraceful insults previous popes who had even murmured, Calixtus recalled to their proper use, that is to the public purposes of the ruler of the holy see. No ambition in his breast for the acquisition of money, nor any love of it when he had it, could deflect him from doing good. He therefore urged English pilgrims to go to St David's rather than to Rome, because of the length of the journey, [saying that] those who went to that place twice would obtain the same amount of blessing as they would have if they went once to Rome. [William of Malmesbury, *Gesta Regum*, ed. W. Stubbs (2 vols, RS 90), 2, pp. 507–8.]

12. A liturgy for departing pilgrims: From the Missal of Vich, 1038

Prayers for those undertaking the journey

Oh Lord who brought Abraham your servant out of Ur of the Chaldees and guarded him through all the paths of his pilgrimage, deign to guard with the shield of your protection these your servants[66] who are voluntarily going abroad (*sponte peregrina petentes*) for the love of your name. Be for them, Lord, a defence in emergency, a harbour in shipwreck, a refuge on the journey, shade in the heat, light in the darkness, a staff on the slippery slope, joy amidst suffering, consolation in sadness, safety in adversity, caution in prosperity, so that these your servants, under your leadership, may arrive where they are boldly going, and may return unharmed, and the church which laments their absence may experience the joy of their safe and prosperous return …

Or

Oh Lord Jesus Christ who through your blessed apostle Paul has taught us that we have here no abiding city, but must always seek the one to come, hearken to our supplications, which we humbly pour out for these your servants, on whom, going forth on pilgrimage in the desire of eternal salvation, we confer the habit of the pilgrim. Give them, we ask, oh Lord, your grace, appointing your holy angel to guard them waking and sleeping and direct their path. Pour out the Holy Spirit into their bowels, Lord Jesus, penetrating and cleansing all that is within them, defending their hearts from all superfluous thoughts, and so disposing their present pilgrimage with the refresh-ment of continual consolation that, through your most merciful goodness and [that of] the almighty father and the Holy Spirit, they may when they shed the burden of the flesh, freed from all the bonds of sin, deserve to become eternal citizens of the heavenly Jerusalem …

The Blessing

(As they rise from the ground, the bishop or the priest shall put the satchels on them and give them the staff, saying), In the name of our Lord Jesus Christ, take this satchel, the garb of your pilgrimage, so that chastened and saved and corrected you may arrive at the shrines of the blessed apostles Peter and Paul [or other saints] where you desire to go, and having completed your journey return to us safely. … Receive also this staff, the support of your jouney and the labour of the path of your pilgrimage, so that you may overcome all the traps of the enemy and arrive safely at the shrine of the blessed apostle Peter and Paul [and others] which you desire to reach, and having completed the appointed course return to us joyfully. With the aid of Our Lord. [*Peregrinaciones*, 3, pp. 146–7.][67]

PART TWO

. . . .

European Pilgrimage
c.1100–c.1500

CHAPTER 2

· ·

Penitential Pilgrimage

Pilgrimage as penance and punishment remained a weapon in the hands of both ecclesiastical and secular authorities in the later middle ages. From the mid-thirteenth century onwards, the inquisition of Languedoc worked with a list of pilgrimages, 'major' and 'minor', on which convicted heretics were sent according to the gravity of their offence. Given that they were dealing with a population located in southern France, it was not unreasonable that the inquisitors should classify the shrines of Becket at Canterbury and the Magi at Cologne as demanding goals for their penitents, along with Compostela and Rome. The minor pilgrimages were all French, with the addition, in the fourteenth century, of the shrine of St Dominic at Bologna, fittingly in view of Dominican prominence in the inquisition [3]. The Holy Land constituted a category on its own.

In the early fourteenth century, the Dominican Bernard Gui enumerated these pilgrimages, and described the procedures of the Inquisition of Toulouse, including form letters for use in a variety of situations.[1] When undertaking a pilgrimage, penitent heretics might be permitted to remove the crosses which they were otherwise obliged to wear prominently displayed on their garments; this was a prudent measure to avert the risk of public hostility and thus increase the chance that the pilgrimage would actually be completed. Bernard Gui provided a form of monition to be used against those 'who mock or molest crucesignatos doing their penance'.[2] The crosses would be resumed when the pilgrim returned and exhibited the certificate of completion of the pilgrimage, which had to be obtained at the shrine [3,a]. Financial or other commutation of the penalty was a possibility, but if a convicted heretic died without performing the pilgrimages imposed and without having made such an agreement, his or her heirs and executors were liable to pay compensation [3,c,d].

Date	Offence	Penance
1321 (I, p. 217)	Adultery	Every year for six years to: St Thomas of Canterbury, St Thomas of Hereford, St Edmund of Bury, and St Richard of Chichester; plus a three-pound candle annually for six years on the feast of St Andrew at Rochester; and almsgiving.
1322 (I, pp. 113–14)	Poaching in my Lord's park at Halling	To Rochester Cathedral on three Fridays, barefoot and in woollen garments.
1325 (I, p. 200)	Adultery	Every year for seven years to: St Thomas of Canterbury, St Thomas of Hereford, St Edmund of Bury and St Mary of Walsingham.
1325 (I, p. 224)	Adultery with godmother	To Santiago.
1326 (I, p. 196)	Disturbing the peace	To Rochester to offer a half-pound candle in the week of Pentecost.
1326 (I, p. 196)	Violating the liberty of the church	To Rochester in three successive years to offer a half-pound candle on the feast of St Andrew.
1327 (I, pp. 233–4)	Slander	Three times to St Thomas of Canterbury; once to St Richard of Chichester; once to St Edmund of Bury, and a one-pound candle at the altar of St Andrew in Rochester Cathedral.
1330 (I, p. 245)	Adultery	The female to be whipped around the church and marketplace and to visit on foot Canterbury, St Edmund's and Walsingham. (The male seems to have been imprisoned.)

1330 (I, p. 439)	Fornication	[Both parties] Once each to the chapel of the Holy Cross at Greenwich and the church of St Thomas at Lesnes.
1332 (I, pp. 467–8)	Malpractices in connection with the farm of the fruits of the church of Ryarsh; and adultery	To St Thomas of Canterbury, offering half a mark, and to St Thomas of Hereford, offering 40d, barefoot, and bringing back certificates of performance.
1332 (I, p. 476)	Renewed adultery	To Canterbury and to St William at Rochester, barefoot and naked but for breeches; certificates of performance.
1332 (I, p. 477)	Fornication	[The male] On foot to Canterbury and to St William of Rochester, in both places offering a one-pound candle. [The female] Barefoot to the church of St Mary at Chatham, offering a candle to the image of the Virgin.
1347 (II, p. 938)	Habitual fornication	To Walsingham and to King Edward at Gloucester, bringing back certificates of performance.
1347 (II, p. 961)	Clerical incontinence	To Walsingham.
1347 (II, p. 962)	Clerical incontinence	To Canterbury [this penance was bought off].
1348 (II, p. 977)	Clerical incontinence	To Walsingham, distributing 6s 8d in alms along the way and bringing back testimonial letters [this penance was bought off].
1348 (II, p. 999)	Fornication	To St Edmund, offering a one-pound candle, distributing half a mark in alms along the way and bringing back a certificate of performance.

The option of imposing pilgrimage as penance was of course also available to bishops. In the course of his visitations, Eudes Rigaud, archbishop of Rouen, sent various penitents, lay and clerical, to Compostela, St Gilles, Rocamadour and Mont St Michel; an esquire who had obstinately contracted a clandestine marriage, against which he had been warned by the archbishop's official, merited stern measures and was sent to Rome and to St Nicholas of Bari with instructions to return by way of St Gilles, bringing with him testimonial letters from all those places.[3] The Franciscan John Pecham as archbishop of Canterbury inflicted a rather extensive programme of pilgrimage on an incorrigibly fornicating parish priest; his decree sheds some light on the measures that had to be taken to safeguard the cure of souls in such a case [4]. It is fairly explicit that the sentence was not merely corrective, but was intended to get the offender out of harm's way. Urban V was similarly motivated when he proposed penitential pilgrimages for repentant members of the military companies which were terrorising France [9].

Hamo de Hethe, bishop of Rochester from 1319 to 1352, used English shrines, often very local ones, almost exclusively.[4] The table on pp. 52–3 shows how he proportioned pilgrimage to offence. The bishop was clearly sometimes acting as lord of the manor rather than, strictly, as spiritual authority. The stipulation that the penitent give money in alms along the path of his pilgrimage reinforces the concept of the 'good work' by virtue of which he was expiating his fault. The one overseas pilgrimage required was for the grave sin of adultery with a godmother, which was tantmount to incest. Hamo also registered the sentence imposed by the papal penitentiary on John Laurence clerk of London, for involvement in the murder of Walter de Stapledon, bishop of Exeter. When a 'general passage' to the east next took place, he was to join it; and he was to go not only to Compostela, but to the shrines of the Virgin at Le Puy and Boulogne, and also to Canterbury, all of which could obviously be effected in one return journey. He was also obliged to do public penance in the churches of Rochester.[5]

Penitential pilgrimage was not exacted by ecclesiastical authorities alone. In 1305 Philip IV of France imposed on the rebellious Flemish a treaty of peace which included among its terms his right to send 2,000 citizens of Bruges on pilgrimages in recompense for the massacre of the French carried out in that city in 1302. In 1316, after the death of Philip's immediate successor Louis X, Count Robert de Béthune agreed with the regent, the count of Poitiers (the future

Philip V), that his son would undertake these pilgrimages, which he did, although not for another five years [6]. The courts of the Flemish cities themselves used pilgrimage as a punishment for criminal offences, drawing up lists of shrines, each with its price, on payment of which the convicted person might be able to buy off the need to make the pilgrimage. These lists could be very extensive indeed: the example which is translated here, from Oudenarde [7], is considerably shorter than those of Ghent, Aalst and Dendermonde, which are also printed by Van Cauwenbergh, though longer than the 1484 list from Leuven.[6]

The Oudenarde list is richest, as we might expect, in shrines located in the Low Countries and in France, but its view extends to Scotland in one direction, Germany in another, Bari to the south, and of course Galicia to the west. Though the shrines are listed in no particular order, the sums to be paid in monetary composition seem roughly proportional to the distances that would otherwise have to be traversed. Most of the shrines mentioned occur also on other, longer lists. Compostela seems to have been the most commonly nominated destination, appearing on twenty-five lists that Van Cauwenbergh examined; others to be named nine times or more were Our Lady at Aardenburg, St Servatius at Maastricht, St Josse in Picardy, Rocamadour, St Martin of Tours, Vendôme, Cologne, the Holy Blood at Wilsnack, St Nicholas of Bari and of course Peter and Paul at Rome. The magistrates of Ghent, Aalst and Dendermonde were among the most demanding, on paper at least, in that they were prepared to contemplate sending delinquents to such far-flung spots as Cyprus, Constantinople and the shrine of St Thomas in India. Here, one feels, the line between penitential pilgrimage and exile is very fine indeed. The specialised commercial knowledge of the Flemish urban patriciate may help account for the presence not only of numerous shrines in eastern England,[7] but for places like Lübeck, Königsberg, Danzig, Breslau and Riga, in some of these lists.

The crimes for which penitential pilgrimage was imposed varied considerably in seriousness. Where murder was in question, the pilgrimage might be carried out not only as punishment, but for the benefit of the soul of the defunct, as a certificate addressed in 1354 to the *scabini* of Ghent by the prior of St Peter's at Rome testifies.[8] Slander and disorderly conduct sent some culprits on their travels. In 1428 a painter of Tournai who was identified as a troublemaker, perpetually abusing other people and endangering the peace, was fined and more or less thrown out of the city to go to Rocamadour

[11]. One inhabitant of Lier, near Antwerp, was sent to St Martin of Tours because of 'verbal injuries' [10] and another to the cathedral of Milan (where the certificate of performance was issued by a civic, not an ecclesiastical, official) for 'threatening Henrich de Mol with injurious words'. The vicar and treasurer of Our Lady of Halle, just south of Brussels, certified in 1479 that one Michael Douwe, also from Lier, had performed his pilgrimage 'because of certain excesses committed by him'. Whatever these were, they cannot have been too serious, considering the modest distance he had to travel.[9]

DOCUMENTS

1. Alexander III to the archbishop of Uppsala and his suffragans, on the penance to be exacted from those guilty of certain offences: 1171, September 9th

Since it is appropriate to punish with adequate severity the abominable presumption of these excesses, you must take care to impose the yoke of a strict penance on those aforesaid who kill their own children, and also those who either advocate or consent to this crime, and all parricides, or those who couple with mother, daughter, cousins-german or grand-daughter, or with beasts; and unless they are stricken by old age, or bodily broken by weakness or want, you should compel them to come to the apostolic see, and to visit the shrines of the apostles Peter and Paul, that in the sweat of their brow and the labour of the road, they may avoid the wrath of the heavenly Judge and earn His mercy. [*PL* 200, cols 880–1.]

2. Innocent III to the prior of Oseney: 1203, February 25th

Mandate to enjoin a fitting penance on the bearer of the present letter, who, having married a wife, committed incest and adultery with her sister, and says he is too poor to go to Jerusalem. The wife is to be admonished not to cohabit with him and to remain continent during his life. [*Die Register Innocenz' III*, ed. O. Hageneder and A. Haidacher, 6, n. 2 (Graz/Köln 1964–), pp. 5–6.]

3. Sentences of the Inquisition of Carcassonne

(a) *1250, November 30th*

Permission was given to Pierre Pelha of Couffoulens to remove the crosses imposed on him for heresy until he returns from France, where he wants to go; and after his return he must within eight days present himself to the lord bishop of Carcassonne and must then willingly resume those crosses, or others, without more ado; and he must show him the testimonial letters of the pilgrimages which he has completed. And he has sworn to uphold and perform these things and agreed that a public record should be made. No change has been made in the other conditions imposed on him. [M. Douais, *Documents pour servir à l'histoire de l'Inquisition* (Paris 1900), pp. 135–6.]

(b) *1251, October 5th*

It was ruled by the inquisitors in the church of St Michel du Bourg of Carcassonne, that the men of Preixan, Couffoulens, Cavanac, Cornèze, Leuc and Villefloure on whom crosses have been imposed for heresy and who have received remission of those crosses, shall begin the minor pilgrimages imposed on them for the said crime within eight days, the major pilgrimages within fifteen days; and those who are so obliged shall cross the sea on the first sailing. [Ibid., p. 159.]

(c) *1256, February 19th*

Bernard Algay, Arnaut Guillaume, Pons Cerda and Guillaume de Marcelleux were cited and appeared; they were requested to make satisfaction, from the goods of the late Raimonde Barbairane, once *crucesignata* for heresy, because she did not complete the pilgrimages imposed on her for that crime in her lifetime, and they replied that they were willing for the goods of the said Barbairane to be noted and enrolled, which was done ... [Ibid., pp. 228–9.]

(d) *March 7th*

Algay, of Rennes-les-Baines, and on his behalf and by his instructions Bernard de Cavanac, tailor, and Amblard Celler, promise that they will give 40 *sous* before Easter on account of the goods of the late [Raymonde] Barbairane, because she did not complete the pilgrimages imposed on her for heresy in her lifetime. But the official of Carcassonne must have 20 *sous* from the preceding sum, because, as he says, the aforesaid Barbairane was in debt to him; and the said

Algay must indemnify his pledges aforesaid on this matter; and when the sum has been paid, the aforesaid goods shall be quit on the part of the inquisition. [Ibid., pp. 229–30.]

4. Archbishop Pecham of Canterbury disciplines a fornicating clerk: 1283, July 15th

Carrying out a metropolitan visitation of the diocese of Chichester we found that Roger, rector of the church of Hamme in that diocese, had on another occasion been arraigned in the court of the ordinary on a charge of incontinence and fornication with various women, and had promised, and indeed sworn, to maintain continence in future, on pain of deprivation of his church above-mentioned. Nevertheless he had afterwards sinned again like a dog returning to its vomit. Wherefore, submitting himself entirely to our will and direction, he has promised and given his oath on the holy gospels of God, to obey our will and ordinance in this matter and to carry out the punishment and penance inflicted on him by us for these sins. Having therefore weighed the matter and taken counsel with the experts, and wishing to take thought for the salvation of both the rector himself and the souls subjected to him, lest by his presence he should infect the Lord's flock committed to him with the example of his usual conduct; and although we could, if we wished, on this occasion exact justice and deprive him of his church as incorrigible, considering the nature of his offence; wishing nonetheless to mingle mercy with rigour we ordain and enjoin on the said rector a three-year penance for his sins, starting from the present date, in the following manner: that he should go on pilgrimage, in this present year, to St James. The following year, he is to visit the shrines of the blessed apostles Peter and Paul and perform the customary pilgrim stations at Rome (*Romae peregrinetur in stationibus consuetis*). In the third year following he shall do pilgrimage to Cologne for the remission of his sins. We ordain further that for the said three years, Ralph rector of the church of Barewe, in whose fidelity and diligence we repose trust, shall have custody of the church of Hamme, and by these presents consign the said church to his custody for that period, on the clear understanding that he will each year bestow on the aforesaid rector, for the necessities of life, 100 shillings sterling from the goods and rents of the church. The said Ralph shall receive another 100 shillings as his stipend. He is to expend the rest on the purposes of the church and the poor of the parish, in each of the three years aforementioned. [*Registrum Epistolarum Fratis Johannis Peckham Archiepiscopi Cantuariensis* (RS 77) 2, pp. 385–7.]

5. The Inquisitor Bernard Gui lists the 'major' and 'minor' pilgrimages: *c.*1320

[In the margin of the Ms, 'The four major pilgrimages'] Item, the pilgrimages of the apostles Sts Peter and Paul at Rome, and there for forty days visiting the shrines of the saints in that city; item, [of] St James of Compostela, St Thomas in Canterbury, and the Three Kings of Cologne.

[The minor pilgrimages] Item, [of] St Mary of Rocamadour, Le Puy, Vauvert, *Notre-Dame-des-Tables* in Montpellier, of Sérignan, St Guillaume-du-Désert, St Peter of Montmajour, St Martha of Tarascon, St Mary Magdalen at St Maximin, St Antony of Vienne, St Martial and St Leonard in Limoges, St Denis and St Louis, Blessed Mary of Chartres in France, St Severin in Bordeaux, Blessed Mary of Soulac, St Foi of Conques in the diocese of Rodez, St Paul of Narbonne and St Vincent of Castres, and St Dominic in Bologna; and from each place they shall bring back with them testimonial letters from the persons in charge on those places, that they have completed the aforesaid pilgrimages, which letters we require and exhort N. to be given without difficulty; and he shall begin these pilgrimages within three or four months of the present and persevere in their completion in virtue of the oath taken by himself ...

It is to be noted, concerning the contents of the aforesaid letter, that having weighed the nature and the greater or lesser seriousness of the offence, and also the condition of the offender, pilgrimages can according to the judgement of the inquisitors be modified, diminished or even increased, with the proviso that [all of] of the first, four pilgrimages, which are commonly called 'major', shall not be imposed, but only two or one of them, let us say the pilgrimage of St James of Compostela, which has very often been imposed for this purpose with the other minor [pilgrimages] aforesaid. Increase can be effected by doubling the pilgrimage and saying that 'he shall go twice to such and such'. Item, concerning the other pilgrimages which are called 'minor', those can be omitted which are in the more distant and remote places, like those in France, or Bologna, or Vienne, and so on for the others, according as it shall seem good to the inquisitors. [*Practica Inquisitionis Hereticae Pravitatis*, II.3, ed. M. Douais (Paris–Toulouse 1886), pp. 37–9.]

6. The Count of Flanders comes to terms with the French

(a) 1316, September 1st

And the said messieur de Poitiers said that the said count Robert of Flanders shall go to the Holy Land with him, or with whoever shall be king of France, when a general passage takes place, if he is in a condition in which he can go; and messieur Robert, his son, shall within a year go on pilgrimage to St James of Galicia, to Our Lady of Rocamadour, to Notre Dame of Vauvert, to St Gilles in Provence and to our Lady of Le Puy. And if he cannot do all this within one year, he shall do it within two ... [Rupin, p. 213.]

(b) 1321, July 17th

Be it known that on the Friday before the feast of St Mary Magdalen the noble and powerful lord Robert of Flanders, son of the great count of Flanders, in order to make peace between the most illustrious lord king of France on the one part and the aforesaid great count of Flanders and his people on the other, humbly and devoutly visited the shrine of the Blessed Virgin Mary at Rocamadour and there made his offering on the altar of the blessed Virgin Mary aforesaid. And we granted the said lord Robert, pilgrim of the Blessed Virgin, the indulgences written herein. In witness of which fact the seal which we use for such purposes is appended. And we notify by this present letter all whom it concerns or may concern. Given at Rocamadour on the aforesaid Friday, in the year of our Lord 1321. [Ibid.]

7. The penitential tariff of Oudenarde, 1338

To St Nicholas of Bari, or 20 pounds of Paris
To St Peter's and St Paul's at Great Rome, or 12 pounds
To St James in Galicia, or 12 pounds
To San Salvador in Asturias, or 10 pounds
To St Peter's at 'Meorke', or 8 pounds
To St Francis at Assisi, or 10 pounds
To Our Lady at Pisa, or 12 pounds
To St Martin's at Lucca, or 12 pounds
To St Andrew's in Scotland, or 8 pounds
To Our Lady at Salisbury, in England, or 6 pounds
To St Ambrose of Milan, or 12 pounds
To Our Lady of Pietra Santa, or 12 pounds

To Our Lady of Rocamadour, or 8 pounds
To St Gilles of Provence, or 8 pounds
To St Nicolas-du-Port, or 4 pounds
To St Matthias at Triers, or 3 pounds
To the Three Kings of Cologne, or 40 shillings of Paris
To Our Lady of Aachen, or 30 shillings
To Saint-Josse [Picardy], or 30 shillings
To St Martin of Tours, or 4 pounds
To Our Lady of Chartres, or 3 pounds
To Vendôme to Our Lord's Crown, or 3 pounds
To St Maur at Paris, or 40 shillings
To Our Lady of Mussi [near Chatillon], or 4 pounds
To Saint Guilhem-le-Désert [Montpellier] or 7 pounds
To St Eutrope in Poitou, or 6 pounds
To Our Lady of Gottesbüren, or 6 pounds
To Our Lady of Vauvert, or 8 pounds
To the Two Maries by the Sea [near Arles], or 9 pounds
To St Florent at Orange, or 8 pounds
To St Maximin [St Mary Magdalen], or 9 pounds
To St Mary Magdalen at S. Baume, or 9 pounds
To St Victor at Marseille, or 9 pounds
To the Holy Cross at Strumberg, or 5 pounds
To St Thomas of Canterbury in England, or 6 pounds
To Our Lady of Hulsterloo, or 12 pounds
To Notre Dame de la Treille [Lille], or 12 shillings
To the Church of Utrecht, or 20 shillings
To St Eloi at Noyon, or 30 shillings
To Our Lady at Reims, or 40 shillings
To Our Lady of Aardenburg, or 12 shillings
To St Julian at Brive, or 5 pounds
To St George in Distel, or 10 shillings
To Our Lady of Alet, or 8 pounds
To St Lambert at Liège, or 30 shillings
To St Servatius at Maastricht, or 24 shillings
[Van Cauwenbergh, pp. 222–3.]

8. Urban V to the bishop of Liège: 1364, March 20th

On the petition of Renier de Thorèle de Berneau and Catherine, widow of Renier de Quoedeu. The last-named was murdered by friends and kin of Catherine as a result of which there was a long armed feud. When this was settled she married the other Renier, and they have contravened the laws, being kin in the third degree. Dispensation is conceded on condition that Renier go within two years to St James, and they can then contract matrimony anew. In the meantime they are to separate. [Urban V, *Communes*, n. 10832.]

9. Urban V recommends to the archbishop of Bordeaux that pilgrimages be imposed on members of the military companies who desire absolution from excommunication: 1366, November 18th

... Also, that those able to sail should within a year of absolution set sail and spend as long on pilgrimage, visiting the Lord's Sepulchre and other holy places overseas, as they have been members of the companies aforesaid; and if in the meantime a general passage should take place, those who are fit should be obliged, instead of those visits, to fight against the infidel for the stated time. The weak and those permanently incapable of sailing should be instructed to go within six months to Rome and to stay there for a year, and every week of that year to visit the shrines of the blessed apostles Peter and Paul and the other places in the City which penitents are accustomed to visit, and then they should visit the shrine of St James in Compostela ... [Urban V, *Communes*, n. 20130.]

10. The dean, treasurer and chapter of St Martin of Tours certify performance of pilgrimage: 1406, July 16th

We certify that John Daple, of the town of Lier, diocese of Cambrai, has come in person to our church and visited as a pilgrim the holy tomb and shrine of the most glorious confessor of Christ, blessed Martin, our patron, as was recommended to him by his judges, with appropriate authority, as he informed us on his own oath, in penance or expiation imposed on him by reason of verbal injuries perpetrated by him. ... The said pilgrim has stated on his oath, in the name already given, that he performed this pilgrimage on his own behalf and not for anyone else, and this we certify to all whom it may concern by these presents, sealed with the seal which we use on various occasions. [Van Cauwenbergh, p. 216.]

11. A delinquent painter of Tournai, 1428

Henri le Mieri, painter, according to information received and otherwise, has always been accustomed to abuse and quarrel with others, and even to utter seditious and slanderous words, trying to creatre trouble and discord, and among other things has untruthfully and without cause maliciously accused the officers, elected and otherwise, of the commune of having been the cause of punishments and executions which have been inflicted on several people, in fact for their demerits, asking whether more officers were wanted to cut off heads as they had done, and stirring up the indignation of the people of the town against them, and other words tending to discord, disturbing and impeding the goods of peace and justice. And he will not be able to come back to the town unless with the agreement and consent of the whole people and community, assembled by colleges and banners for the purpose, and he will pay a fine of twice ten pounds, and make a journey to Our Lady of Rocamadour. [Rupin, p. 215.]

· ·

CHAPTER 3

Indulgences and Jubilees

In the course of the twelfth century, the granting of indulgences for pilgrims to churches all over Christendom became commonplace. By this means, shrines and relics were given a more exactly quantitative salvific value than they had previously had. It did not escape notice that the practice was open to over-use if not outright abuse, and in 1215 the Fourth Lateran Council legislated both to subject the verification of relics to the authority of the Roman Church and to restrict the amount of indulgence that bishops could grant to forty days [2]. It was pointed out that even the pope, who possessed the plenitude of power, normally restricted his grants to this level, and for much of the thirteenth century this remained true, as in two grants by Innocent IV to the cathedral of Cologne, in which he enunciated current 'official' views of the rationale of indulgences and the justification of pilgrimage [3].

There is no certain evidence that a plenary indulgence was available to pilgrims anywhere before 1300. It is highly unlikely that the indulgence available on 1st August at the church of Santa Maria degli Angeli just outside Assisi, which enclosed the little church of the Portiuncula where Francis had died, was plenary at this date, but it was, or was believed to be, generous enough to be attracting pilgrims before the end of the thirteenth century.[1] By this time the indulgences available at Rome itself were expanding. In 1289 Nicholas IV issued a confirmation of all the indulgences which he claimed that his predecessors, according to traditions written and unwritten, had granted to the basilica of St Peter. Indulgences of seven years and seven 'quarantines' were available on a long list of major feast-days, principally those associated with Christ Himself and saints Peter and Paul, while three years and three quarantines were obtainable virtually every day in June and July. A distinguished list of saints' days merited one year and forty days. The forty-day indulgence, which early in the century the Lateran Council had nominated as the normal maximum, was now available on every day in the year which was not otherwise provided for.[2]

In 1300, responding it seems to the expectation of pilgrims that something special would be available to them in this centenary year, Boniface VIII offered a plenary indulgence to those who visited the basilicas of the apostles during the year [5]. To earn it, the non-Roman had to spend fifteen days performing the prescribed visits, and the inhabitant of Rome thirty days. In 1291 Nicholas IV had awarded different quantities of indulgence to pilgrims to St John Lateran, according to their place of origin [4], and Boniface himself had employed a similar principle when making a grant to the shrine of St Mary Magdalen at St Maximin in 1295, distinguishing between inhabitants of Provence, who received forty days' remission, and others, who received one hundred days. This principle was, however, inapplicable when, as now, plenary remission was in question, although Boniface's bull somewhat muddied the waters by suggesting that pilgrims could receive the indulgence *more* effectively by doing more than the prescribed minimum.[3]

The success of the Jubilee, according to contemporary observers, was immense, perhaps in part because the scope of the indulgence offered was misunderstood to encompass the sinner's guilt as well as his penance;[4] this was to become an almost commonplace error. Boniface's intention was that the Jubilee would occur once in a century, but early in the first year of his pontificate (1342–43) Clement VI, resident at Avignon, yielded to pressure from the Romans among others, and in the bull *Unigenitus* proclaimed a second Jubilee to be held in 1350 [6,a]. The bull began by explaining the theology of the Treasury of Merits, which provided the rationale of indulgences; recapitulated the provisions of Boniface VIII's indulgence; explained the reasons for narrowing the interval between Jubilees from a century to fifty years; and ended by proclaiming the Indulgence itself. Basically, Clement repeated Boniface's stipulations, but he added the requirement that the pilgrim must visit the Lateran basilica as well as those of St Peter and St Paul.

The circumstances were now very different from those of 1300. Indeed, the circumstances of the fourteenth-century popes were in many respects abnormal. They were absent from Rome from 1305 to 1378, and then the Great Schism began. In 1300 Boniface had capitalised on what he perceived to be the public mood, proclaiming the indulgence only when the year was two months old. Clement gave abundant notice of what was going to happen in 1350. This gave time for other interested parties to make their dispositions,[5] and also for excited and misleading rumours to spread about the conditions of the indulgence. The legist Albericus de Rosate, who himself attended the Jubilee with his wife and three children, transcribed into his dictionary of civil and canon law not only what he wrongly believed to be Clement's bull (his text bore little resemblance to *Unigenitus*), but another variant which he thought 'beautiful', although he was doubtful of its authenticity; he noted that it was not *bullata*, nor were its provisions actually observed at Rome.[6]

This second and particularly garbled version included a lengthy narration of the vision of St Peter which had supposedly inspired Clement to proclaim the Jubilee, and elaborated considerably on the conditions of the indulgence. Some of its emendations clearly served the interests of the other greater Roman churches which had for centuries been on the pilgrim itinerary. Not only Roman residents, but the inhabitants of all Italy, from Calabria to Piedmont, were to stay in the city for a month and visit every day not only St Peter's, St Paul's and the Lateran, but Santa Maria Maggiore, San Lorenzo fuori le Mura, Santo Croce in Gerusalemme, San Sebastiano and the cemetery of Calixtus with its 174 martyrs and seven martyr popes. Foreigners also had to perform this enlarged circuit, but they had to stay for only fifteen days. When the faithful had completed their visits, the *sudarium* of Jesus Christ would be shown to them and at the sight of it the plenary indulgence would take effect, returning the pilgrim to the state he was in on the day of his baptism. The *sudarium* was the cloth preserved at St Peter's, sometimes called the 'Veronica', on which Christ had miraculously imprinted an image of his face.[7] In *Unigenitus*, Clement VI had mentioned not the *sudarium*, but the equally miraculous image of Christ preserved at the Lateran. The exhibition of the Veronica, which had been growing in celebrity in the course of the thirteenth century, had, however, been a feature of the 1300 Jubilee, and in 1350 Clement issued a string of instructions to his officials at Rome to permit private views of the relic to distinguished visitors.[8] To what extent was their eagerness to see it a reflection of contemporary Christ-centred piety, of a belief in its special efficaciousness as advertised in the bogus bulls, or both?

If these 'bulls' imposed additional burdens on the pilgrim, at least in terms of the number of churches he had to visit, they also offered more than Clement VI genuinely intended, and more than the theologically (or historically) well-educated could have sanctioned. The version which Albericus believed to be authentic urged that everyone could 'achieve *more* merit and obtain the indulgence *more effectively*' by visiting Santa Maria Maggiore and San Lorenzo as well as St Peter's, St Paul's and the Lateran. (Here, however, the forger may have taken his cue from the rather dubious clause already noted in Boniface VIII's bull, to which nothing in *Unigenitus* corresponds; Clement evidently knew better.) In the longer, still more fantastic, version, 'Clement' confirmed all the indulgences allegedly granted by the 203 popes from St Peter onwards, and finally promised that, if anyone returning from obtaining the indulgence were at diabolical instigation to fall into sin and so die, he would automatically be absolved.

The real Clement went so far as to concede, in *Unigenitus*, that the confessed and penitent pilgrim who set out on his journey but was unavoidably prevented from reaching Rome, or, having arrived there, died before he could complete the prescribed visits, would still receive the indulgence; but in a letter of March 1350 to Philip VI of France [6,c] he insisted that it could not be granted, as the king and others had requested, to the old, the sick, or to persons such as enclosed nuns who for other reasons could not personally make the journey.[9] The fictitious bull was much more lenient, requiring of those impeded by 'broken-down old age or unavoidable infirmity' that they say instead 350 Paternosters with the Salutation of the Blessed Virgin. Secular clergy could free themselves to come by placing a substitute in their benefices for the duration of a year, without any need for episcopal permission. The monk, black or white, received a special concession: if his abbot refused to grant him leave of absence, he could demand it in the presence of three senior monks, together with the cost of his victuals, clothing and footwear for a year.

Clement did in fact issue a number of mandates, during and after 1350, directing abbots to re-admit monks who had attended the Jubilee without licence: sometimes they were to exact no penalty, sometimes they were to apply 'the ordinances touching apostates'.[10] The pope never implied that the conduct of these monks was covered by a blanket prior permission, but misunderstanding was not un-natural. Even the forger, however, stopped short of according a like licence to nuns, contenting himself with providing that if they could not obtain permission from their superiors to make the pilgrimage, they should say the psalter every week instead.

These false bulls were widely influential, not least in England. A reader of the very compressed account of the Jubilee in the chronicle of the Cistercian abbey of Meaux in Yorkshire [6,b] could be forgiven for thinking that the sight of the *sudarium* alone was sufficient to convey the indulgence. The versified English guide-book called *The Stacions of Rome* repeatedly stressed the antiquity of the indulgences available there.[11] The belief that Clement had issued a general permission for monks to attend the Jubilee even without the licence of their superiors was still current when preparations for the 1450 Jubilee were in hand. William, abbot of Bury St Edmund's, Henry VI's proctor at the Roman court, represented to Nicholas V 'the perils of Clement VI's statute allowing religious to go to Rome without licence of their superiors in order to gain the Jubilee indulgence'. The pope in response declared the conditions on which monastic personnel, from abbots down to servants, farmers and tenants, could receive the indulgence without stirring from home.[12]

Clement VI's attempt to insist on the physical performance of the pilgrimage had in fact soon broken down, at least retrospectively. On 8th January 1351 the queen of Hungary was awarded all the benefits of the indulgence as if she had personally been to Rome, and on 14th May Edward III of England, his wife, his mother, Edward prince of Wales, and Henry earl of Lancaster received the same privilege. On 6th September 1352 the pope awarded the indulgence to the inhabitants of the island of Majorca on condition of a payment of 30,000 florins, which the bishop was to collect.[13] In themselves, these concessions merely paralleled what had happened when, for slightly different reasons, the crusading indulgence was conceded to persons who sent a substitute or provided finance for a crusading expedition. The belief that pilgrimage (or other pious exercises) could be performed vicariously, and the merit due to it acquired thereby, underpinned the practice of late medieval testators who left money for this purpose.[14] When exercising their prerogative of permitting the commutation of vows, or delegating that power to the subject's confessor, the popes were answering a real need which could be created by old age or sickness, but they were also contributing to what might now be termed a 'culture' in which one good work was interchangeable with another. By a variety of means a wedge was inserted between the physical performance of the pilgrimage vow and the acquisition of its spiritual benefits.

The popes had now set their feet on a road which seemed to lead in two quite different directions. On the one hand, they had many reasons, even when themselves resident at Avignon, to promote pilgrimage to Rome. They were the living representatives of the apostles who were thus venerated; they had to consider both the interests of the Romans and the demands of pilgrims. On the other hand, the popes derived benefit also from the grant of generous indulgences to churches elsewhere in Christendom, in response not merely to 'popular' pressure, but to the interests of bishops, abbots and clergy everywhere. The circumstances of the Great Schism increased the pressure in both directions. Urban VI, his position threatened by an anti-pope, decided in one of his last acts that Jubilees should be held every thirty-three years in honour of the age of Christ, and announced one for 1390, which he did not himself live to see. According to the English chronicler Walsingham, the pretext was 'the diminished life-span and strength of men'.[15] Having presided over this Jubilee, Urban's successor, Boniface IX, offered the indulgence to numerous persons throughout Christendom on terms which closely resembled those on which the popes usually permitted the commutation of vows to go on pilgrimage.[16] The stipulation, sometimes but not always made, that the beneficiary must physically visit certain churches preserved something of the principle that pilgrimage should involve not merely expense but bodily effort. Meanwhile, Boniface was notoriously lavish with grants of indulgence to other churches, frequently plenary and described as the equivalents (*ad instar*) of the indulgences available on certain days at the Portiuncula (the most frequent choice), St Mark's Venice, or St Mary's Aachen.[17]

Boniface's grant to the city of Cologne in 1394 is of particular interest for a number of reasons [7]. This was a replica of the Roman Jubilee indulgence (the terms of which Boniface recapitulated), solicited by the urban magistrates, on behalf, not just of the cathedral, but of the numerous churches in the city which possessed celebrated relics. Boniface conceded the indulgence, and the offerings made by actual pilgrims, to those churches, but the offerings made in order to obtain the indulgence by those who were unable or unwilling to come in person were divided between the rebuilding of the abbey church of St Heribert, in Deutz just across the Rhine from Cologne, and the repair of the churches of Rome. The involvement of the urban magistrates, in soliciting and in administering the indulgence, is conspicuous; their representations were rewarded with further grants of indulgence in September of the same year.[18]

By the middle of the fifteenth century, the papacy had weathered the schism and, now established at Rome with reasonable security, had embarked on the long-suspended task of creating a fitting capital city for the Vicar of Christ. A Jubilee was accordingly celebrated in

1450, and the decision (which still holds) was taken to hold the Holy Years at intervals of a quarter of a century thereafter. The quantities of indulgence available at Rome, and not only in Jubilee years, had grown extravagantly; already before 1400 the author of *The Stacions of Rome* could assure his readers that there was absolutely no need to put themselves out to go to Jerusalem ('over the see') or Compostela in order to obtain 'pardon'.[19] It might not even be necessary to go to Rome. A Parisian diarist in 1446 sagely commented that the indulgence that had just been made available at Notre Dame de Pontoise (which had been badly damaged in the wars with the English) was the same as the one to be had at Rome, but did not take as long to get.[20] The popes had to try to orchestrate the situation, particularly if churches arrogated to themselves the power to award plenary indulgences, as Martin V complained Canterbury did in 1420 for the second centenary of Becket's translation [9]. More circumspect fifty years on, the Canterbury authorities successfully obtained such an indulgence from Paul II.[21] The popes sought to ring-fence their own Jubilees: in 1473 a plenary indulgence was conceded to St Andrew's, to be obtainable on the feast of St Andrew and throughout the octave, in every one of the next seven years and once every three years thereafter, 'the Jubilee year always excepted'.[22]

The exception was probably intended as much to safeguard a source of revenue as to guarantee a stream of pilgrims to Rome. The rebuilding of Rome was an expensive preoccupation, and the advance of the Ottoman Turks in the eastern Mediterranean gave additional point to the established practice of marketing the Jubilee indulgence after the event. In November 1450 Nicholas V made the current Jubilee indulgence available to James of Scots and his whole kingdom, on conditions which included the transmission of one-third of the oblations received to Rome for the repair of the basilicas, while in 1454 he was advertising its continued availability in order to raise money for the support of the overstretched order of St John of Jerusalem. In May 1476 the Pope appointed John abbot of Abingdon papal nuncio to Edward IV and collector of the monies from those who had not been able to go in person to Rome for the 1475 Jubilee, the proceeds to go to the war against the Turk; the offer was renewed in 1478.[23] In 1520 the Canterbury authorities were struggling through their diplomatic representatives in Rome to obtain their latest Jubilee indulgence, but negotiations foundered, partly on the pope's determination to have half the proceeds for the rebuilding of St Peter's.[24]

The indulgence as fund-raising device was now well established. A mobile and well-informed person, at most times of the year, could have been assured that a plenary indulgence was available at a church somewhere near him. Minor indulgences, which it was in the power of bishops to grant, continued to be obtainable at churches all over Christendom, as they had been since the twelfth century. These too were frequently available not only to to those who went in person to the church, but to those who sent money for its restoration.[25] Indulgences were of course also available in respect of many pious activities other than pilgrimage, for example, the devout recitation of certain prayers, and the popes also granted to individual Christians the power to choose a confessor who would administer plenary remission to them on their deathbed. What impact did this apparent inflationary spiral have on the physical performance of pilgrimage? Did the volume of, say, Holy Land pilgrimage (at its height surely only undertaken by relatively few) decline from what it might have been because it was perfectly possible to obtain comparable indulgences elsewhere?

It has been suggested that 'down to the middle of the thirteenth century pilgrims above all sought to venerate the relics of a saint and to beseech his protection, while from the later thirteenth century the earning of indulgences came clearly into the foreground'.[26] Whatever truth there may be in this view, it would be rash to think that late medieval pilgrimage was monothematic. Fra Niccolo da Poggibonsi, who went to the Holy Land in 1346, frequently remarks, in his *Libro d'Oltramar*, that 'Here there is great indulgence', 'Here there is indulgence of guilt and punishment', 'Here' (more prosaically) 'there is indulgence of 7 years and 70 days'. When, however, his party penetrates to the monastery of St Catherine at Sinai, and stands before the tomb of St Catherine, he strikes a different note: 'For great joy and devotion everyone began to weep, like people who had found what they had longed for; and for a long time we had longed to come to that blessed body.'[27] That there was an element of emotional release here, after the arduous journey across the desert, hardly alters the fact that more was in question than indulgences.

Margery Kempe went not only to Rome, the Holy Land and Compostela, but to Assisi, Wilsnack and Aachen, as well as to numerous shrines in England. She was, undoubtedly, aware of indulgences and believed in their efficacy. She went to Syon Abbey 'for to purchase her pardon through the mercy of the Lord'.[28] Yet no reader of her story could doubt that she had many other motives for her peregrinations, not least her love and devotion for the person of Christ, who after all had gone far to assure her personally of her salvation. Her description of her visit, or visits, to the Portiuncula is instructive in this respect. 'She was there also on Lammas Day, when there is great pardon of plenary remission, for to purchase grace, mercy and forgiveness for herself, for all her friends, for all her enemies and for all the souls in Purgatory.' On another occasion, however, she 'was shown our Lady's kerchief which she wore here on earth, with great light and great reverence. Then this creature had great devotion', which she expressed in her characteristic manner. For the devout and excitable Margery the first-hand experience was irreplaceable, and for many the experience of beholding with one's own eyes the locations of the birth, life and death of Christ had (and has) a value all its own.

There can be no doubt that what may be termed the culture, even the commodification, of the indulgence was influential. There are widespread testimonies to the belief that the benefits of pilgrimage could be shared, as it were by prior agreement, by persons who were not themselves going but had contributed to support the journey. It can hardly be doubted that for centuries benefactors who had underwritten pilgrimage costs had hoped to benefit spiritually from the prayers of the pilgrims, or from their own 'good work' in supporting an act of devotion. Now the dissemination of itemised lists of the indulgences available at Rome and elsewhere gave the pilgrim and his stay-at-home well-wishers a more precise notion of what it was they had to share. One prospective member of the party with which Leonardo Frescobaldi (a member of one of the most prominent Florentine banking families) went to the Holy Land in 1384 was prevented by family and political cares from going: Leonardo and his remaining companions each agreed 'gladly' to give him the third part of the indulgences they acquired: 'May it please God to make them valid for him and for us.'[29]

Criticism of these developments is hard to distinguish from the criticism of pilgrimage in general which, partly reworking old-established themes, takes on new vigour in this period.[30] The report of one man's criticism that is given by a highly interested party, a monk of Canterbury, is revealing in its very tendentiousness. In 1370, the ill-fated Simon Sudbury, bishop of London, allegedly told a party of pilgrims on the road to Canterbury for the Jubilee indulgence that they would derive no benefit from it. His indignant hearers accused him of impugning the merits of St Thomas himself, and their prophecies that Simon would meet an evil end were fulfilled when (as archbishop of Canterbury) he was murdered by the rebels of 1381.[31] We are not in fact told on what grounds the bishop based his judgement. If he was really questioning the intrinsic value of the indulgence, he was impugning papal authority, not the merits of St Thomas, who theologically speaking had nothing to do with the case. It is perhaps more likely (if in fact he said what is attributed to him) that Simon was sceptical of the penitence and contrition of the pilgrims, which alone could validate the indulgence. It was not, perhaps, a point on which pilgrims or the custodians of shrines always insisted too scrupulously. Leonardo Frescobaldi, however, seems to have been aware, at least in theory, that indulgences might or might not be effective.

The mere influx of large numbers of pilgrims, who required hospitality and many of whom might be too poor to make really substantial offerings in return, did not necessarily guarantee a profit to the shrine. Woodruff long ago calculated that despite the large sums received at Canterbury Cathedral in both the Jubilee years of 1320 and 1370 the cellarer's expenditures were correspondingly large, and the accounts show a considerable adverse balance.[32] The chapel of St James in the cathedral of Pistoia obtained a plenary indulgence from Boniface IX in 1395; the receipts from offerings over the next decade suggest diminishing returns after a highly profitable beginning.[33] The quest for indulgences on the part of churches may have originated as much in the desire to maintain prestige, to obtain what befitted the church and its saints, as it did from scientific calculations of advantage, although hope doubtless sprang eternal. A greater proportional profit may well have gone to the lay population of a city which housed a celebrated shrine. As for the pilgrims themselves, people continued to need help in the trials of life; and the journey doubtless retained its lure for many. The late medieval Christian could have been forgiven for thinking that he needed all the indulgences he could get, but as a human being he remained subject to a variety of impulses that could lead to pilgrimage.

DOCUMENTS

1. Eugenius III to the church of San Frediano, Lucca: 1149, December 19th

As we believe has come to your notice, we with our own hands and at the instigation of God (*Deo auctore*) have consecrated the church of blessed Frediano, out of reverence for his body which is believed to repose there, and, trusting in the merits of blessed Peter and Paul, have granted an indulgence of forty days of enjoined penance to those who come there for the annual celebration of that consecration. We also grant that anyone who, for any reason, cannot be present there on that day and who shall come within the octave of that dedication, shall receive this remission, on the part of almighty God and blessed Peter and Paul His apostles. [*PL* 180, cols 1404–5.]

2. The Fourth Lateran Council, 1215: From *c.* 62

... In addition, since because of the indiscreet and excessive indulgences which certain prelates of churches grant, the keys of the Church are belittled and not feared, and penitential satisfaction is weakened, we decree that, when a church is dedicated, the indulgence may not extend beyond a year, whether it be dedicated by one bishop or several; and subsequently, on the occasion of the anniversary of the dedication, the remission of enjoined penance granted shall not exceed forty days. We also direct that letters of indulgence granted for any cause whatsoever shall observe this number of days, since the Roman pontiff, who holds the plenitude of power, has been accustomed to observe this norm in such matters. [Alberigo, pp. 263–4.]

3. Two grants by Innocent IV to the cathedral of Cologne

(a) 1245, July 30th

If the people of Israel, who lived under the shadow of the Law, went frequently to the place where the Lord had chosen to plant his name, and offered many vows and offerings, the Christian people, to whom the benevolence and humanity of the Saviour have been made manifest, are as much the more obliged to frequent with due honour the churches in which Christ, immortally and incorruptibly alive, is daily sacrificed in order to erase the stain of our crimes, and there to make offerings in purity of heart, as the experience of reality is more certain than the riddles of symbols. Since therefore in the church of Cologne especially the relics of saints repose in reverent safekeeping, we ask, advise and exhort you in the Lord, enjoining it upon you for the remission of your sins, that you come to the aforesaid church with devotion and reverence and in purity of heart. We, desiring that this church should be frequented with due honour, grant forty days of enjoined penance every year, out of the mercy of Almighty God and by the authority of the blessed Peter and Paul, His apostles, to all those who are truly penitent and confessed and who visit that church annually on the day of its consecration. [*Quellen zur Geschichte der Stadt Köln*, ed. L. von Ennen (6 vols, Cologne 1860–79), 2, p. 244.]

(b) 1247, April 6th

Although He, by whose gift it comes about that He is well and laudably served by His faithful, out of the abundance of His pity, which exceeds the merits and vows of the suppliants, repays those who serve Him well with much more than they are able to merit, we nonetheless wish to render the people acceptable to the Lord, and invite the faithful of Christ to be pleasing to Him, with certain enticing gifts, indulgences and also remissions, that they may thereby be rendered more receptive to the divine grace. Desiring therefore that your church, in which the bodies of the Three Magi, resplendent with many miracles, are conserved under reverent guard, should be frequented with due honour, we mercifully concede forty days of enjoined penance each year to all, truly penitent and confessed, who reverently visit that church on the annual feast-day of those saints, out of the mercy of Almighty God and by the authority of the blessed Peter and Paul, His apostles. [Ibid., n. 256, p. 258.]

4. Nicholas IV awards indulgences to pilgrims to St John Lateran: 1291, March 23rd

He concedes indulgence to all those truly penitent and confessed who visit the Lateran basilica, in which the heads of the saints Peter and Paul are bestowed, on each day on which the holy image[34] is exposed, [that is, the feasts] of the Saviour, saints Peter and Paul and blessed Agnes; to Romans, and inhabitants of the Campagna, the Marche and other adjacent regions, four years and four quarantines;[35] to Tuscans, Apulians and Lombards, five years and five quarantines; to those from beyond the mountains and those crossing the sea, seven years and seven quarantines. To those who visit it on every feast of the blessed Virgin Mary, and also of saints Bartholomew, Matthias, Laurence, the Forty Martyrs and Euphemia, and during the eight days following, two years and two quarantines. On every [remaining] day of the year, one year and forty days. [*Les Registres de Nicholas IV*, ed. E. Langlois (2 vols, Paris 1905), 2, p. 677.]

5. Boniface VIII proclaims the first Jubilee: 1300, February 20th

It is the reliable report of our ancestors that great remissions and indulgences of sin have been granted to those who come to the honourable basilica of the Prince of the Apostles at Rome. We therefore, who in pursuance of the duties of our office, seek and willingly provide for the salvation of all, ratify, confirm and approve all of these by apostolic authority, and also add to them and by means of the present writing make this known. So that the apostles Peter and Paul should be the more greatly honoured by the devout attendance of the faithful at their basilicas in the City, and the faithful themselves should know that they are fortified by the boon of spiritual benefits as a result of their attendance, we, out of the mercy of almighty God and relying on the merits and authority of His Apostles, by the advice of our brothers and in the fullness of apostolic power, grant to all who in this present year 1300, beginning from the feast of the Nativity of Our Lord Jesus Christ just past, and in every hundredth year following, come reverently to those churches, truly penitent and confessed or about to do penance and confess, in this present year and every hundredth year to come, not only full and complete, but the most total forgiveness of all their sins; stipulating that any who wish to participate in this indulgence granted by us, must come to those churches for at least thirty days, continuously or at intervals, and at least once a day, if they are Romans; if however they are foreigners or non-Romans (*peregrini aut forenses*) for fifteen days in a similar manner. Everyone however, who frequents the basilicas more often and more devoutly will merit more and obtain the indulgence more effectively. [*Les Registres de Boniface VIII*, ed. G. Digard (4 vols, Paris 1907–39), 2, n. 3875.]

6. The Jubilee of 1350

(a) 1343, January 27th: Clement VI proclaims the indulgence: From the bull Unigenitus

... Decreeing, by the common consent of our brothers aforesaid and in the apostolic fullness of power, that all the faithful of Christ who, truly penitent and confessed, in the year from the Nativity of the Lord 1349 next and thereafter for all time from fifty to fifty years, shall in the prescribed manner and out of devotion visit the aforesaid basilicas of the apostles Peter and Paul and the Lateran Church (which we read Constantine of illustrious memory built in honour of the Saviour when through the blessed Silvester, as through the apostles themselves, by God's revelation he acknowledged them, and was reborn in the baptismal font and cleansed of the contagion of leprosy, and blessed Silvester dedicated it with a new manner of sanctification and chrism; on the walls of which church the painted image of the Saviour first appeared to the Roman people, to be devoutly venerated; which church, for these and other reasonable causes, we order to be honoured so that it shall be adorned with the same privilege of indulgence, and the devout people may receive from the Saviour, whose wondrous nature is proclaimed in the Apostles, by their merits and prayers, the bounty of indulgence) shall receive the fullest forgiveness of all their sins (*plenissimam omnium peccatorum suorum veniam consequantur*); in this manner, as follows, that whoever wishes to obtain the indulgence, if a Roman, shall be bound to visit the aforesaid Basilicas and Church at least once a day for at least thirty days, continuously or at intervals; foreigners and non-Romans for at least fifteen days in like manner; with the addition that those also who, coming to the basilicas etc. in order to obtain these things, and having set out on their journey, are genuinely prevented from reaching Rome, or die on the road or in Rome before they have completed the prescribed number of days, if truly penitent, as aforesaid and confessed, shall obtain the indulgence. Each and every indulgence granted by us and our predecessors as Roman pontiffs, both to the basilicas and churches aforementioned and to others in the said city, we confirm and approve and renew, by apostolic authority and make known by the force of the present writing. [Grandisson 1, pp. 154–5.]

(b) A popular version

In the Year of our Lord 1349, there appeared in a vision to the lord Pope Clement VI at Avignon a venerable person, holding two keys in his hands, who said to the pope, 'Open the door, and send fire forth from it, by which the whole world may be warmed and illuminated.' And when the pope hesitated about whether this was a true vision or a phantasm, he saw a similar vision for a second time. Whereupon the pope summoned together the cardinals and the clergy, and considering the condition of human beings of great age, that because of the decrepitude of age they cannot survive for the full indulgence of sins once established in the city of Rome by pope Boniface VIII at hundred-year intervals, wherefore many remain frustrated of their desire for the aforesaid indulgence, he changed the indulgence, established at every hundred years, to every fifty years. So he made available to all Christians who came to the holy city of Rome in that fiftieth Jubilee year indulgence and remission of sins. And he granted that whoever resolved to set out on pilgrimage to that holy city, on the day that he set out from his home, should be able to choose a confessor on the way who should have full power of absolution of all papal causes; and if, being truly confessed, he was overtaken by death on the way, he would be free of all his sins and completely absolved. The said Pope also directed the angels of Paradise to take his soul, totally absolved in purgatory, immediately to the joys of Paradise. The *sudarium* of our lord Jesus Christ would be shown to those arriving at the said holy city, and having seen this they would be absolved of their sins, and would have indulgence of them, restoring them to the state they were in on the day on which they received holy baptism. He also confirmed all the indulgences granted by 200 supreme pontiffs, which are innumerable. Wherefore, from every part of the world, countless people of both sexes flocked to Rome, because of these indulgences, in that fiftieth year of Jubilee. [Meaux 3, pp. 88–9.]

(c) 1350, March 3rd: Clement VI to Philip VI of France

... Concerning your request that we should concede the indulgence as granted in the fiftieth year to those visiting in the prescribed manner the aforesaid basilicas and church [of the Lateran] to the old, crippled and sick, and to those afflicted by personal danger or disease, and enclosed nuns; just as many kings and princes, when the indulgence was first proclaimed, asked that it be granted to them without their visiting the basilicas, putting forward many reasons why this should be done; it has been decreed, by the common consent of our brothers the cardinals of the Holy Roman Church, that no one, of whatever status, condition, religious order or rank, no matter with what dignity they be invested, may obtain this indulgence except by personally visiting the basilicas ... [Clement VI, *France*, n. 4426.]

7. Boniface IX grants the Roman Jubilee Indulgence to Cologne: 1394, April 16th

The most devoted city of Cologne, faithful daughter of the Roman church, by the virtues and merits of the Three Kings, who in the flesh offered three gifts to Christ the King and, it is said, rest there bodily; of the most holy eleven thousand virgins; of the holy Thebans Gereon and his companions (these virgins and Thebans and Moors shed their precious blood there for Christ);[36] of the archbishop St Severinus, a contemporary of St Martin; and saints Cunibert, Ewald, Felix and Nabor, Gregory of Spoleto, Hippolitus, Felix and Audactus, Vitalis, Albinus and many other martyrs and confessors, whose bodies and relics similarly repose in various monasteries and churches in the same place; worthily merits that the apostolic see, which as a loving mother always seeks the salvation of souls, should gladly provide that the faithful of those regions may abundantly obtain the divine mercy and pardon for their sins in the aforesaid city. Some while ago Pope Urban VI of happy memory, our predecessor, moved by certain reasonable considerations, and with the consent of his brothers, the cardinals of the Holy Roman Church (of whom we were then one) and out of the fullness of apostolic power, decreed and ordained, that all truly penitent and confessed Christians, who in the one thousand three hundred and ninetieth year from the nativity of our Lord Jesus Christ (then to come, now past), and thereafter in perpetuity every thirty-three years, who personally and out of devotion visited the basilicas of the blessed apostles Peter and Paul, and the Lateran, and Santa Maria Maggiore, at Rome, should receive the fullest possible forgiveness of their sins, on condition that anyone wishing to obtain that indulgence, should be bound to visit those basilicas and churches for at least thirty days, continuously or at intervals, if a Roman, and for at least fifteen, if a foreigner or non-Roman, as in the letters composed by our said predecessor is more fully contained. Since therefore, as we hear, many people of both sexes in the aforesaid city and diocese and province of Cologne and the surrounding areas, who did not obtain that indulgence because they did not come to Rome in that year, desire to become sharers in it and obtain it, and since we have been humbly petitioned, by the magistrates, citizens and consuls of that city, that we should with apostolic generosity take action on these matters, we, like a merciful father taking profitable thought for the salvation of the souls of these people, and hearkening to the supplications of the above magistrates and consuls, trusting in the mercy of almighty God and the authority of the blessed Peter and Paul His apostles, by these presents mercifully grant, that a confessor (out of twenty or more suitable confessors, if it should be necessary, of the secular or regular clergy, whom our venerable brother the archbishop of Cologne or his vicar in spirituals, and our beloved son the collector or sub-collector of the debts of the Apostolic Camera in those parts shall think fit to appoint for the purpose) may choose to grant, that any person of the city, diocese or province of Cologne, or of regions within three days' normal journey surrounding that province; together with foreigners, nobles, merchants and others who happen to be or to come there during the period of this grant; or has otherwise obtained this indulgence by apostolic authority; of either sex and of whatever status, dignity, religious order or condition they may be, even if they enjoy the episcopal dignity, and who humbly seeks it, truly penitent and confessed; who, thus penitent and confessed, [visit] the major church of Cologne, and the churches of St Martin and St Pantaleon, of St Maria im Kapitol, of the monasteries of the order of St Benedict, of St Severinus, of the Twelve Apostles, of Gereon, of the 11,000 Virgins and of St Cunibert, for at least fifteen days if they are of Cologne, and for at least seven, continuously or at intervals, if they are an outsider or foreigner, at least once a day within a year reckoning immediately from the first day of September next. That is, those of the aforesaid persons who can conveniently do it; they however who are impeded by old age, weakness, ill health, considerations of religion or other just cause, in place of these visits may, according to the judgement of a suitable confessor whom they shall appoint for the purpose, choose prayers, or send another person in their place who may perform these visits on their behalf, or other works of piety, and may each of them obtain this indulgence and remission of sins, as if they had, within the year prescribed by our predecessor aforementioned, visited the the basilicas and other churches of Rome in person, on this condition however, that their confessor commute into other works of piety the physical labour which they would have undergone if that had come to Rome on this account in the said year; and that each of these persons shall be bound to hand over the expenses which they would have incurred in making the journey to Rome, staying there and returning home, according to their status (*secundum earum decentiam*), and the offerings they would have made to the aforementioned churches, to two trustworthy and suitably qualified clerical receivers (of whom the aforementioned collector or sub-collector shall appoint one, and the magistrates and consuls the other), in full or as the collectors according to their judgement shall think fit, on which point we grant them the power of judgement according to their conscience; of which expenses, offerings or pledges on account of them half shall be faithfully spent, at the direction of the magistrates and consuls, on the rebuilding and repair of the church of the monastery of St Heribert of Deutz near Cologne, of the aforementioned [Benedictine] order, recently, as we hear, entirely destroyed; the other half shall be faithfully transmitted to the aforementioned city [Rome] to be spent on the fabric of the churches and basilicas of that city. The other offerings which these people make in visiting the churches of the city of Cologne shall be spent on the purposes of those churches by their rectors, faithfully and in their entirety, on the conscience of the collectors and sub-collectors of the magistrates, consuls and rectors. [*Quellen Zur Geschichte der Stadt Köln*, 6, pp. 221–4.]

8. 1402, January 1st

Boniface IX grants to penitents who at stated times visit and give alms for the conservation of the church of the Augustinian priory of Kyrkeby super Wrethek, dioc. Lincoln [Kirby Bellars, Leics.], 'the same indulgence as is granted for visits to St Mark's Venice on the feast of the Ascension from the first to the second Vespers. The prior and six or more priests may hear confessions and grant absolution, except in reserved cases, and commute vows of pilgrimage and abstinence. Penitents who are detained by infirmity or otherwise lawfully hindered, and who send their alms, may gain the indulgence as if they had made their visits in person.' [*CEPR* 5, p. 489.]

9. 1423, March 19th

Mandate to James bishop of Trieste and Master Simon of Teramo, doctor of canon and civil law, collector for the *camera* in England, papal nuncios, to make diligent enquiry as to the truth of what the Pope has learned, namely that archbishop Henry and the prior and chapter of Canterbury appointed for the year 1420 a Jubilee, after the manner of the Jubilees ordained by the Popes, with promise to all who should visit the church of Canterbury of the plenary remission of sins gained in time of Jubilee by visit to the shrine of the Apostles at Rome, and appointed penitentiaries to give absolution from all sins, or rather to ensnare simple souls and extort from them a profane reward, thereby setting up themselves against the apostolic see and the authority of the Roman pontiff, to whom alone so great a faculty has been granted by God. [CEPR 7, p. 12.]

10.   1434, August 28th

Licence that in the chapel of St Thomas the Apostle within the parish of St Ludgvan, situated in Cornwall, divine service may be celebrated by any suitable priest, with indulgence of forty days for all faithful Christians visting that chapel by reason of pilgrimage or contributing goods to the upkeep of the said chapel. [Register of Edmund de Lacy, Bishop of Exeter 1420–1455, ed. G. Dunstan (3 vols, CYS 60–66) 1, p. 279.][37]

. . . .

CHAPTER 4

Help and Hazard: The Pilgrim's Experience

The hazards of pilgrimage were many and in some cases obvious. Some were the hazards of all travel, generated by nature and man: wind, wave and weather, on the one hand, and everything from brigandage to bad inns on the other. In so far as pilgrimage arguably created crowds where they might not otherwise have been, and increased the numbers of people traversing certain routes at certain times, it had the potential to aggravate these basic problems, not least because it attracted malefactors. Robbers knew that at certain times there would be large numbers of people, possibly unarmed, on the road to Rome; swindlers and mountebanks of all kinds knew that at any popular shrine there was a promising market of possibly credulous people, eager to have their money changed, desperately in need of accommodation at almost any price, willing to buy the shoddiest goods. Already in the earlier twelfth century, the 'sermon' known as *Veneranda Dies*, falsely attributed to Pope Calixtus II, denounces the villains who defrauded or otherwise endangered pilgrims.[1]

If successfully publicised, indulgences held out the promise to the custodians of a shrine, and to local traders, of larger than normal numbers of pilgrims; but these numbers would be concentrated on to a day or into a period of a few days in a year, with the consequent impact on problems of order and security and also on the supply of basic living requirements for pilgrims. This was not, of course, entirely new. A saint's major feast-day (perhaps accompanied by a local fair) was always a high point in the year, and there had long been a seasonal dimension to the movements of pilgrims, for example at Easter. Disasters such as occurred at Rome in 1450 when the Ponte Sant'Angelo collapsed under the weight of pilgrims moving to and

from St Peter's [B1,d] had older precedents; in 1018 fifty people had
died in a crush at the church of St Martial in Limoges on the saint's
feast-day.[2] Devout women were easy game: a Perugian statute of
1343 lamented that women, including 'foreigners', attracted by the
indulgence lately granted to the church of San Domenico by Benedict
XII, were subjected to all kinds of insult.[3] Pilgrims were also quite
capable of causing trouble themselves. Riots at a shrine could result
in the shedding of blood (and more than blood, according to Innocent
IV on one occasion), and necessitate the reconsecration of the church,
a process which the popes agreed to ease for the benefit of several
important shrines [A10].

To travel at all meant (if one was prudent) taking thought both
for the security of one's person and property on the road, and for the
safeguarding of the interests one left behind. Preparations would be
both secular and spiritual, from raising the money for the trip, making
a will and appointing attorneys, to participating in the valedictory
rites provided by the local church.[4] Seemingly distinct in character,
these diverse types of preparation were synthesised in the minds of
some contemporary observers, for whom the liturgical farewell
possessed a defining legal value. 'He is understood to be a pilgrim
who publicly, with the knowledge of the priest and [his fellow-]
parishioners, departs from his place ... and according to the custom
of the country leaves an attorney.' Again, 'Solemn pilgrimages are
said to be when the pilgrims, having received leave in their parish,
with cross and holy water, are escorted or accompanied processionally
out of the parish on their way to Jerusalem, Rome or St James.'[5] The
concept of the pilgrimage as a publicly certified undertaking is evident
in the reluctant concession embodied in Norman custom, that if a
woman were disseised, or otherwise suffered a wrong during her
husband's absence outside the province on 'a known pilgrimage (in
celebri peregrinacione)' or on business abroad, she might be heard in
court, lest her husband's delay should deprive her of the inquisition
within a year and a day provided in such a case; if her husband was
in the province, however, she was by no means to be heard in his
absence.[6] Some of these legal privileges the pilgrim shared with
others, such as merchants. Others were special; for example, at St
Gilles he theoretically enjoyed a remarkable freedom to withdraw
from a contract to buy or sell, and was also specially protected in
matters of money-changing [A7]. The pilgrim's ceremonial leave-
taking differentiated him from other types of legitimate traveller, as
did his reason for setting out, whether this was a sentence of peni-

tential pilgrimage, a vow, or a less binding voluntary intention, devout or otherwise.

Illness, injury or other problems (real or alleged) could prevent an intending pilgrim from ever setting off, and this might mean seeking a dispensation from vows, or even from a sentence of penitential pilgrimage.[7] Some of our documentation in fact has to do with pilgrimages that were never performed. It is easy to get the impression that extravagant vows of pilgrimage were made which had little prospect of fulfilment, or that occasionally pressing claims of other business (royal service, for example) were used as an excuse not to fulfil them. This is unlikely, however, to have been the whole truth. Not only may fighting men have been moved to make such vows in moments of remorse, or at least pessimism about their eternal prospects, but, however ill-thought-out, the project of an arduous and itself dangerous journey to a spiritual goal fitted well into what we may imagine to have been their general culture.[8] The vow of pilgrimage (like the crusading vow) was appropriate to the self-image of the man of rank who wished to advertise his orthodox piety and his awareness of the duties of his station. Explanations of a different order are perhaps needed for the backsliding of many ecclesiastical dignitaries who also had to be absolved from pilgrimage vows that they later perceived to be inconvenient. Humbler folk might sometimes plead inconvenience too, but they could of course experience genuinely difficult personal circumstances, and ill-health could afflict anyone.

Papal dispensations and absolutions thus amplify our picture of pilgrimage, and pilgrimage vows, as elements in a total religious culture. The papal power of dispensation was part of the armoury of 'help' available to pilgrims, and the pope's responses to such requests sometimes give us moving glimpses of personal and domestic predicaments. Occasionally pilgrims *manqué* seem to have been so desperate to be absolved from ill-considered vows that they presented the pope with alternative excuses, either of which would have sounded more convincing without the other. There was, for example, the party from Lautrec, in 1367, who had vowed to go to Jerusalem; deterred by stories of 'the savagery of infidels in those parts', they added for good measure that they were anyway far too poor to go.[9] A father and son from Salerno simultaneously claimed, in 1363, that the former was suffering from gout and the latter from piles.[10]

Like so much else in the later middle ages, dispensation and commutation became to a large degree systematised. The pope frequently granted petitioners the right to choose a confessor who could absolve them from their vows, but usually vows to adopt a life of continence or chastity, to enter religion or to perform the 'major' pilgrimages to Rome, Jerusalem or Compostela, were excepted and reserved to the pope's own dispensing power. Pilgrimage vows might be commuted into 'other works of piety' or 'a salutary penance' imposed, or both; the petitioner could be required to send to the shrine the offering he would have made or, not infrequently, to contribute its value to another fund currently dear to the pope's heart, normally the crusading subsidy. The Lautrec party above-mentioned had to give the cost of their abandoned pilgrimage to the fabric of the church of Lautrec. These procedures closely resembled those used when Jubilee indulgences were granted to persons who had not in fact made the journey to Rome.[11] In addition, the pope (like other superior authorities) facilitated actual pilgrimage. Occasionally he solicited alms and good will on behalf of particular pilgrims [A27]. He might dispense (male) religious to make pilgrimages with or without the consent of their superiors, or intervene to obtain access for women pilgrims to shrines from which they would otherwise have been debarred.

A not uncommon feature of the papal registers in the fourteenth century was the issue of permissions to pilgrims to visit the Holy Sepulchre. Papal concern about improper commercial dealings (for example, in slaves) was virtually as old as Christian–Muslim relations, but this attempt to regulate the Holy Land traffic was more specifically rooted in concerns which dated from the loss of Jerusalem, first to Saladin and again after Frederick II's brief negotiated tenure of the holy city ended in 1239. In c. 71 of the Fourth Lateran Council in 1215, Innocent III prohibited dealings with the infidel and imposed a four-year moratorium on the sending of ships to the Holy Land while Christendom mustered its forces for a new Crusade. These provisions were echoed by Gregory X at Lyons in 1274, where the moratorium on shipping was extended to six years.[12] Popes thereafter periodically reaffirmed the anathema on those who flouted the trade embargo. These declarations did not specifically mention pilgrims, but it did not escape notice that illicit commerce could be carried on under the guise of pilgrimage and that pilgrims themselves contributed to Muslim prosperity (as commentators had been aware already in the eleventh century).[13] The French pope Urban IV (1261–64) laid the foundations of a policy which cast the count of Anjou not only as papal champion in Italy, but as the spearhead of a crusade to reassert Latin control of Constantinople and ultimately the Holy Places. In

October 1263 Urban reissued the provisions of c. 71 of the Fourth Lateran Council. A few days before, he had conferred a variety of powers on Walter bishop of Worcester, who was to preside over the preaching of the Cross in England. Among them was the authority to absolve, either personally or by deputy, 'those who contrary to the prohibition of the holy see or of its legates have visited the Lord's Sepulchre and those who have conveyed iron, arms, timber and prohibited goods to the Saracens, and others who have given them counsel, aid or favour against Christians'. Urban's successor Clement IV exactly echoed these words when on 7th May 1265 he granted the archbishop of Tyre power to absolve such people.[14]

Evidence for the continuance of this policy is afforded by the permissions issued in the fourteenth century and the very much less numerous references to absolution of those who had flouted it [A15,d]. In about 1350 Leopold von Suchem wrote:

> He who would go to the said Holy Land must beware lest he travel there without leave from the Apostolic Father, for as soon as he touches the sultan's country he falls under the sentence of the Pope, because from the time the Holy Land came [again] into the hands of the sultan, it was, and remains, excommunicate, as are likewise all who travel there without the pope's leave, lest by receiving tribute from the Christians the Muslims should be brought to despise the Church. For this reason, when any traveller receives his license to go there from the Apostolic Father, in addition to the leave which is granted him, there is a clause in the bull to the effect that he shall not buy or sell anything in the world, save only victuals and clothes and bodily necessaries, and if he contravenes this he is to know that he has fallen back again under sentence of excommunication.[15]

A workable, if somewhat precarious, normalisation of the situation was achieved from the middle of the century onwards, with the Franciscans, as official guardians of the holy places, responsible for the supervision of pilgrims, and the Venetians running a regular package-tour business. From this period date the numerous guidebooks and first-hand narratives which survive in both manuscript and early printed editions. Leonardo Frescobaldi's account of his embarkation from Venice in 1384, quoted here [A21], is but one (though one of the earlier) of such accounts.[16]

Pilgrims, like other travellers, might fall sick and die while performing a pilgrimage. Meritorious this might be, but it was also inconvenient, not least if the pilgrim found himself surrounded on his deathbed by strangers eager to lay hands on his property; efforts were therefore made, by the popes and others, to outlaw this abuse [A4]. Both Alfonso X of Castile[17] and the commune of Siena [A13] legislated to safeguard the testamentary rights of pilgrims. The 1308 Lucchese statute prescribed that all 'hosts' in the city must take a comprehensive oath to treat their guests 'of any condition whatsoever, *peregrini*, merchants or others' with every care and consideration, benignly recommending to them, if they fell sick, that they should take care of both their souls and their goods.[18] Sometimes special burial-places were provided for *peregrini*, though this, even at a relatively late date, could simply mean 'foreigners' and not necessarily 'pilgrims' in the narrow sense. Hospital foundations, which dealt with a transient population of sick as well as pilgrims, often possessed their own burial facilities. Archbishop Diego Gelmírez of Compostela in 1128 granted land to the hospital of St James for the construction of both a church and a *sepultura* both for those already buried there and for future use, and Innocent IV in 1252 similarly authorised the order of St Antony of Vienne to build four oratories, with as many cemeteries, at its houses at Marseilles, Bourges, Aubenas and Montferrand, for the use both of the brethren and passing *peregrini*.[19] It might be deemed necessary to make it clear that a proposed cemetery was solely for *peregrini*, who stood outside the parochial structure [A,3]. A *peregrinorum sepultura* existed at Broni, between Piacenza and Pavia, where Contardo d'Este, on his way to Compostela in 1233, was for a time buried until he was recognised to be a saint and translated to the church itself. The story of his sickness and death amounts to a *novella* illustrating the trials of the moribund pilgrim, left behind (with his consent) by his companions who wanted to fulfil their vows, and inhospitably ejected from his lodgings because his sufferings were troublesome to his fellow-guests.[20]

If death represented the extreme hazard a pilgrim might expect to encounter, there were others, from bad roads and broken bridges to rascally innkeepers and surly alewives, which do not just appear in miracle collections. Vested interests might obstruct the provision of more effective services. The holy man Allucius of Pescia (d. 1134) founded one of his hospitals on the 'public road' near the Arno, at a site probably to be identified with Ponte a Signa. Pilgrims frequently came to grief in the 'great river' nearby, but when Allucius asked the bishop of Florence to build a bridge there, he discovered that local notables were making a handsome profit out of a ferry service, and it was they whom he had to persuade to permit a bridge to be built.[21]

Isolated or wooded stretches of road along major routes were always problematical. A Becket miracle story tells how a man called Fretus built a *xenodochium* on the eastern side of a hill seven miles from London, where robbers were wont to prey upon travellers, but he needed miraculous assistance to locate the necessary water-supply.[22] A statute enacted around 1330 at Modena, on the old Roman highway across northern Italy, required anyone who owned land along speci-fied stretches of the road to build a house there and cause it to be inhabited 'so that pilgrims passing along the Strata Claudia may go in greater safety and not be interfered with by anyone'.[23]

The more developed society that was now coming into being had a wider range of potential remedies for old problems, but could not always guarantee their effectiveness. It was easier to meet a short-term demand for lodgings and basic foodstuffs than to achieve permanent improvements in the state of roads and bridges. The sudden flow of pilgrims to Rome in 1300 alerted the Bolognese authorities to the deplorable state of the roads 'by which pilgrims pass from Bologna via Florence to Rome', and the *capitano* thereupon instituted a system of inspection of bridges and bridge hospitals, but in 1380 they were found to be in a dilapidated condition. One of them, which should have been staffed by three lay-brothers, had one, who had been there for about forty years.[24]

The Bolognese, situated at a nodal point on what had always been a major thoroughfare, were bound to be aware of the pilgrim traffic which passed in both directions. In 1321 and 1324 the commune handed out doles of grain to poor pilgrims to Compostela; in both years, hospitals were being built to cater for pilgrims among others.[25] In 1378, the *Compagnia di San Giacomo* in the church of the Augus-tinian Hermits was 'by ancient custom' giving a dinner for departing Santiago pilgrims on Easter Monday. The Company had a firm grip on alms-gathering by pilgrims: 'it was not permitted ... for any pilgrim during Holy Week, nor during Easter, to go about begging alms on the pretext of his [pilgrimage] vow, if he had not previously received written permission and been admitted by the said Company, which collected the names and surnames of pilgrims at a table set up for the purpose in the cathedral.' At the behest of the Company, the *capitano* proclaimed penalties, on 19th April, for anyone falsely claim-ing to be going on the pilgrimage. In 1407, 522 departing pilgrims were entertained to dinner by the Company; there were processions, triumphal cars 'and many spiritual representations', and the rich and noble gave generous alms to the pilgrims.[26]

Everywhere a variety of brotherhoods offered support services for pilgrims, both their own members and others. Some achieved considerable fame, holding property and raising funds on an international scale. The order of Altopascio possessed property all along the roads to Compostela. Already, by the end of the twelfth century, the celebrity of the mother-house was such that in a record of the itinerary of Philip II of France on his return from the Holy Land in 1191 it was called simply 'the Hospital'. The Order possessed a house just to the south of Paris, known as St Jacques de Haut Pas (a Gallicization of 'Altopascio') which was a first stop for pilgrims departing from the French capital.[27] The equally famous hospital of Roncesvalles in the Pyrenees and the order of St Antony of Vienne, already mentioned, also possessed networks of dependencies and conducted fund-raising tours, in England as elsewhere. The king of England took such orders and their property under his protection, and also, from time to time, issued edicts against bogus alms-gatherers who were collecting in their name.[28] A poem written in praise of the hospital of Roncesvalles around the beginning of the thirteenth century declared that: 'Here man performs the six works which God orders lest, when the day of Jubilee should come, he be adjudged guilty and thus a Pharisee by the faithful.'[29] In 1321 Edward II granted protection for messengers sent to England to collect alms on behalf of the hospital of St Mary Roncesvalles 'in consideration of the benefits constantly given in that hospital to poor pilgrims visiting the shrine of Santiago'.[30]

More localised brotherhoods were involved in the administration of hospitals, and there were also pious confraternities reserved for past or intending pilgrims, to Compostela or elsewhere, some of which were similarly active. There was a 'society' of 'men and persons who have gone to the church of St James of Galicia' at Assisi early in the fifteenth century. Twenty such people met on 18th September 1418 and appointed a proctor to oversee the creation of a hospital. In the previous July, a testator had left his own house for this purpose: there were to be beds there for the accommodation of the 'poor of Christ'. In 1424 the bishop united this new hospital with another already existing, and in the following year it was referred to as the 'recently created hospital of St James and St Antony'. In 1439, thirteen members of 'the society of the hospital of St James and St Antony of Assisi' met to elect proctors. The hospital oratory, splendidly frescoed later in the century with stories of both saints, still exists.[31]

Hospitals as such catered increasingly for the sick and the genuinely indigent rather than for the average pilgrim. Raimondo 'Palmario' of

Piacenza had been an enthusiastic, even an over-enthusiastic, pilgrim in his earlier life, but when at Christ's command he turned to charit-able works in his own city his concern was for the poor and the infirm; pilgrims benefited if they were otherwise vulnerable. The house he established near the church of the Twelve Apostles in Piacenza was 'excellently suited to receive the poor of both sexes, whether they were *peregrini* or sick'. Subsequently feeling the need to make separate provision for women, he set up another establishment nearby, staffed by chaste matrons, which was more luxurious but also more secluded: 'Here he admitted not only woman pilgrims but also poor [female] citizens, devoid of all means of support.'[32] His follower Gualtiero of Lodi, similarly, was himself a practitioner of pilgrimage, but his many hospital foundations were 'for the honour and glory of God and the refuge of the poor'; it is their location, on main roads along well-established routes certainly used by pilgrims, which sug-gests that they catered for pilgrims among others [A6].

It was consistent with this tendency that when hospital provision was made for pilgrims, it might be hedged by conditions. The revised statutes of the Eastbridge Hospital at Canterbury in 1342 provided that priority was to be given to the poor sick pilgrim over the healthy one, who was accommodated for one night only [A18]. At Hildesheim too, in 1440, the hospital of St John would offer only one night's lodging to the healthy pilgrim. Here the authorities required that the pilgrim established his *bona fides* by showing his 'letter', and enforced strict segregation of male and female pilgrims into separate chambers. The sick pilgrim was assured of nursing until 'he got better or died'; his clothes and valuables were taken from him and carefully inven-toried and stored, to be returned to him on his recovery; if he died, they were absorbed into the common stock of the hospital.[33] Pilgrims came from every stratum of society, and at one end of their socio-economic range could still be identified, as in the earlier medieval centuries, as a species of God's poor. The party with which Margery Kempe rather reluctantly travelled to Aachen surely qualified: they begged their way, and before entering a city deloused themselves [A23,d], a detail which suggests the appropriateness of the bequest made in 1474 by a widow of Hildesheim for the provision of two 'soul-baths' for pilgrims on their way to and from Aachen [A26].

Some pious guilds, not specifically dedicated to pilgrimage, in-cluded among their statutes the provision that a brother or sister going on pilgrimage should receive a small subsidy from the other members, and that he or she should be escorted out of the town on departure, and if possible, greeted on his or her return. It might be explicit, in such a case, that the guild members were in fact investing in the pilgrimage and expected to share in the spiritual benefits obtained [A22,a].[34] Apart from their good wishes, and this small measure of material help, there was little such brotherhoods could do to ensure the success of the pilgrimage. The dangers of seafaring were unalterable, and the saints were kept busy rescuing their devotees, on the way to and from the Holy Places, as well as on other sea journeys. Land routes were periodically rendered hazardous by local warfare which bred brigandage, not least the Anglo-French conflict of the fourteenth and fifteenth centuries; the fragmented landscape of Italy also presented problems. In 1349, planning for the Jubilee, Clement VI urged the cities of Italy, as well as Edward III and Philip VI, to make peace so as to ensure access to Rome. He also wrote to the Roman nobles urging that they take action against highwaymen, but to judge from the experience of two Sienese pilgrims in 1333 the highwaymen were often working for the nobles [A17]. One would-be pilgrim to Rocamadour, a mariner of Bordeaux, was deterred from going because of the presence of the English and of brigands along the way: arangements were made for him to deposit his offering with a merchant of Bordeaux.[35] High-ranking pilgrims sometimes disguised their identity to avoid unwelcome attentions, as the bishop of Rodez did when he went to the Jubilee in 1350 [B1,b].

Increased pilgrim traffic generated opportunities for profit: pilgrims had money which others wanted to get. There were both violent and non-violent means of getting it. The manufacture and sale of special pilgrimage souvenirs seems to have begun in the west in the twelfth century, but the association of pilgrimage churches with marketplaces and with sundry opportunities for profit was certainly not new, as examples of commercial activity around the shrine of Ste Foy at Conques in the tenth century attest.[36] The supply of wax and the manufacture of candles was an important ancillary activity generated by churches in general in their need for lighting: pilgrims often made offerings of wax, including models of affected body parts, or even of whole children, in thanks for healing miracles. The early twelfth-century oath of the money-changers, inscribed in the portico of the cathedral of Lucca, was exacted also from the 'spicers' (*spetiarii*), who provided wax.[37] This oath covered transactions in private lodgings as well as in the *curtis* of the cathedral, but later in the century at St Gilles, money-changers were forbidden to do business with pilgrims in their lodgings [A7,a]. The author of *Veneranda Dies* included both

Lucca and St Gilles, with Le Puy, Tours, Piacenza, Rome, Bari and Barletta, in a list of academies of fraud, where tricksters allegedly sent their apprentices to learn the trade. Clearly this author believed that wherever there were pilgrims there was chicanery, adding the names of Leonard (Noblat), St Mary Magdalen (Vézélay), St Michael (Mont St Michel), John the Baptist at St Jean d'Angély and Bartholomew at Benevento to the list of saints who were aggrieved by the treatment their pilgrims received.[38]

Authorities lay and ecclesiastical tried, probably with limited success, to protect the pilgrim from over-pricing and other sharp practice. The town council of Hildesheim was much concerned with the welfare of pilgrims who passed through the city on their way to Aachen; in 1517 and again in 1527 they issued proclamations against the over-pricing of provisions, lodging and money itself, stipulating, in 1517, a rate of exchange for the Hungarian penny.[39] The authorities also, however, tried to ensure what they regarded as legitimate profits. One common way of trying to secure both was to proclaim safe-conduct and freedom from toll for all peaceful and legitimate travellers to major feasts and indulgences and to the fairs which frequently accompanied them, in the expectation, as the Perugian authorities said in 1433, that both public benefit and private profit would accrue [B2,f]. Intervention on the part of higher authority to prevent the exaction of tolls from pilgrims remained necessary [A11].

The 1300 Jubilee took almost everyone by surprise, from the pope downwards, and hospitality for pilgrims had, to a large extent, to be improvised. By contrast, it was possible to plan for 1350; the pope and his officials at Rome did so on their part, and other prospective beneficiaries on theirs. At Siena on the *Via Francigena* in Tuscany,[40] a special levy was exacted from innkeepers who stood to profit from the flow of pilgrims. In April 1400, when pilgrims were flocking to Rome although there was no official Jubilee, special controls were instituted on the measuring of wine to avoid deception by wine-sellers, 'seeing that in this present time of Jubilee [*sic*] much wine is being sold retail in the city of Siena and in the suburbs'. At the same period, certain 'poor citizens' who made a living from the passage of travellers by offering lodgings and other 'refreshment' claimed that they were willing to pay the *gabella* to the commune, but sought to avoid the additional imposts of the guild of innkeepers, since they did not have an annual turnover of 25 *lire*.

In 1449 the Sienese government decided to review the *gabelle* exacted along the 'road to Rome', 'inasmuch as the time of the indulgence and the Jubilee approaches next year, during which time, it is thought by the majority of citizens, many people will be passing by ... and by many it is said that in time past it was usual at the time of indulgences to double the gabelles ... '. In December the officials of the *gabella* were, on the same principle, given full powers to increase the proceeds of the tax on bread, wine, meat and fish granted to places of resort along the *Via Francigena*. Innkeepers had to obtain licences to sell food retail. New food-shops and hotels sprang up; in 1465 the commune of Abbadia San Salvatore authorised the construction of an *albergo* on the *Via Francigena* which was to be exempt from the payment of *gabella*, *except* in Jubilee years. The efforts of local authorities were not, however, always sufficient to ensure an adequate supply of food and lodging. In 1350, because of the failure of supplies, it proved necessary to curtail the length of stay the pilgrim was supposed to make in Rome in order to obtain the Jubilee indulgence, but in 1450, according to one chronicler, the visitors wanted for nothing [B1,d]. A grain shortage during the winter of 1389–90 caused the Perugian authorities to forbid anyone to give bread to pilgrims, and indeed to close the gates against them. In 1450, however, they were endeavouring to ensure that pilgrims on their way to Rome from the direction of Gubbio proceeded by way of Perugia: a craftsman of Gubbio was remunerated for setting up a '*Maestà*' as a signpost, and an *interpres* was also hired to point pilgrims in the right direction.[41]

The selection of sources which follows makes no claim to cover every aspect of this vast and various area. It is a miscellany, which aims merely to give a picture of the problems faced by pilgrims and of the efforts made to ease their path and provide protection and support. It includes some extracts from two personal accounts of the pilgrimage experience, by the Florentine Leonardo Frescobaldi, a pilgrim to the Holy Land in 1384 [A21], and Margery Kempe of Lynn, a pilgrim everywhere that she could manage [A23]. A second section comprises some material relating to certain 'special occasions' on which an abnormal local concentration of pilgrims exacerbated routine problems: the Roman Jubilees and the annual Indulgence of the Portiuncula at Assisi, as seen from neighbouring Perugia.

DOCUMENTS

A. Privilege and Assistance for Pilgrims

1. The First Lateran Council, 1123

c. 16 That *Romipetae* and those visiting other sacred places, are not to be molested. If anyone lays hands on *romipetae* and *peregrini* visiting the shrines of the apostles and the oratories of other saints, or despoils them of the things they are carrying, or tries to inflict novel tolls and taxes on merchants, they shall abstain from Christian communion until they have made satisfaction.[42] [Mansi, 21, col. 285.]

2. Raimondo Palmario and his mother set out for Jerusalem, *c.*1160

Then, to fulfil their vows, they prepared the things necessary for their pilgrimage; and having taken leave of their friends and kin, as they should, they went to the most venerable bishop of Piacenza and addressed him thus: 'Most reverend father and pastor, we have determined to go hence on pilgrimage to the Holy Sepulchre: therefore, with our hands place crosswise we beg [permission] as is the custom of pilgrims.' When the holy bishop heard the mutual request of the mother and son, he placed a red cross on the breast of each of them, and said, 'Behold the sign which will guard you from all danger. May the most merciful Saviour guide you and bring you safely back. When you pray, be mindful of your homeland.' [Raimondo, p. 647.]

3. Foundation of a hospital church and pilgrim cemetery, 1168

Be it known to all both present and to come that I, Rodrigo by the grace of God bishop of Calahorra and Nájera, grant to you, lady Isabel, that you may build an oratory in the hospital which you are building in the town which is called Azofra and a cemetery for the burial of *peregrini* only, saving in all things episcopal rights. And the grant is on these conditions, that the chaplain shall be presented to us, and that he shall profess obedience, and he shall receive the cure of souls of pilgrims only, and shall be replaced by us, or our successors or vicars. You shall not receive there our parishioners alive or dead for burial. ... If however anyone wants to become a *conversus* in the service of the pilgrims, you shall receive him with our licence, on condition that his parish church does not lose tithes or first fruits. [*Peregrinaciones*, 3, p. 60.]

4. Alexander III to the clergy, judges and whole people of Benevento: 1169, July 24th

A custom, or rather abuse (*usurpatio*) is said have arisen in your city which is well known to be inimical to divine and human laws, and puts both the perpetrators and those who consent to it in danger of divine vengeance. That is to say, that merchants, travellers and pilgrims, who are lodged with someone in the city, if it happens that they become ill, are not permitted to leave the house, to make a will [disposing] of their goods, or to choose their place of burial if they should die, although the laws and the canons direct that the last will of the dying as to their burial and the disposition of their property is to be upheld. In fact, their goods are dispersed, part to our court, part to the church, and part to their hosts. Wherefore several people suspect that it sometimes happens that the sick are so badly treated by their hosts that, as a result of their cupidity, their death is hastened by their wishes and actions. Whence, our predecessor of blessed memory, pope Eugenius, fired with the zeal of his office, lest the Roman pontiff should be said to permit what he ought to censure and correct in others, abolished this vile abuse, which by long passage of time had become accepted as custom at Benevento, and decreed that it was bereft of force. But, after our predecessor went the way of all flesh, the pestiferous custom revived, thanks to human cupidity, and the root of bitterness germinated again out of greater negligence and dissimulation. We by the common consent and assent of our brethren condemn this custom, which rests not on any law but on simple cupidity and long usage, with a prohibition of permanent validity, and decree that it is without any effect, placing both burial and the disposition of goods in the free will of the departing, and removing from our court as from the city as a whole all taint of such immense avarice. The aforesaid persons in the city of Benevento shall henceforth have the right of leaving their lodgings and returning as they wish, and of changing their place, and choosing their burial, and willing their goods ... .[*PL* 200, cols 595–7.]

5. Trouble on the road from Santiago, 1188

It happened after a few days that two knights of the household of the king of England, whose names were Robert Poore and Ralph Fraser, crossed the land of the Count of St Gilles, returning from St James, which they had visited on pilgrimage, going via Toulouse; scouts of the count laid hands on them and arrested them and brought them bound to him and he imprisoned them. Much later the count negotiated with them, saying, 'If the count of Poitiers will release my servant, whom he has in captivity, free and unharmed, I too will permit you to go free and unharmed.' So, one of them, namely Ralph Fraser, was allowed to go to Richard count of Poitiers concerning their release and that of the servant of the Count of St Gilles. Count Richard, hearing that they had been captured on pilgrimage, returning from St James, told him that they would not be released by his agency, whether by his request or his money. He said that he would offend God and his blessed apostle James more if he gave something in return for their release, because respect for pilgrimage (*peregrinationis reverentia*) alone sufficed for their liberation. When they could get no other reply from him, they went to the king of France, who had come to that region to make peace between Count Richard and the Count of St Gilles, and told him all that had occurred, how they had been captured and held on their pilgrimage. On hearing this, the king of France commanded the aforesaid Count of St Gilles to let the pilgrims go, not for the love of the king of England, or of his son Count Richard, but out of reverence and love for the blessed apostle James. [*Gesta Henrici Secundi* (RS 49), 2, p. 35.]

6. Gualtiero of Lodi: hospital foundation in the early thirteenth century

When he had been fully instructed in works of hospitality, he observed a certain isolated place where many evils were committed, and which no one could traverse with safety or dared to, and decided in reverence of God and in honour and memory of the blessed apostles Philip and James to build a house there to be a perpetual refuge and assistance for passers-by. The land belonged to the commune of Lodi and the holy and upright man of God sought the Commune's help to undertake this task, that is, he asked for the property on which to build the holy house ... [Permission is obtained] ... He built the hospital, with a church, which is called the Misercordia, on the Milan road not far from the city of Lodi. ... Similarly, he built other hospitals in remote places, to the honour and glory of God and as a refuge for the poor: one at Vercelli, another beyond Tortona on the Genoa road, another at Crema, and the last on the river Vettabia, near the Milan road, not far from Melegnano. [A. Caretta, 'La Vita di S. Gualtiero di Lodi', *Archivio Storico Lodigiano*, ser. 2, 17 (1969), p. 18.]

7. Twelfth–thirteenth centuries: Legal privileges and protection of pilgrims at St Gilles

(a) 1178, October: Statute of Raymond count of Toulouse and the councillors of St Gilles concerning money-changers

... It is decreed that for a period of five years changers may lawfully change money for pilgrims, provided that they weigh their gold, silver or coin correctly and count their pennies, and their own which they are going to give them, without deception, and neither steal their money nor permit it to be stolen by their employees or others. And if they see that anyone is deceiving them, they are to denounce the offenders to the court or the consulate.

It is also decreed that the changers may carry out no exchange for pilgrims in inns, or in houses or shops. It is, however, conceded that they can lawfully carry out exchange for pilgrims in the house of the Hospitallers, of the Knights of the Temple or in the cloister of St Gilles; and if in weighing or counting they unknowingly make a mistake of one penny in a quarter-mark (*in denario uno de firtone eos ... fefellerint*), they shall not be held to account for it ... .

Also, the innkeepers of the town of St Gilles have sworn that they will not lead pilgrims into any houses, workshops or shops to change money, and that they will not change money for them, and that they will not permit them to be defrauded in exchange, and that they will uphold the exchanges of the town of St Gilles as lawful. If they slander them, or, by reason of any ill intention, deter pilgrims from them, they will incur the full penalty, in person and money, according to the present regulations. [*Layettes de Trésor des Chartes*, ed. A. Teulet (5 vols, Paris 1863–1909), 1, p. 119.]

(b) Twelfth-century customary of St Gilles, revised in the thirteenth century

c. 12 On any criminal or pecuniary charge which does not involve a public accusation of crime nor a question of real property (*ad immobilis rei questionem*), no one can claim legal privilege, whatever their origin and whatever the jurisdiction to which they are subject, unless by chance they are merchants or dealers or carters who are hiring their animals to transport goods, or pilgrims. With all such persons, because their patrimonies are situated far away, compensation is impossible. [*Les Coutumes de Saint Gilles (XIIe–XIVe siècles)*, ed. E. Bligny-Bondurand (Paris 1915), pp. 69–70.]

c. 17 ... It must not be omitted, that the the pilgrims whom we call *romevi*, who in order to fulfil vows to God have left their own homes, may, even after something has been handed over to them and the price counted out by them, rescind the contract and, having given back what they have bought, may recoup the price that they have given, to the extent that, even if something has been cut or otherwise removed from the whole quantity which they bought, they can nevertheless rescind the agreement and recoup the price, the seller making no deduction from the price on account of what has been removed. The same applies to things sold by them, if they change their minds. But the buyers who have contracted with them, even if they change their minds, cannot withdraw from the agreement. This privilege pilgrims can exercise while they are in the town and for two days after they have left it. [Ibid., p. 80.]

8. Norman legal practice in the thirteenth century[43]

(a) From Le Très Ancient Coutumier de Normandie

c. 42 Of Essoins. There are several ways of essoining: for illness which is contracted on coming to the court; for prison; for war; for pilgrimage to the saints; for being out of the country on secular business.

c. 43 Of Delays. For pilgrimage overseas [i.e. to Jerusalem] a year and a day; for pilgrimage to Rome, two months and two days; for pilgrimage to St James, two months and two days; otherwise to St Gilles, one month and one day, and for other [places] according to the manner of the pilgrimage. (*Coutumiers de Normandie: Textes Critiques*, ed. E.J. Tardif, 1, pt 2, *texte français et normande* [Rome–Paris 1903], pp. 32–3.]

(b) From the Summa de Legibus Normanniae in Curia Laicali

c. 94 Concerning those who have set out to Jerusalem, or on another pilgrimage or on business far away, it is to be understood that if a year and a day have not yet elapsed when they return, they shall have recognition of the seisin they had on the day and in the year when they set out from their homeland. [Ibid, 2, (Rome–Paris 1896), pp. 235–6]

c. 98, v. It is also to be observed that if someone dies overseas, at Jerusalem, or in Galicia, or in other pilgrimages or on business outside Normandy or in it, within a year and a day after his death is made publicly known at his place of residence, even if he died a long time previously, the heir shall have recognition of the seisin which he had on the day and at the hour when he left his home or country, and for as long as he is not of age he can have this recognition. [Ibid., p. 240.]

9. Gregory IX to the archbishop of Rouen: 1233, September 9th

We have received a grave complaint from the abbot and monks of St Michael-in-Peril-of-the-Sea [Mont St Michel], in the diocese of Avranches. Their monastery is built on a high cliff and is no small distance from land, and entirely surrounded by sea, which, its surface rough and the spirit of the tempest swelling, day and night with a double tidal motion advances to the place where the monastery is built and retreats to its accustomed station. It forbids safe access to those wishing to go to the monastery and for those wanting to leave makes departure excessively difficult and dangerous. When it happens that there is legal dispute between the monks and our venerable brother the bishop of Avranches on pecuniary or other matters, and they, summoned by his authority to appear in court, are not infrequently prevented, by the stormy sea or other canonical impediment, he does not consider that it is not in their power, constrained as they are by necessity, to appear in his presence whenever they wish, unless, when the time comes for the hearing, the Lord commands the sea and winds and favourable weather allows them a secure passage. It is not contempt of his mandate which forbids them to obey, but, although he could coerce them by means of the churches and other property which they are known to possess on the landward side, he passes sentence of excommunication or suspension on them for contumacy and as executor of his own judgement places the monastery under interdict. Thus it frequently happens that when pilgrims arrive thither from different parts of the world, there to obtain forgiveness of their sins, they are in no small measure scandalised and their ardour cooled when they find the monks, by whose prayers they believed they would be helped in the sight of the Lord, excommunicate and suspended from the divine office. Wherefore the same abbot and monks have urgently besought us to see fit to provide a remedy with paternal solicitude ... . [*Les Registres de Grégoire IX*, ed. L. Auvray (4 vols in 3, Paris 1896–1953), 1, n. 1519.]

10. Innocent IV to the abbot of St Gilles: 1246, March 29th

It has been put to us on your part that, since a multitude of pilgrims flows from different parts of the world to your church, in which the body of the most glorious confessor, the blessed Giles, reposes, because of the glorious miracles which the Lord frequently performs there, often because of quarrels and fights, which very frequently arise, the church itself is violated by the spilling of both blood and seed (*effusione tam sanguinis quam seminis violatur*). Wherefore you have humbly requested that we come mercifully to your aid in this matter. Bowing to your supplicatons, therefore, we hereby concede to you the entire faculty of having the church reconciled with holy water by any bishop you prefer, and as often as it shall for this reason seem to you necessary, without prejudice to the constitution which prescribes that this is to be done by [several] bishops.[44] [Innocent IV, 1, p. 266, n. 1781.]

11. Innocent IV to the queen of France: 1251, March 18th

We believe that you think it important that no injury should be done to anyone in your kingdom. However, the prelates of the kingdom of Denmark have passed to us a grave complaint, that certain tax-gatherers in certain places of your kingdom compel the messengers of the prelates themselves, travelling to the Apostolic See, and clerks of the kingdom of Denmark going to the schools, and the messengers of those clerks, and pilgrims passing through those regions to pay taxes and tolls on their horses and the things they are carrying with them, like merchants, although they are not merchants at all, and although they are prepared to swear that they are not bringing horses and goods in order to trade; wherefore the aforesaid prelates have humbly asked us to provide a remedy with paternal care. [Ibid., n. 5163, 2, p. 207.]

12. John cardinal priest of San Lorenzo in Lucina to the abbot and convent of Pontigny: 1255, April 9th

We deem it right that fitting honour should be paid by the faithful to the saints of God, and that devotion should enjoy the attraction of certain spiritual privileges. Since, therefore, some women from England, and even from more distant parts of the earth, inflamed by the zeal of faith and devotion, come in pilgrimage to visit the place where the most precious body of Blessed Edmund, Archbishop of Canterbury, reposes in your church, in consideration of their devotion, the length of journeys which they undertake, and the labours and difficulties they undergo, in order that such may obtain therefrom gladness of spirit, by the command of the Lord Pope, given to us by word of mouth, we permit, by the authority of these presents, that all such women, when accompanied by other women of good repute, may enter the said place and there in humility of spirit offer to God the sacrifice of the prayer of their lips, any contrary custom or statute of the Cistercian Order or of our monastery, whether confirmed by apostolic authority or in whatsoever way, notwithstanding. ... It is our will, however, that the said women, even though they be of the nobility, should not appear in the presence of the convent in the cloister, and should neither eat nor sleep within the precincts of the monastery. It shall be lawful, however, for them to enter the chapter room of the said monastery for the sake of asking the suffrages of your prayers. We have caused the foregoing to be done for the increase of the glory of the Confessor and the devotion of the faithful, and we confirm it with the authority of our seal. [Bernard Ward, *St Edmund, Archbishop of Canterbury: His Life as told by Old English Writers* (London 1903), pp. 210–11.]

13. Statutes of Siena, 1310–11

Dist. II, r. lxi. Item, we decree that if any merchant, *romeo*, pilgrim or other legitimate traveller dies in the house of any innkeeper or indeed any other person, in the city or *contado* of Siena, and that person has made disposition of his goods and the things he has with him, of which disposition there is a public document, or it is attested by three male and law-worthy witnesses, that disposition must be observed. And if he dies without making a will, the landlord, or he in whose house he dies, shall be bound to report and consign the goods and things that remain in his house to the lord and rector of the house of the Misericordia of Siena and the chamberlain of the consuls of the Mercanzia of Siena, so that they can be restored to a person who has the right to them. And if he has made a will, as has been said, the said will must in similar manner be delivered to the master of the Misericordia and the chamberlain of the consuls of the Mercanzia, so that it can be executed. This clause was enacted in 1292, the fifth indiction, in the month of May.

r. lxii And every pilgrim shall be free to lodge in whatever place he wishes and to leave the inn. [*Il Costituto di Siena volgarizzato nel MCCCIX–MCCCX*, ed. A. Lisini (2 vols, Siena 1903), 1, p. 409.]

14. Dispensations granted by John XXII from vows of pilgrimage to Compostela

(a) 1323, December 19th: To the bishop of Ösell (prov. Riga)

His vow personally to visit St James, made before his promotion when he was in peril on the sea, may be fulfilled by someone else, provided that he sends thither, in honour of the saint, what he would have spent over and above his necessary expenses, and in place of the bodily effort which he would have undergone on the journey, gives alms to the poor. [John XXII, *Communes*, 5, n. 18639.]

(b) 1331, July 28th: To the bishop of Paris

Hugh de Boville, knight of the diocese of Sens, when his wife Marguerite de Barri was gravely ill, uttered a vow that if she was cured of that grave sickness, they would visit the shrine of the blessed apostle James together, and Marguerite consented; but the aforesaid Marguerite, weighed down both by many childbirths (about twenty) and by the fact that she is getting on in years, and is in too delicate a state, cannot fulfil this vow, wherefore it is requested that it be commuted into other works of piety. [Ibid., n. 54378.]

(c) 1331, September 24th: To the archbishop of Rouen

Raoul, constable of France, 'vowed personally to visit the shrine of St James, and relying on the fact that several magnates and other nobles were undertaking an armed expedition against the Saracens in the kingdom of Granada, and agreed to go with the said constable, he vowed he would not bear arms until he had reached the goal of that journey; then, however, a truce was made between the king of Castile and the king of Granada and therefore the said magnates and nobles did not undertake the said journey. Wherefore the said constable has petitioned for the commutation of the aforesaid vows into other works of piety.' [Ibid., n. 55087.]

(d) 1331, November 20th: To the bishop of Paris

Jean le Mire, layman, when Joanne de Pacy, his wife, a woman of Paris, was labouring gravely in childbirth, so that men despaired of her life, vowed that if God delivered her happily from childbirth, he would go together with her to the shrine of the blessed apostles James, and she agreed to this vow. Although he has set out to fulfil this vow, the aforesaid Joanne, because she is normally pregnant every year, as she is at present, cannot without great bodily peril personally fulfil the vow; wherefore Jean begs that as his wife, to fulfil her vow in part, has sent a woman to visit that shrine at her own expense and cost, [the Pope] will deign to commute the vow, so far as it concerns Joanne, into other works of piety. [Ibid., n. 55710.]

15. John XXII and Benedict XII: Holy Land pilgrimage

(a) 1329, February 8th

Otto de Cauqualis, priest and professor of laws, living in the diocese of Narbonne, was born in the Holy Land of Jerusalem and brought up for some time in Cyprus; he came to the regions this side of the sea (*cismarinas*) and has lived here for several years. He is granted licence to visit the Holy Sepulchre and other holy places there, with six companions, taking with them those things without which they cannot complete the journey, but nothing else to the profit or advantage of the enemy. [John XXII, *Communes*, n. 44281.]

(b) 1329, April 24th: To Guillaume bishop of Mende

At the request of Louis duke of Bourbon the pope has conceded to him that he and his household may set out for the Holy Land, and that at the point of death his confessor may give him plenary absolution of his sins, and that he and his household may receive the indulgences which are normally granted to pilgrims to that land. But, if it should happen that he or members of his household should die, it is conceded to them that the bones of the dead, separated from the covering of flesh and the entrails, may be taken to wherever the dead have chosen to be buried. [Ibid, n. 45027.]

(c) 1329, July 19th: To Louis duke of Bourbon

He may escort his daughter Maria, betrothed of Guy, firstborn of

Hugh of Cyprus, there with a fitting escort in four armed galleys, and all those in the said galleys may visit the Holy Sepulchre etc., and merchants in the party may do business there and at Alexandria in non-prohibited goods. [Ibid., n. 45766.]

(d) 1337, May 7th: To the archbishop of Nicosia

He is authorised in the name of the pope and of the Roman Church to receive an oath from Villano of Tuscany (*de Tuscia*), servant of John de Lusignan and man at arms, who for fifteen years has served personally against the Saracens, that he will abide by the commands of the aforesaid church; he is then on this occasion to absolve the said Villano from the sentence of excommunication incurred by him because he visited the lands of the Saracens with prohibited goods and did business with them (although he made no profit) and also visited the Holy Sepulchre and paid tolls to the aforesaid Saracens against the apostolic constitutions and prohibitions.[45] [Benedict XII, *Lettres Communes*, ed. J.-M. Vidal (3 vols, Paris 1903–11), 2, p. 78, n. 6063.]

16. From the Statutes of Arezzo, 1327

Lib. III, r. lxxxi. That reprisals are not to be taken from those who come to shrines.

It is decreed that those who are visiting the shrines of any saints reposing in the city of Arezzo or its district, or at Rome, St James or the Holy Angel [i.e. St Michael on Monte Gargano, Puglia], and also ambassadors, shall have free passage through the city and district of Arezzo, nor can anyone seize them while they are passing, nor anyone coming to perform military service or to the funeral of anyone dying in the city or district of Arezzo, or coming to the festival of San Donato, or to the fairs ... . [*Statuto di Arezzo (1327)*, ed. G. Camerani (Florence 1946), III.81, p. 189.]

17. Petition before the Consiglio Generale of Siena: 1333, February 19th

Meo di Corario and Vanni di Gratia, citizens of Siena, submit 'that this year [i.e. 1332] in Lent, relying on the safe-conduct of the Romans, which safe-conduct and free licence the Commune of Rome notified and publicly announced by many heralds and proclamations to all those wishing to go to Rome, we actually set out to the aforesaid city to obtain the indulgences, and when we had got to within six miles or thereabouts of the city the people of Jacopo Savelli, citizen of Rome, on horse and foot ambushed us like robbers and attacked us on the public highway leading to Rome, and striking us and inflicting insult and violence on us took us captive by force to a certain castle of the aforesaid Jacopo Savelli and kept us there for several months in chains, both of us in one pair of fetters. Jacopo questioned us about our power and resources and not content with our replies, put us to torture and inflicted various torments on us, seeking the promise of a larger sum of money. At last he imposed a ransom on us, which we paid so as to obtain our release, thanks to a loan from our friends, namely, I Meo seventy gold florins and I Vanni 250, including the expenses we incurred to obtain our release. Wherefore, since the commune of Rome was the cause of our detention, because of our reliance on its proclamation of safe-conduct, by which we were deceived, and because they refused to give us any help when we asked for it, but totally refused it, like Jews devoid of all charity and brotherly compassion, and so that we may not be left bereft, we have recourse to your paternal care and that of the commune of Siena, seeking help and favour with filial devotion, asking and humbly supplicating you that it be resolved and decreed by you and the appropriate councils that by the authority of the said decree we be permitted freely and without penalty, ourselves and through our kin and friends and others, to seize, imprison and cause to be seized and imprisoned, in person and property, all Romans and *contadini* of Rome and property and other things belonging and pertaining to Romans and *contadini* and *distrettuali* of Rome. And that by the present authority of this decree we may have and be understood to have [the right of] reprisals ... .[46] [Siena, Archivio di Stato, Consiglio Generale 113, fol. 32v.]

18. From the revised statutes of the Eastbridge Hospital, Canterbury, issued by Archbishop Stratford: 1342, September 23rd

Poor and sick pilgrims, who have been seized by illness on their journey, but not lepers, may be received in the hospital. If they should die they may be buried in the cemetery of our church of Canterbury, in the place of old allotted for the purpose. Healthy pilgrims arriving there may be received for one night only. For the subsistence (*ad vitae subsidium*) of these pilgrims, both well and sick, we will and ordain that up to four pence be spent daily from the goods of the hospital. However we wish poor and sick pilgrims, arriving with the healthy, whether to stay or to receive subsistence at the above rate, to be given priority over the healthy. If it should happen, on any day, because no or few pilgrims arrive, that the sum is not spent, we wish that on other days, or at times when a large number of pilgrims, according to the norms noted above, [the expenditure] be supplemented with the result, that in this pious and laudable employment of the hospitals' goods, up to four pence is faithfully spent according to the number of days in the year.

We order that twelve beds shall be perpetually available in the aforesaid hospital for the use of the poor pilgrims flocking thither; and we wish that some woman of honest life, who exceeds forty years of age, shall serve as minister to the pilgrims, attending to both the beds and the necessaries of life as aforesaid. This woman is to be provided from the goods of the hospital with an adequate subsistence for all her needs ... . [*LC* 2, pp. 251–7.]

19. Dispensations issued by Pope Urban V

(a) 1363, April 17th: To his Vicar at Rome

We have been informed that although the holy Veronica and many other relics of the saints whose bodies repose in the City are shown to the Romans and to pilgrims to Rome (*Romipedis*) at Easter and at other times, nevertheless the most venerable image of our Saviour, which is kept in our chapel at the Lateran which is called the *Sancta Sanctorum*, begins to be exhibited on the day of the Resurrection of our Lord, the day when the pilgrims customarily leave Rome; and wanting to see that image, they lament that they are deprived of the sight of it; wherefore, wanting to satisfy their pious desires, we command your fraternity to show the said image every year, beginning on Palm Sunday and throughout Holy Week at the times at which, after the day of the Resurrection, it has been customary to show it, and thenceforward until the usual day of closure of [the exhibition of] the blessed image. [Urban V, *Secrètes*, n. 363.]

(b) 1364, May 18th: To Francisco de Yaronto OFM

He is licensed to go with one companion of the Order of Friars Minor, whose teacher he is, to visit the Holy Sepulchre and the other oratories of the Holy Land and to stay in the houses of the Orders of Friars Minor established on Mount Sion and at Bethlehem for as long as he wishes. [Ibid, n. 11276.]

(c) 1364, December 21st: To the archbishop of Milan

Luchina de Vuliano, relict of Spingesio de Cambasides, a widow of Milan, in her husband's lifetime was pregnant and vowed that if she gave birth to a live child she would visit St James of Compostela; she then bore the child which however died after a year, and she is neither able nor willing to fulfil the vow because of the dangers of the sea, and has sent ten florins to the apostolic *camera* for the Holy Land subsidy. If the facts are thus, the widow's vow may be commuted into other works of piety, provided that she faithfully send to the said church of St James the offering which she would have made if she had gone in person. [Ibid., n.14297.]

20. Joanna of Naples to the seneschals of Provence and Fourcalquier and their lieutenants, on behalf of the Dominican prior and convent of St Maximin, 1365

... It has been reverently expounded to our Majesty that it was once decreed by the lord King Charles II of happy memory, our grandfather, the first founder and benefactor of the aforesaid monastery, 'to the glory and honour of God, and the reverence of the most blessed saints, Maximin and Mary Magdalen, whose holy relics rest in Christ in the said monastery', that the portal, or great gate of the aforesaid town of St Maximin should be so constructed, right in front of the entrance of our church of St Maximin aforesaid, that travellers and pilgrims passing along their way should from the road see it close at hand and enter the church and more conveniently obtain the indulgences there available. ... At present, the citizens of the said town of St Maximin, in contempt of the said royal ordinance, seem to have done the opposite, deciding to build the gate far from the entrance of the said church, to the detriment and prejudice of the church; in that these travellers and pilgrims, who both coming and going would willingly visit the church and the shrine of the blessed Magdalen, fail to do so because they have to make a tedious circuit of the town to the aforesaid gate, which, as already stated, is far from the church. Wherefore we have been earnestly petitioned, on behalf of the said religious, that with due regard for the aforesaid lord king Charles, we will deign to command that the portal be constructed there where that great king envisaged it ... . [Faillon, 2, cols 975–8.]

21. Leonardo Frescobaldi embarks for the Holy Land, 1384

... We found at Venice many French pilgrims and some Venetians, among whom was Messer Remigi Soranzi, who one evening gave a dinner party for all those who were going to the [Holy] Sepulchre, of whom there was a large number, and they made him their chief. ... The Florentines we found there going to the Holy Sepulchre were Santi Ricco, Simone Sigoli,[47] Antonio di Paolo Mei and a priest from the Casentino. All these Venetian and foreign pilgrims wanted to go to the Holy Sepulchre in Jerusalem, without going to St Catherine [Sinai] or to Egypt, except for us three, who were travelling together with a servant and also a bursar (*spenditore*). All the others wanted to sail in galleys and make port every evening. We decided to disembark in Alexandria and then begin our quest in Egypt; we were hiring a new cog of twelve *botti*,[48] paying seventeen ducats a head. When the [other] Florentine pilgrims saw that we were making a bigger tour of the Holy Land and beginning at Alexandria, they gained courage, came to an agreement with us and decided to do what we were doing.

Then I fell ill, and as the time for departing approached, the doctors refused to allow me to embark. So Giorgio [Gucci] and Andrea assembled certain Florentine merchants and several Venetians who were friends of the Florentines and after discussion with the doctors decided that this time they would go no further, but that we would return to Florence. And they came all together to the house of the Florentine Filippo di Jacopo Filippo, where I had gone to get better nursing because there were his mother and wife there, and there were no women in the Portinari household. Here messer Remigi Soranzi said, 'You Florentines are not used to the tempests of the sea as we and other maritime peoples are; and even the healthiest seafarer, entering on the stretch of water between here and Alexandria, finds the strongest body torn to pieces. So we are all agreed in advising you not to embark and not to tempt God.' To which I replied that I was not tempting God by placing myself in His mercy; and for Him, not just making a sick man well, but a dead man live, was easy; and I was minded to see the gates of the Sepulchre before I saw those of Florence; and if God had decided that the sea should be my tomb, I was content. The doctors who were caring for me were present at all these discussions, and so was the master of the new cog on which we were going to Alexandria, whose name was messer Lorenzo Morosini, and the name of the cog was Pola. Seeing my determination, he offered me his cabin, which was next to the helm. The doctors made arrangements for my regimen and food and medicine and everything a sick man needs, telling me to make my bed as if I was in my room in Florence. The priest from the Casentino who was with us had also fallen ill in Venice; seeing me embark, he resolved to do likewise.

In Venice we provided ourselves with many things, among which Filippo di Jacopo Filippi bought a barrel of good *malvasia* ['malmsey' wine], and among the other things we bought was a chest to keep certain useful things in, like the Bible, Gospels and *Moralia*, and silver cups and other fragile things. And from this chest we removed one of the bands which was fixed to the underside of the lid, and with a file hollowed part of it out, so as to conceal in it six hundred new-minted ducats, two hundred for each of us; and I carried two hundred silver Venetian ducats and a hundred in gold, and an advance of seven hundred ducats altogether in letters to Guido de' Ricci in Alexandria and to Andrea di Sinibaldo da Prato in Damascus; they were there for the Portinari.

On the 4th September 1384, early in the morning, all the pilgrims took communion of the true Body of Christ, mostly at St Mark's; at churches nearer at hand the priest communicated us, including me because of my illness, and we were fourteen in all. That morning, they brought the cog three miles off Venice, and there they anchored and loaded her with a cargo mostly of Lombard cloth, silver ingots, copper, oil and saffron. In the evening, at the hour of vespers, we embarked on a sixteen-oared brigantine with our many Florentine and Venetian friends and went out to the cog; and making the sign of the Holy Cross we and our company went abroad; and when we had had a drink with our friends they disembarked from the ship and returned to Venice. And in the name of Almighty God we set sail; and because the deck and quarterdeck of the cog were not yet finished, many craftsman came along who were still working; the master employed fifteen good young bowmen, as well as the crew. So, between merchants and pilgrims and soldiers and crew, it seemed a gallant company.

So, sailing with gentle winds through the Gulf of Venice close to Lussino, we had good fortune. Because the ship was new and large it seemed to make light of the sea. But an unarmed galley, laden with pilgrims who were coming from the Sepulchre, split apart because it was old, and about two hundred were drowned, all poor people; it's the usual case that in order not to pay high transport costs only the miserable goods of poor men are put on to such a wretched ship. But according to our holy faith, they will have made a better bargain than we, for I think they are at the feet of Christ. [*Pellegrini Scrittori*, pp. 171–3.]

22. English guilds

(a) 1389: Returns made to the King's Council by order of parliament, describing the foundation and character of English guilds

The *Fraternitas Sancti Cristofori* of Norwich prescribes prayers for all order of society, including 'for all trewe shipmen, and trewe pilgrymes, yat godd for his grace yeve hem wederung and passage, yat yei mowen savely commen and gone'. [J. Toulmin Smith, *English Gilds: The Original Ordinances of More Than One Hundred Early English Gilds* (EETS 40, 1870), p. 23.]

Gild of the Holy Cross, Lynn: And if any brother or sister be in pelgrimage, he schale have a galoun of ale to his drinke. [Ibid., p. 84.]

Gild of the Blessed Virgin Mary, Hull: But if any brother or sister of the gild wishes, at any time, to make a pilgrimage to the Holy Land, then, in order that all the gilde may share in his pilgrimage, he shall be fully released from his yearly payment until his return. [Ibid., p. 157.]

Gild of the Tailors Lincoln: If anyone wishes to go on a pilgrimage to the Holy Land of Jerusalem, every brother and sister shall give him a penny; if to St James's or Rome, a halfpenny, or more; and they shall go with him outside the gates of the city of Lincoln; and on his return they shall meet him and go with him to his mother church.[49]

If a brother or sister dies outside the city, on pilgrimage or elsewhere, and the brethren are assured of his death, they shall do for his soul what would have been done if he had died in his own parish. [Ibid., p. 182.]

The Gild Merchant, Coventry keeps 'a lodging house with thirteen beds to lodge poor folks coming through the land, on pilgrimage or any other work of charity. And there is a Governor of this house, and a woman to wash their feet, and whatever else is needed.' [Ibid., p. 231.]

(b) Certificate of the Gild of St James in St Peter's church, Burgh, Lincolnshire

There is a certain gild of St James in the church of Burgh which is ordered by the devotion of the parishioners of that church in honour of St James and has existed for 24 years and still continues. In this manner, namely, that certain men vowed to go on pilgrimage to

the land of St James, that is to say John Magnus the elder, William
Galt, William Curry, Hugh atte Trapp, Thomas atte Bele the elder,
who fulfilled the aforesaid vow and while they were returning were
imperilled by storm and tempest and made a vow to almighty God
and blessed James that if they might by the intercession of blessed
James escape the storm and return home, they would build and
dedicate an altar in his honour in the church of St Peter at Burgh and
to the best of their ability support and administer the divine office
there in honour of the aforesaid St James; and when they had made
their vow the storm abated and they came to the longed-for harbour
by the intercession of St James, and when they got home they were
asked about their health and how they had fared, and told their
neighbours and families about the storm and the vow they had made.
Then, wanting to fulfil the vow, to the praise of God and St James
they built the altar with their neighbours and had it dedicated to St
James for the administration of the office and the celebration of
masses. And similarly every brother promised a measure of barley to
the fabric of the aforesaid church, which act of devotion it has pleased
them to uphold for a long time, so that all the brothers and sisters,
once a year, eat together and there elect an alderman to govern on
their behalf as aforesaid and this is the form of the aforesaid guild and
it was ordained for this devotion. [*The Medieval Lindsey Marsh, Select
Documents*, ed. A.E.B. Owen, *Lincoln Record Society* 85 (1996), n. 10.]

23. Early fifteenth century: Margery Kempe

(a) She prepares to go to Jerusalem

When the time came that this creature should visit the holy places
where our Lord was quick and dead, as she had by revelation before,
she prayed the parish priest of the town where she was dwelling to
say for her in the pulpit that, if any man or woman claimed any debt
of her husband or of her [they] should come and speak with her
before she went, and, with the help of God, she would make satisfaction to each of them, and so she did. [Margery, p. 60 (slightly
modernised).]

(b) Delay at Bristol en route to Santiago

And then she remained in Bristol, by the bidding of God, awaiting
shipping for six weeks, inasmuch as there were no English ships that
might sail thither, for they were arrested and taken up for the King.
And other pilgrims were there at Bristol, desiring to speed their

journey, [who] went about from port to port and got on no faster ... [She meets Thomas Marchale of Newcastle] ... He said to this creature, 'Mother, I have here ten marks. I pray you that it be yours, as your own, for I will help you to St James with God's grace. And what you bid me give to any poor man or woman, I will do your bidding, always a penny for you and another for myself.' Then, as it pleased our Lord, he sent a ship out of Brittany into Bristol which ship was made ready and arrayed for to sail to St James. And then the said Thomas Marchale went and paid the master for himself and for the said creature. [Ibid., pp. 106–8.]

(c) Trouble with a 'worshipful doctor' at York

Then said the worshipful doctor to her, 'Woman, what do you in this country?' 'Sir I come on pilgrimage to offer here to St William.' Then said he again, 'Have you a husband?' She said, 'Yes'. 'Have you any letter of record?' 'Sir', she said, 'my husband gave me leave with his own mouth. Why do you this with me, more than you have done with other pilgrims that are here, which have no letter any more than I have?'[50] [Ibid., p. 122.]

(d) Trouble on the way from Wilsnack to Aachen

When she came there, she saw a company of poor folk. Then she went to one of them asking whether they were purposed to go. He said, 'To Aachen.' She prayed him that he would suffer her to go in their company. 'Why, dame,' he said, 'hast thou no man to go with thee?' 'No', she said, 'my man is gone from me.' So she was received into a company of poor folk, and when they came to any town, she bought her meat and her fellowship went on begging. When they were outside towns, her fellowship took of their clothes and, sitting naked picked themselves [i.e. of lice]. Need compelled her to stay with them and prolong her journey and be put to much more expense than she would have been otherwise ... .

When they were come to Aachen, the said creature met with a monk of England, who was on his way to Rome. Then was she much comforted inasmuch as she had a man she could understand. And so they abode there together for ten or eleven days, to see our Lady's smock and other holy relics which were showed on St Margaret's Day. And in the meantime it chanced that a worshipful woman came from London, a widow with many people with her, to see and worship the holy relics. The said creature came to this worthy woman, complaining that she had no fellowship to go with home to

England. The worthy woman granted her all her desire, and had her eat and drink with her and made her right good cheer. When St Margaret's Day was come and gone and they had seen the holy relics, the worshipful woman sped out of Aachen with all her people. The said creature, hoping to have gone with her, and defrauded of her purpose, was in great despondency. She took her leave of the monk who was going to Rome, and got herself a wagon with other pilgrims and pursued the aforesaid woman as fast as she might to see if she could overtake her, but it was not to be. Then it happened that she met with two men of London going to London. They said, if she could stand going as fast as they, she should be welcome, but they could not tolerate much delay; nevertheless they would help her forward in her journey with a good will. So she followed after them with great labour, till they came to a good town where they met pilgrims of England who were coming from the court of Rome and were going home again to England. She prayed them that she might go with them, and they said shortly that they would not delay their journey for her, for they had been robbed and had but little money to bring them home, wherefore they must needs make a sharper journey. And therefore if she could bear to go as fast as they, she should be welcome and otherwise not. She saw no other succour but to abide with them as long as she might, and so left the other two men and stayed with these. Then they went to their meat and made merry. The said creature looked a little to one side of her and saw a man lying and resting on a bench-end. She enquired what man that was. They said it was a friar, one of their fellowship. 'Why eateth he not with you?' 'Because we were robbed as well as he, and therefore each man must help himself as well as he may.' 'Well', said she, 'he shall have part of such good as God sendeth me.' She trusted well that our Lord should ordain for them both as was needful for them. She gave him food and drink and comforted him very much. Then they all went forward together. Soon the said creature fell behind; she was too old and too weak to keep up with them. She ran and leapt as fast as she might till her strength failed. Then she spoke with the poor friar whom she had cheered before, offering to meet his costs until he came to Calais, if he would stay with her and let her go with him till they came there, and that she would reward him for his labour. He was well content and consented to her desire. So they let their fellowship go on, and they two followed gently as best as they could. The friar, being very thirsty, said to the creature, 'I know this country well enough, for I have oft-times gone this way to Rome, and I know that there is a place of refreshment a little hence. Let us go thither and drink.' She was well pleased and followed him. When they came there, the goodwife of the house, having compassion of the creature's labour, counselled that she should take a wagon with other pilgrims and not go thus with a man alone. She said that she had firmly intended and planned to go with a worshipful woman of London and she was deceived. When they had rested for a while and conversed with the goodwife of the house, there came a wagon with pilgrims. The goodwife, knowing the pilgrims in the wagon, when they passed her house called them back again, beseeching them that that creature might ride with them in their wagon for more speed of her journey.[51] [Ibid. pp. 237–9.]

24. **1462, December 26th: Robert Chelmyston and William Thornden, monks of Christ Church Canterbury and by the authority of the archbishop penitentiaries of that church, certify that ...**

... 'a certain Robert Almer, of the province of Canterbury, who has in time past made a vow of pilgrimage to the shrine of the apostles and also to the Holy Land of Jerusalem, and has come to our presence asking to be signed with the cross and for benediction according to the custom of the holy Roman Church; according to the manner of the holy Roman church as known and practised by us, we have signed him with the cross and blessed him, in virtue of the authority committed to us, in favour of the performance of his pilgrimage.' [*LC* 2, p. 239.]

25. **From the revised statutes of the Confrérie de Saint Jacques, Tournai, 1469**

Item, it is ordained that at the said hospital there shall be received the poor people of God, and especially pilgrims passing every night. From the night of St Martin (November 11th) until the following Easter each poor inmate shall receive a loaf of mixed grains (*blé de gollené*) weighing fourteen ounces, a pint of Hamburg [beer], a bowl of bean soup and a slice of pork flesh or a herring, according to what is available on the day, and to warm themselves a large bundle of firewood.[52]

Item, it is ordained that the twelve masters can receive no man or woman into the said Confraternity if they have not made the journey to St James in Galicia at their own expense and out of pure devotion,[53] without constraint, fraud or deception, according to the content of the second bull obtained from the Holy Father Sixtus IV. And if in the future it comes to be known that anyone has not done so, they shall no longer be regarded as brother or sisters and shall be deprived of all the benefits of the said hospital and expelled from this Confraternity without any possibility of being readmitted, nor of reclaiming the costs they have expended by reason of their admission or otherwise. [*Bulletins de la Société Historique et Litteraire de Tournai*, 9, 1863, p. 320.]

26. 1474: Geseke, widow of Hinrick Oldekoppes, leaves money to the hospital of the Holy Trinity at Hildesheim …

… 'and establishes two "soul-baths" [*zelebaden*],[54] to be provided always on the occasion of the Aachen pilgrimage [*der Akenevart*], of which one shall be provided in the Osterstoven [bath-house] on the way out, and the other shall be provided in the Steinstoven on the return journey, when the pilgrims come back from Aachen, and the gatekeepers before the Eastgate and the Damgate shall publicise these baths widely to the pilgrims, and therefore to each of the said gate-keepers shall be given sixpence of our new pennies, and at each bath shall be given: for thirteen shillings and four pence of our new pennies, bread; for one new pound, bacon and also two barrels of beer. And the aforementioned elders and their master shall go to the aforesaid two baths and with the bathhouse-keeper and his servants see to it that the pilgrims are well and efficiently treated, and to each of the said servants therefore shall be given two shillings of the aforesaid new pennies. … When the two baths aforesaid have been provided and paid for, if there is any money over, it shall go to the poor people of the aforesaid Holy Ghost [hospital].' [*Urkundenbuch der stadt Hildesheim*, 7, p. 529.]

27. Innocent VIII to all the faithful: 1489, January 17th

Whereas Peter, a friar preacher of the convent of St Thomas in the diocese *Partheniensis*,[55] and John, a canon of the monastery of St Antony of Vienne, and George, a layman of the diocese *Partheniensis*, came from India to Jerusalem, and stayed there for several years, and have come to Rome in order to visit the basilicas of the Apostles Peter and Paul and other basilicas, and intend to visit the church of St James in Compostela and the churches of St Mary Finisterre, Mont-St-Michel in Normandy and St Thomas of Canterbury in England, and then to return to Jerusalem and thence to India; and whereas they have not the means to make the said pilgrimages, and the alms etc. of the faithful are very useful to them, the pope grants to all faithful who being penitent, and having confessed, give alms etc. to the said Peter, John and George, or any one of them if the others are absent or deceased, until they return to India, a relaxation of three years and three quarantines of enjoined penance; the present letter, which the pope forbids to be carried about by 'pardoners' [*questores*], to hold good for three years only from the date thereof. [*CEPR* 14, p. 312.]

B. Special Occasions

1. The Roman Jubilees

(a) 1300: Chronicle accounts

(i) In the year 1300, after Christ's Nativity, as many people said that in every hundredth year the pope of that time granted a great indulgence, Pope Boniface VIII, who was then pope, in reverence for the Nativity of Christ granted a great and supreme indulgence in this manner: to every Roman, throughout the whole year, who visited the churches of the blessed apostles Peter and Paul, continuing for thirty days, and to all other people who were not Romans, [who did so] for fifteen days, [he granted] full and entire pardon of all their sins, being confessed or if they confessed, both of guilt and punishment. And for the consolation of the Christian pilgrims, every Friday and solemn feast-day the Veronica of the *sudario* of Christ was shown in St Peter's. Wherefore, a large number of Christians then living made this pilgrimage, men and women alike, from distant and different countries, from far and near. And it was the most remarkable thing that ever was seen, that during the whole year there were in Rome, besides the Roman people, 200,000 pilgrims, not counting those who were coming and going along the roads, and all were adequately provided with victuals, both horses and people, and with great patience and without disturbance or dispute; and I can bear witness, for I was there and I saw. And from the offerings made by the pilgrims great treasure accrued to the church and to the Romans; all were made rich by their takings.[56] [Giovanni Villani, *Nuova Cronica*, ed. G. Porta (3 vols, Florence 1990–91), 2, pp. 37–8 (Lib. 9, cap. 36).]

(ii) Be it known to all faithful Christians that in the year 1300, from the East and from the West, there came both men and women without number, of every Christian race, rushing to Rome, who said to Boniface, then supreme pontiff, 'Give us your blessing before we die. We have heard from our fathers that every Christian, every hundredth year, who visits the relics of the blessed apostles Peter and Paul, shall be liberated both from guilt and punishment.' Then the aforesaid Boniface and his cardinals assembled their council, investigated the law but found no notice of this; whence they decreed that every Christian who that year and throughout the year should stay at Rome for fifteen days, visiting the churches of the blessed apostles Peter and Paul, should be free, [as] from the day of their baptism, of every sin, both from guilt and from punishment [*tam a culpa, quam a poena*]; and this indulgence was confirmed by Boniface and his cardinals in every hundredth year for ever. It was marvellous, how men and women went about everywhere who were that year in Rome; for I was there and I stayed there for fifteen days. Bread, wine, meat, fish and oats were cheap there, but hay and also lodgings were extremely expensive, so that my bed and hay and oats cost me a *gros tournois*. Leaving Rome on Christmas Eve I saw a crowd so big no one could number it, and it was said among the Romans that there were more than twenty hundred thousand men and women there. Several times I saw both men and women trampled under the feet of others and on several occasions I myself escaped the same danger. The pope received an infinite amount of money from them, for day and night two clerics stood at the altar of St Paul holding rakes in their hands and raking in endless money. Future Christians should know that the aforesaid Boniface and his cardinals confirmed the said indulgence for every hundredth year for ever, and issued a decree, of which I took a copy back to Asti, and I have made a copy of it at the end of this book. And I, Guglielmo, when I was at Rome, was fifty years old and more. It is therefore highly advisable and praiseworthy for all faithful Christians that the same should be done every hundredth year. [*Chronicon Astense: Memoriale Guilielmi Venturae civis Astensis*, in L.A. Muratori, *Rerum italicarum Scriptores* 11, cols 191–2.]

(iii) For the whole of the year 1300, from the beginning of the year to the end, a general indulgence of all sins (*generalis indulgentia omnium peccatorum*) was granted by the lord pope Boniface VIII who lived at that time, to all those truly penitent and confessed who visited at least once the churches of Saints Peter and Paul; and this was made public to the greater part of Christendom in solemn papal letters. Wherefore, a large and almost infinite number from the city and district of Parma, men, women, clerks, laymen, religious male and female, and nuns went to Rome, and from all of Lombardy, France, Burgundy, Germany and from other provinces and regions in every part of Christendom, and numberless barons, knights and great ladies, and others without number of both sexes and every condition, status, order and dignity, went to Rome for this reason. Every day it seemed as if a general army was passing every hour along the *strata Claudia*, in and out, and there came barons and ladies of France with mounted escorts of forty and fifty and more; and all the houses on the *strata Claudia*, both in the city and outside it, both the usual hospices and taverns and others, were for the most part full of guests, and they gave food and drink for money, and every day they were full of people. And there was good abundance of all victuals. And the sound of this indulgence went out through the whole world. [*Chronicon Parmense, RIS* 9. ix, pp. 80–1.]

(b) 1349–50: Letters of Clement VI

1349, 10th April: To the clergy of Rome: To abate discords and hatreds in the city, so that the joy of pilgrims wishing to receive the indulgence shall be unimpaired. [Clement VI, *Lettres*, n. 1977.]

To the nobles of Rome: To restrain highwaymen 'with the bridle of justice'. [Ibid., n. 1978.]

To the council and people of Rome: *Inter alia* 'that hospices should be made fit for the reception of so many people in good time, with victuals and all things necessary, so that pilgrims suffer no want or shortage when the time comes, but, just as they will be fully refreshed spiritually, so your direction and forethought will provide abundantly for their bodily wants.' [Ibid., n. 1979.]

1350, January 5th: To the Pisans: 'Although we have before now hoped to pacify quarrels and disturbances in every part of the world, and especially the region around Rome, which are in a continual state of instability because of the sins of their inhabitants and individual hatreds, and have devoted our efforts to improving their condition, we are the more concerned at the present salutary and acceptable time, that is in the year of Jubilee, in which we have granted the full indulgence of all their sins to those who, on certain conditions, visit the venerable basilicas of the apostles Peter and Paul and the church of the Lateran at Rome, that the seeds of dissension and discord be totally uprooted and the tranquillity of peace everywhere diffused, inasmuch as the whirlwind of disorder may prevent many from obtaining so great a mercy.'[57] [Ibid., n. 2117.]

February 20th: To the cardinals Annibaldo of Tusculum and Guido of S. Cecilia; also Poncio, bishop of Orvieto, vicar in Rome: Grants them the faculty of granting the indulgence to non-Romans (*forenses*) even if they have not visited the basilicas for fifteen days; this because of the shortage of victuals and lodgings which pilgrims are experiencing.[58] [Ibid., n. 2142.]

February 21st: To Poncio of Orvieto: He is instructed to place trustworthy men as altar-keepers in the basilicas to receive and keep offerings safely. [Ibid., n. 2144.]

May 17th: To Napoleone Orsini: 'We have learned with pleasure from the account of our venerable brother Pierre, bishop of Rodez, our kinsman, and Jean Maurelle, dean of the church of St Croix at Liège, auditor of the chamber, that when they were returning from Rome, where they had gone to obtain the indulgence, and had reached your town of Sant'Antimo, in the diocese of Sabina, they could not easily find accommodation, as you had arrived with a large entourage and also because of the large numbers of pilgrims. Hearing that the aforesaid auditor was there, you recognised the bishop (although he was suppressing his name and rank and called himself Bajasse) as our kinsman, and received and treated him most kindly, out of reverence for us, lavishing the fullest honours upon them, and at last, as they have told us, provided them with the necessary safe-conduct, without any request on their part, detaining with you certain people who had been plotting to set upon them and impeding their plans. [Clement VI, *France*, n. 4512.]

August 11th: To Jacopo di Gabriele: Instructs him to take particular care of the roads in this year; the bishop of Orvieto will give him the necessary money out of the offerings, but he is not to claim excessive expenses. [Clement VI, *Lettres*, n. 2276.]

September 12th: To the seneschal of Rodez: Instructs him to release certain pilgrims from the dioceses of Bordeaux and Périgord, seized by him 'as English' on their way to obtain the indulgence. [Clement VI, *France*, n. 4717.]

(c) 1350: Two chronicle accounts

(i) There was a great pardon at Rome, which was ordained for a hundred years, and now, because that was too long, it was ordained for fifty years, and so the pope proclaimed it throughout the world, and a preaching friar came to Siena. In January the commune of Siena gave the said friar 50 florins, and the pardon was to begin in March (*sic*) and continue until next March 1350 [1351]. The Sienese imposed a levy on the innkeepers of Siena, that is on whoever kept an inn or tavern, on account of the said pardon; and they paid 2,000 gold florins. And an enormous number of people passed by because of the said pardon, of every tongue from all over the world. And considering the numbers of people who passed, things weren't dear. Whoever kept an inn, or did business, or used the roads, got rich. [Agnolo del Tura, in *Cronache Senesi*, RIS 15.vi, p. 561.]

(ii) In the said year my lord the Pope held the pardon at Rome, and it was said that *bolognini* and *grossi*, that is the old ones, had the greatest currency, greater than any other money spent in Rome and thereabouts.[59]

The said pardon began at Christmas and lasted for a year; and people guessed that the Holy Father must need money, for the said pardon was usually at the end of a hundred years and was reduced to fifty. [*Corpus Chronicorum Bononiensium*, RIS 18.i, 2, pp. 599–600.]

(d) 1450: A disaster at Rome

In the year of our Lord 1450, that is the Holy Year, Pope Nicholas with great care and attention, and with the aid and counsel of no one else, made provision that in the said year of Jubilee nothing should be lacking, and all the thousands of people who came to Rome never lacked for anything ... .

In the said year, on the 19th of December, which was a Saturday, the *sudario* was shown to the pilgrims who were in Rome, and the pope gave his blessing to all the Christian people who were the piazza of St Peter's, and when the people wanted to return, there was a great crush on the Ponte Sant'Angelo, and there was a mule, some say it was from San Marco, and some say it was carrying two baskets and two women who were coming for the indulgence, and the mule panicked and because of the crowd people tumbled down, and there was such great pressure on the bridge that two hundred people and three horses were drowned, and the mule and many people fell into the river. Some of the dead were taken to Santo Cello and part to the Campo Santo, where eighteen cartloads full of dead people were carried. Never was such a thing seen or heard of, such a horrible event. [*Diario della Città di Roma di Stefano Infessura, FSI 5*, pp. 48–9.]

2. The Indulgence of the Portiuncula: Measures taken by the Perugians

(a) 1277, July 31st

It is resolved by the authority of this council, and out of reverence for God and the Blessed Virgin Mary, that the Lord Captain, with those of his household whom he wishes to take, may absent himself from the city to go to the feast of the Blessed Virgin Mary which is celebrated at Assisi, staying there until Tuesday, so that on that Tuesday he is again present in Perugia [notwithstanding any Perugian statute to the contrary].[60] [Fantozzi, p. 246.]

(b) 1288, August 22nd

[The council meets to consider] letters sent by the lords Podestà and Captain and the commune of Borgo San Sepolcro, containing that certain inhabitants of that land were attacked and robbed of their goods in the territory of Perugia as they returned from the feast of Santa Maria degli Angeli in the district of Assisi. [Ibid., p. 247.]

(c) 1321, July 28th

[It is resolved that] all the brethren of St Francis may and should go to the procession of the church of Santa Maria degli Angeli. And they shall each have a large candle in their hands, at the expense of the commune of Perugia. And the treasurer of the said commune is bound to pay for this out of the money of the commune, to the shame and opprobrium of the commune of Assisi. [Ibid., p. 249.]

(d) 1321, August 1st

[It is resolved that] the treasurer of the commune of Perugia, without authorisation, shall pay Betto di Lapo Cacile, so that he can pay the men and women from whom he bought bread to send to the pilgrims and those going to the church of Santa Maria degli Angeli for the indulgence (*ad veniam*), to the shame and opprobrium of the commune of Assisi and its followers, for 6,500 loaves at the rate of 2d per loaf, and for 185 loaves at the rate of 3d per loaf: [a total of] £56 6s 9d. [Ibid., p. 249.]

[An exactly similar decree the same day authorised payment for 313 loaves at a cost of 52s 2d.]

(e) 1326, August 3rd

[It is resolved that] the Treasurer shall be instructed without any further authorisation to pay Massolo Nereolo, for himself and his associates, £4 for the care they took of the water-fountain in the piazza, to prevent a water shortage for the pilgrims to the general indulgence of Santa Maria degli Angeli of Assisi. [Ibid., p. 250.]

(f) 1433, October 11th

... Since in the month of July and on the first of August foreigners, outsiders and strangers from various parts and regions of the world pass through the city, *contado* and district of Perugia on pilgrimage to the Indulgence of Santa Maria degli Angeli in the Portiuncula in the diocese of Assisi, and many more would do so, and foreign merchants and others would in transit bring to the aforesaid city, *contado* and district their merchandise, animals and goods, and would take away merchandise, animals and goods from the Perugians, if they were free and exempt from the exaction of tax and duties and tolls on the import and export of this merchandise, animals and goods and from any other tax, exaction or duties of the city, *contado* and district of Perugia; and since both the public benefit and the evident profit of individuals would result from the business of foreigners and their presence at this time if the present Council, should take appropriate action on the aforesaid ... [It is resolved that all foreign merchants and others shall be exempt from taxes, tolls, duties etc. on all goods except certain woollen cloths which remain prohibited merchandise.][61] [Ibid., pp. 254–7.]

. . . .
Remembering Pilgrimage: Souvenirs

'People bring a cross back from Jerusalem, a Mary cast in lead from Rocamadour, a leaden shell from St James; now God has given St Thomas this phial, which is loved and honoured all over the world, to save souls; in water and in phials he has the martyr's blood taken all over the world, to cure the sick. It is doubly honoured, for health and as a sign.'[1]

This passage from Garnier's French life of St Thomas Becket bears witness to a new development in twelfth-century pilgrimage, which reflects the economic development of western society. It was the making and marketing of such souvenirs in the west which was new; it had a long history in the Byzantine east.[2] Naturally occurring objects might also serve, for example the palms which were blessed and distributed at the Palm Sunday services in Jerusalem and became treasured mementoes. Beatrice tells Dante to commit to memory what she is telling him as pilgrims bind palm about their staffs in remembrance of their pilgrimage (*Purgatorio* XXXIII, 76–8). The scallop-shell emblem of Compostela too began its career as a natural object which came to be identified with the shrine and which some enterprising craftsman or entrepreneur must have seen the possibilities of reproducing in tin or pewter. The earliest reference to the marketing of pilgrim 'signs' in the west occurs in the description in the *Pilgrim's Guide* of the stalls in the plaza before the church of St James, where they were sold, together with a lot of other useful items. The words *cruscille piscium* suggest that these were natural shells.[3] Towards the end of her life St Bona of Pisa (d. 1207), a passionate devotee of St James, was transported by the saint himself on a last pilgrimage to Compostela; bringing her back by the same miraculous means, he was careful to supply her with 'those things, which pilgrims are accustomed to bring back from St James of Galicia'.[4] We are not told whether these were natural or man-made shells, but by this time, on Garnier's evidence, they were clearly being reproduced in metal. Innocent III's letter conceding to the chapter of St Peter's the rights over the production and sale of badges of Sts Peter and Paul that, he said, the popes themselves had hitherto enjoyed, suggests a similar time-scale [2,a]. Gerald of Wales tells how, after a visit to Canterbury, he went to Southwark to wait upon the bishop of Winchester, who recognised by the *signacula* hung from the necks of Gerald's companions where they had been.[5]

As Garnier implies, these objects were more than just souvenirs. Like the Holy Land ampullae of an earlier age, the Becket ampullae were made to contain a miraculous, or at least potentially miraculous, substance. Count Boso of Aosta was cured of a quartan fever when he drank a little Becket water from the *ampullae* that were being brought back through that region (a well-trodden pilgrim thoroughfare) by pilgrims.[6] 'Souvenirs' made in other forms were also believed to carry with them the wonder-working properties of the shrine from which they originated. One of the miracle stories collected at Rocamadour in the twelfth century related how a priest of Chartres, who was grievously sick, was cured when his mother placed upon his body a *signum peregrinationis*, invoking as she did so the Virgin of Roc-amadour.[7] In this respect, medals and *ampullae* resembled the 'relics' of an earlier age, which included any object which formed part of or had been in contact with the shrine.

Signa also identified the pilgrim, as the crusader's cross had identified him and as the pilgrim's garb and staff had in a general way already done for centuries. Perhaps the best-known testimony to the identificatory function of pilgrim 'signs' is a satirical one, the description in *The Vision of Piers Plowman* of the pilgrim who had never heard of a saint called Truth: 'on his hat were perched a hundred tiny phials, as well as tokens of shells from Galicia, cross-ornaments on his cloak, a model of the keys of Rome and on his breast a vernicle.'[8] The scallop-shell came to be emblematic of pilgrimage in general, as well as of Santiago in particular. A pilgrim was buried in Worcester Cathedral, probably in the late fifteenth century, with a cockle-shell (superficially similar to the scallop in general aspect though smaller and more concave), which was pierced for attachment by a thong to a staff (a fine ash staff was also found in the grave).[9] It is not clear whether this was intended to indicate that the dead man had been to Compostela, or simply that he had been a pilgrim. The manufactured scallop-shell, like other badges, absolved the pilgrim from the need to drill holes for attachment by providing loops for sewing as part of what was often, though not always, an openwork structure. There was regional variation in styles of manufacture: English makers favoured a brooch style, with a pin cast as an integral part of the badge, whereas in southern Europe the predilection was for 'a solid, medallic form of badge'.[10]

In our own time these technical aspects of the trade have attracted an increasing quantity of scholarly attention. A miracle story of St Thomas Becket vividly evokes the manufacturing process [1], but it was not this aspect that most interested contemporaries. The documentation largely concerns the legal rights that were claimed and contested by different parties who wished to control or to have some share in a profitable business. Monopolies were often claimed by the authorities of the church where the cult was located, who were, however, often dependent on lay craftsmen actually to produce the objects. There was potential here for conflict, especially if the clergy attempted to obtain a monopoly of what had first been, or had become, an unregulated trade. In some places the result was a modest chapter in the history of conflict between ecclesiastical institutions and the urban societies which so frequently grew up around them and serviced them. At Le Puy legal process, excommunication and the threat of excommunication were periodically deployed in a battle which continued into the fifteenth century. Here, it seems to have been believed that the *signum* had to be touched by a priest to the altar of the shrine to acquire its virtue, and the refusal to do this became a weapon in the hands of the clergy. At Le Puy as elsewhere, souvenirs of different designs and materials were sold, which complicated the argument over rights and privileges, while the right to manufacture and the right to sell could in principle be distinct issues.[11]

At Rocamadour, Elie de Ventadour got himself elected abbot on the death of his uncle, Abbot Bernard VI, in 1235 and proceeded to despoil the possessions of the monastery, *inter alia* conferring on the townsfolk the right 'of selling to passing pilgrims the emblems which they call *Carcanelli*', as Gregory IX complained in a letter to the archbishop of Lyon on 20th October 1237. In the fourteenth century, the bishop of Tulle evidently had some control over sales, at least in so far as he licensed the stalls which stood in the significantly named 'platea del Senhals'. Rocamadour badges were used as a sort of passport during the Anglo-French wars, and it may be that this added to the value of the trade in the early fifteenth century, when we again hear of conflict over rights of sale and manufacture. In 1423 Jean de Valon compounded his alleged right to manufacture badges for an annual payment of 8 *livres tournois* and 100 *signes sive senhales* which he could have either in cash or kind. He was not the only one in the hunt, however, and in 1425 the bishop conceded to the inhabitants of Rocamadour the right to sell badges of all kinds, for a period of two years only: thereafter he would regain his monopoly of the sale of those which bore the image of St Amadour. Meanwhile Jean de Valon's heirs did not let the matter rest, and in 1488, at a hearing before the seneschal, Antoine de Valon won recognition of his entitlement (which he had possessed 'from all time') to half of the entire sale of 'signs of lead or pewter on which the image and figure of the glorious Virgin Mary is imprinted'.[12]

If by all accounts the battle to retain control of the traffic in pilgrim signs at Compostela, Rocamadour and Le Puy was ongoing or at least intermittent, the Dominicans who in 1295 were installed in the church of St Maximin in Provence, where the relics of the Magdalen had been rediscovered in 1279, seem to have had no bother before the Black Death. The king and queen of Naples, reaffirming their monopoly in 1354, said that they had enjoyed it undisturbed for forty-three years, but precisely which period of forty-three years is not made entirely clear [3]. Nor is it explained exactly how the plague had affected the issue: had mortality among the Dominicans led to a breakdown of their authority over the local community, or had pilgrimage so increased that the prospects for profit became irresistible to the laity? No one on the production side of the business would have benefited from the sort of pilgrim behaviour described by a continuator of Chaucer, who imagined the Miller and the Pardoner shoplifting Canterbury tokens, presumably with a view to resale.[13] At the end of the fourteenth century, the problem of the badge-makers of Mont-St-Michel was not that any higher authority was trying to stop them working, but (so they said) that the living they made was so poor that they could not afford to pay the tax on sales [4].

Finds of pilgrim souvenirs all over Europe have helped to amplify the picture of pilgrimage given by written sources. In Scandinavia, for example, they give an independent, if necessarily rough, impression of the relative popularity of shrines. Santiago is in an overwhelming lead with more finds (125) than all other destinations, Scandinavian and non-Scandinavian, put together, and is followed at some considerable distance by Vadstena (37) Trondheim (21) and Kliplev (14) in

Scandinavia, Maastricht (15), Cologne (13), Thann (12) and Rome and Einsiedeln (11 apiece) from outside Scandinavia. Aachen, which to judge by written evidence ranked only after Rome, Jerusalem and Santiago as the most popular of destinations for Scandinavian pilgrims, musters only three souvenirs altogether. Furthermore, the finds 'testify to pilgrim journeys to places which do not appear in the written sources: Thann, Neuss, Königslutter, Marburg, Elende, Fritzlar, Trier, Düren, Niedermünster and Eichstätt in the German-speaking world, Tours, Noblat and Paris in France, as well as Lucca in Italy.' As to finds in pilgrim graves, Krötzl points out that only one such Scandinavian find originated from a Scandinavian shrine, this suggesting that considerations of the prestige attached to a long-distance pilgrimage influenced the decision to bury a token with a pilgrim.[14]

Pilgrim souvenirs have been found buried with their owners in many parts of Europe,[15] but otherwise the survival of objects which were not very durable, and were made of materials that could readily be melted down, was very much a matter of chance. It is all the more striking then that some of those that have survived bear witness to obscure local and ephemeral cults, like that of John Schorn, rector of North Marston, Buckinghamshire, who died in 1314 and was remembered for having conjured the devil into a boot, an achievement commemorated in the badges made in honour of him.[16] Some souvenirs were made of even less durable materials than tin or pewter. The 'Veronica' of Rome, the veil supposed to be miraculously imprinted with the face of Christ, was reproduced not only as a badge, but as a small cloth replica, which of course could easily be sewn on to a hat or other garment. New methods of reproducing images opened up further possibilities: a cache of devotional objects found in the choir of the monastery of Wienhausen included a sheet of eight woodcuts of the Veronica, not yet cut up.[17]

We are here on the borders of a neighbouring territory, of the (almost) mass-reproduced devotional object which could promote a cult even among people who had never been, and would never go, to its fountainhead. Indulgences were available for the devout saying of prayers, which might accompany gazing upon an image, perhaps (as in the case of the Veronica) a 'reproduction' of a holy original. The pilgrim badge, and other souvenirs, had always of course had this potential, for they could easily be given or requested as gifts and left as heirlooms. Pilgrimage generated vicarious participation by a variety of means.

DOCUMENTS

1. A Becket miracle

A certain Augustine, a citizen of London, skilled in the arts of the founder, was melting down old ampullae so that he could make new ones from the old, to be devoted to the sacred ministry and the divine cult. He added one of the vessels of the new martyr, which people carry about. When everything was liquefying, one ampulla was seen to be floating in the melted tin. The founder, marvelling, took his tongs and pressed the unmelted tin into the liquid. But it did not entirely yield to the heat, retaining a degree of solidity. Marvelling at what he saw, he reasoned that the furnace was ineffective because it was not hot enough, and built up the kindling under the vessel, but he could not overcome the firmness of the metal. Wherefore, investigating the causes of the phenomenon, he realised that something of the body of the holy martyr had infused the container, which conferred strength upon it and repelled the assaults of combustion.[18] [*Materials*, pp. 464–5.]

2. Two letters of Innocent III concerning pilgrim badges

(a) 1199, January 18th: The pope to H[ugolino] archpriest and the canons of St Peter's

[The Pope explains that his many preoccupations make it impossible for him to give the basilica of the apostles the care and attention it requires. Recognising that the responsibility for the beauty and upkeep of churches depends above all on those who serve them, he is making a small gift to the canons, hoping that it will prove acceptable to Him who accepted the widow's mite.] Wherefore, beloved sons in the Lord, we are by the authority of these presents conceding to you and through you to your canons, and fortifying the grant with the protection of this writing, both the proceeds from the emblems of lead or tin *(de signis plumbeis sive stagneis)*, bearing the image of the apostles Peter and Paul, with which those who visit their shrines distinguish themselves, as evidence of their devotion and proof of their completed journey *(se ipsos insigniunt in argumentum proprie devotionis et testimonium itineris consummati se ipsos insigniunt)*, which our predecessors and we ourselves have been accustomed to receive, and the right *(auctoritatem)* to manufacture them or to grant it to those founders whom you choose, who will be responsible to you alone in these matters. [*Die Register Innocenz' III*, ed. O. Hageneder 1, n. 534, pp. 772–3.]

(b) 1207, June 19th: To the bishops of Spain and Gascony

It has come to our apostolic attention that certain people, located in Spain and Gascony, are not afraid to strike bogus emblems of St James, which are called shells (*adulterina insignia beati Jacobi, quae conchae dicuntur ... cudere*), to the peril of their souls. Wishing therefore that such presumption should be restrained by the prudent action of your discretion, we command and direct your fraternity by written apostolic instruction that by our authority you take care strictly to restrain everyone dwelling throughout your provinces, on pain of excommunication, from striking such bogus emblems, which tends to the peril of their own souls. [*PL* 215, col. 1176.]

3. Charter of Louis and Joanna of Naples in favour of the prior and convent of the church of St Mary Magdalen [St Maximin]: 1354, April 29th

... for a long time past it has been the custom, firmly observed, that no one of whatever condition in the said territory of St Maximin should presume to make the leaden images, carved with the image of the said St Mary, which are given [*sic*] to pilgrims for the devotion of that saint, unless by the special licence and mandate of the prior and convent, and on provision of the moulds and other necessary materials (*datis ferris et aliis opportunis*), to those having such licence, by the sacristan of the said church. Continuously, for the past forty-three years, the prior and convent have been in peaceful possession of [the right of] granting this licence to the makers of such images and providing the moulds and other necessary materials. However, several people of the aforesaid territory, or living therein, from the time of the general mortality last past, having no qualms about disturbing the church in this matter, have on their own authority and without the licence and mandate of the prior and convent been making the aforesaid leaden images and selling them to pilgrims; thus audaciously contravening the ancient and observed custom aforesaid, to the injury of the law and the prejudice and detriment of the aforesaid church. [Faillon, 2, col. 964.]

4. Letter of Charles VI of France: 1393, February 15th

We have heard the petition of the poor people living at Mont Saint Michel, making and selling signs of Monseigneur St Michel, shells and horns which are called *quiencaillerie*, and other work in lead and pewter, cast in moulds, because of the pilgrims who flock there: containing, in order to gain their poor livelihood they are accustomed to sell the said signs and others things above-mentioned to the said pilgrims coming on pilgrimage to the said Mont St Michel, and they have no other means of living and know no other trade; which trade is so small, that they have to sell for farthings (*mailles*) and pennies to the pilgrims who come on the said pilgrimage, and in such small quantities that the said petitioners can hardly make a living in the said place of Mont St Michel; also that no grain grows there nor other things which would help to support them, so that they buy at a high price the water with which they work and everything else that they need for their support; the said suppliants being compelled from day to day to pay the tax on the said signs and other things above-mentioned, wherefore they are so burdened that they have nothing to live on; and the suppliants, or some of them, are on the point of leaving the said town and going elsewhere to seek a living, because several of them know no other trade from which they can live; whereby the said pilgrimage to Mont St Michel would be damaged and the devotion of the pilgrims diminished, for these pilgrims, for the honour and reverence of Monsieur St Michel, take great pleasure in having the said signs and other things above-mentioned to take back to their own countries in honour and remembrance of St Michael, as the petitioners say; humbly beseeching that in our joyous visit to the said place of Mont St Michel it should please us to extend our grace to them in the said matter. Wherefore we have given consideration to the matters above stated, and because of the singular and especial devotion which we have to the said Monsieur St Michel and also because of our joyous visit to the said place, we decree by these presents to the petitioners out of knowledge, special favour, and full royal power and authority, that they and their successors, marketing, making and selling the said signs or other things above-mentioned, shall be free, quit and exempt in perpetuity from payment of the said tax of twelve pence in the pound on the sale of the said signs ...[19] [*Ordonnances des Rois de France de la Troisième Race*, 7 (Paris 1745) pp. 590–1.]

5. Souvenir-hunters: *c.*1400

And here they are, arrived at Le Puy in the Auvergne, not without difficulty, and they make their pilgrim devotions. God knows how crushed and pushed about the poor husband is in the middle of the crowd in order to get his wife through! Here she is, giving him her girdle and her beads so that he can touch the relics and the venerated statue of Our Lady with them. God knows that he is well jostled, that he gets some good elbowing and is nicely buffeted! Furthermore, there are among the women there with them some rich ladies, maidens and bourgeoises who are buying beads of coral, jade or amber, and rings and other jewels. So his wife must have them like the others; sometimes, there's no more money, but nevertheless, he's got to get them. [*Le Quinze Joies di Mariage*, ed. J. Rychner (Paris 1967), pp. 69–70 (modern French version by M. Santucci (Paris 1986), p. 90).]

. . . .
Pilgrimage Post Mortem: Wills

We have already seen that from early times benefactors left money, land or goods for charitable purposes, which sometimes included the foundation or endowment of hospitals which had the care of pilgrims among their responsibilities. Wills were also made by departing pilgrims as part of their preparations. Wills of both these types continued to be made throughout the medieval period. Late medieval wills, including those made by the town-dwelling, middle-class testator, often included a lot of small amounts left to different churches and for different purposes. With the growth of the belief in the possibility that pilgrimage, like other good works, could be performed vicariously, testators began to instruct their executors or heirs to effect the performance of one or more pilgrimages for their benefit and often also of ancestors or other kin. Such bequests were also made if the testator had vowed, or even simply wished, to make the pilgrimage in his or her lifetime and had failed to do so. It is with wills of this kind that this section is mostly concerned.

If a specific sum of money is assigned for the performance of a named pilgrimage, it serves as a useful if rough guide to costs (rough, because it may include an allowance for offerings or for the profit of the hired pilgrim). Sometimes a sum had been put aside in a purse or chest with such pilgrimages specifically in mind, although more often property was to be sold for the purpose, or the cost simply to be taken out of the estate. The benefits, too, might be carefully apportioned: this pilgrimage to be undertaken for the soul of my late husband, that pilgrimage to be undertaken for my own. Vicarious pilgrimages were carried out by a variety of people. Men not infrequently asked wives, daughters or other female kin to undertake the journey; sons might be required to undertake a pilgrimage before they could enter into their inheritance. Where executors were instructed to hire another person to perform the pilgrimage, it might or might not be stipulated that that person should be of good moral character. Sometimes a poor person was to be chosen, which may suggest that the sum bequeathed would yield a modest profit. Several wills indicate that the 'professional' pilgrim could be either male or female, while some testators wanted honest clerks who could say masses at the shrine of choice, especially when Rome was the destination. Like the penitential pilgrim, the vicarious or professional pilgrim might be required to bring back a certificate of performance.[1]

Wills, then, had more to do with pilgrimages intended than with pilgrimages that had actually taken place, although occasionally a testator remembered a pilgrimage actually performed by himself in life, perhaps leaving a bequest for a travelling companion, or bequeathing an object which he took with him on the journey [3,e; 9,b]. Taken together, they illustrate what may be termed the mental map of pilgrim sites that the testator (or his spiritual advisers) carried in his or her head. What were the shrines which came to mind as the faithful contemplated death?

When a testator names a number of destinations, it is not unusual for the list to include one or more of the major pilgrimages alongside shrines of largely regional or local interest. In September 1410, Queen Margaret of Denmark made a will which was rather unusual in that the 'executors' had to spend the money allotted within the next two years, whether the queen lived or died (she in fact died in 1412) [5]. The coverage that she envisaged was extensive, beginning with Jerusalem and the Holy Places, including Sinai. Although she paid attention to a large number of biblical saints and ancient martyrs, and was unusual in remembering St Louis of France, Margaret did not ignore Scandinavian shrines: St Magnus comes sixth in the list, Eskil, Olaf, Eric and Knut are named later, as well as the very recent Brigid, and a number of Scandinavian shrines of the Virgin and the Holy Cross are also mentioned. This coverage befitted a formidable woman who managed all three Scandinavian kingdoms for most of the period between 1387 and her death.[2]

Where a significant number of wills survive from a similar place and time, the imaginative 'map' not merely of an individual, but of a local society, can be sketched, and similarities and differences between different maps may emerge. Between 1305 and 1363, five Lübeck testators made wills on the point of their own departure on pilgrimage (to Aachen, in every instance); forty left money for pilgrimages to be performed on their behalf; and four mentioned pilgrimages undertaken by themselves or another. A mother and son separately, in 1357 and 1361, remembered Heinrich Borkan, who 'was with me in Rome', perhaps for the 1350 Jubilee.[3] Thirteen testators wanted two or more vicarious pilgrimages to be performed for them, while one was happy that either Rome or Compostela should be the objective. If we eliminate this permissive testator from the reckoning, it appears that St James, with nineteen definite choices, was the most popular destination, with Aachen, at sixteen, not all that far behind. Rome, Trier and Rocamadour received six choices each, while the shrine of St Olav at Trondheim was stipulated twice. Cologne, despite its long and international celebrity, was mentioned only once, as was St Theobald at Thann in Alsace. The widest-ranging combination of destinations was chosen by a foreigner, the Florentine Niccolò Salimbeni, who, like his father before him, was official mint-master to the city of Lübeck; he was ill when he made his will in 1358 and wanted three persons to be sent on pilgrimage, one to 'great Rome', the second to Compostela and the third to Aachen, St Ildefonsus at Zamora and St Josse in Picardy.[4]

A smaller sample from the immediately succeeding period comes from another Hanseatic city, Hamburg [3], where, between 1360 and 1400, eleven testators made their wills on the point of departure on pilgrimage, fourteen left money for vicarious pilgrimages and one mentioned her own past pilgrimage to Aachen. This small sample is in fact rather heavily weighted towards Rome. Of the eleven wills made before departure, seven were made in 1390, six of them between August and October, and four of these specified that the testator was going to Rome, evidently for the Jubilee; in addition, seven testators wanted a Roman pilgrimage performed on their behalf. Equally popular, however, was Aachen. Three testators wanted pilgrims sent to both Aachen and Trier on their behalf, while one mentioned Trier alone. One widow specified not only Aachen and Trier, but 'zunte Erwolde' (St Theobald at Thann) and 'sunte Yoste', the latter already mentioned by Niccolò Salimbeni of Lübeck.[5] Strikingly absent, by contrast with the slightly earlier Lübeck sample, is any mention of Compostela. Both sets of wills, on the other hand, attest the popularity of Aachen pilgrimage.

Did a Florentine, making his will in Lübeck, share the 'mental map' of his adopted fellow-townsmen? Niccolò Salimbeni's choice of St Idelfonsus at Zamora is unparalleled. Another Italian who had been transplanted into an alien society, Lucia Visconti, countess of Kent, in 1424 included a bequest to her seneschal, in consideration of the fact that he had promised to go to 'St Antony', Jerusalem and St James on her behalf and that of her late husband.[6] A common stopping-place for Italian pilgrims to Compostela, and remembered by Italian testators as we shall see, the shrine of St Antony in the Dauphiné is scarcely mentioned in English sources, although St Hugh of Lincoln visited it in 1200 and the Order had property in England.[7] By marked contrast with countess Lucia, an Englishman of rank, Thomas earl of Arundel, who died in 1415, did not look outside England for his bequests [6,a].

Personal experience, family loyalties and new fashions affected the dispositions made by testators in this as in other areas. Humphrey de Bohun, earl of Essex, whose father had died at the battle of Borough-bridge in 1321 as an adherent of Thomas of Lancaster, desired that a man should go to Pontefract and offer 40s to 'St Thomas' in his name [1]. At a later date and a lowlier stratum of society, a sailor of Hull in 1520 left money for offerings not only to our lady of Walsingham, but to 'the Holy Bloid of Welslayk' [9,k], which must be Wilsnack, also visited by Margery Kempe, another inhabitant of the mercantile east coast, and frequented also by Scottish pilgrims in the fifteenth century.[8] Wilsnack was a new focus of devotion in that century, as was Loreto, which begins to be mentioned in Italian wills, along with another popular shrine of the Virgin, the Annunziata at Florence, and with St Antony of Padua and the newer Franciscan saint Bernardino of Siena, canonised in 1450 and venerated at his tomb in L'Aquila in the Abruzzi.

Wills made by the inhabitants of Assisi, both by people about to depart on pilgrimage themselves and those wanting pilgrimages performed on their behalf, reveal what may be regarded as a typical range of local and far-flung devotions.[9] A number of testators wanted someone to go every day for a stated period to Santa Maria degli Angeli a couple of miles away.[10] The shrine of the Archangel Michael on the Gargano peninsula in Apulia was mentioned occasionally,[11] but there is no gainsaying the superior attractive power of Compostela.[12] The earliest bequest for a pilgrimage to St Antony printed by Cenci dates from 1422.[13] Later in the fifteenth century a widening range of Italian shrines entered the reckoning. In 1469 Nanni di Appollonio, stricken in years, left money for pilgrimages to Vienne, Compostela, Loreto, San Bernardino and St Antony of Padua; in 1485 another testator wanted his son to release his soul from the obligations he had incurred in making vows to go to Vienne and to the Annunziata. In 1496 a carpenter similarly enjoined his sons to fulfil his vows to the Annunziata and to the Virgin 'of the oak' at Viterbo; he had also vowed to go with them to Loreto. Still more local was the vision of the testator in 1520 who had vowed to go and make an offering to 'the glorious virgin Mary of Todi'.[14]

Wills which specifically mention pilgrimage, it must be emphasised, represent only a small proportion of the surviving total, whereas legacies to churches, including lights to burn before favoured images, were numerous to the point of normality. Sometimes these too amplify the picture, in the sense that the images or shrines chosen were in fact celebrated focuses of pilgrimage which were obviously known to the testator at least by repute. Furthermore, when a testator specified offerings, or the gift of garments or jewels to an image, these offerings or gifts had to be conveyed to the shrine by someone. We may not regard such executive errands as pilgrimages, but they are related to it, as part of the day-in, day-out round of recourse to shrines and the maintenance of their popularity and income.

DOCUMENTS

1. Will of Humphrey de Bohun, earl of Essex (d. 1361)

We will also and instruct that our executors hire a chaplain of good condition to go to Jerusalem, chiefly for my lady my mother and my lord my father on whom God have mercy, and that the chaplain be charged to say mass along the way as often as he conveniently can for souls. And also that our executors hire a good and loyal man to go to Canterbury and there offer for us forty shillings of silver. And another such man to go to Pontefract and offer there at the tomb of Thomas formerly count of Lancaster forty shillings. [John Nichols, *Collection of all Wills Extant of Kings and Queens of England* (London 1780), p. 54.]

2. Some Lübeck wills

(a) 1307, Thideman Wise

Leaves 5 marks for one pilgrim to St Olav at 'Drontheim' [Trondheim]; 10 marks for a pilgrim to St James. [*Regesten der Lübecker Burgertestamente des Mittelalters*, ed. A. von Brandt (2 vols, Lübeck 1964–73), I, n. 25.]

(b) 1320, Johann Jode

When the testator went to blessed Mary of Rocamadour [Risse-madun] he settled his account with his landlord Dithmar van Lunden; this settlement is entered in the city register and, having been paid there, has been cancelled. [Ibid., n. 66.]

(c) 1332, Meynekin van Vlenseborg

His son Adam, before he inherits, is to go to Rome to St Peter's; his younger son is to go to 'St Maria Sizemadum' [Rocamadour] if he is able. [Ibid., n. 116.]

(d) 1346, Tale, widow of master Erpo

Her three best overgarments, with linings, are to be sold and [the proceeds] spent on a pilgrimage to Aachen, four payments for *Fasten-speisen* [the Lenten allowance of food] during a year, and masses for the souls of her husband and herself. [Ibid., n. 244.]

(e) 1350, Elizabeth, widow of Otto Spyher

A male or female pilgrim is to go on a pilgrimage to Aachen and Trier, the journey to Aachen for her own soul's health, the journey to Trier for that of her brother Johann Hogheveld. [Ibid., n. 326.]

(f) 1358, Gerhard Hardenacke

In alms, 40 marks of pennies. With these, five women shall be chosen to go on pilgrimage, to Trier, Rocamadour [Rickemedune], Cologne and Aachen. ... Further, his son, before he inherits his paternal estate, shall go on pilgrimage to St James; when he under-takes the journey, he may receive in advance as much as he needs for expenses. [Ibid., 2, n. 701.]

(g) 1359, Johann Gronowe

In his chest lie 27 pounds sterling. These are to be spent to enable [another] Johann Gronowe to make a pilgrimage to St James of Compostela for the testator's soul's health. Johann may have this legacy on condition that he performs the pilgrimage; when the ex-ecutors are satisfied that he is truly setting out, they may give it to him. Otherwise they shall spend it as seems good to them. [Ibid., n. 793.]

(h) 1359, Herman Grambeke

Two pilgrims are go to St James, one for himself, the other for

Ghese Hovedes, from whom he has 10 marks in hand. [Ibid., n. 816.]

(i) 1363, Johan Holenbeke, called van Kaspen

The executors shall appoint at his expense and that of his lord, Hinrik Ryebode, a man to go to 'St Ewald' [St Theobald of Thann] and Aachen, and, at his expense alone, to St James. [Ibid., n. 976.]

(j) 1363, Johan Schof

From his goods his sister Geseke's expenses are to be paid to enable her to undertake a pilgrimage to Rome and to the Blessed Virgin at Aachen for his soul's health, as she has promised him. [Ibid., n. 989.]

3. Some Hamburg wills

(a) 1360, Heinrich Sasse

His niece Beke receives 40 marks of ready money and all his greater and lesser household goods in consideration of the eleven years she has served him. 'Item, the aforesaid Beke for the salvation of my soul shall make two pilgrimages (*reysas*), one to Trier and the other to Aachen. And my executors shall give her sufficient of my money for her expenses.' [*Hamburger Testamente 1351 bis 1400*, ed. H.-D. Loose (Hamburg 1970), n. 11.]

(b) 1375, Reineke Wulfhagen

His wife Abelen receives, before the division of his effects, all her personal garments and all the silverware which they possessed together, all the household goods as they are in the house, and also 40 marks 'with which she will go to *magna Roma* for the salvation of my soul and the salvation of her own soul'. [Ibid., n. 34.]

(c) 1388, Johann Vleteman

I, Johann Vleteman, burgher of Hamburg, have decided to go to holy places (*to wanderne to hilgen steden*), to win God's mercy and comfort to my soul. [Ibid., n. 81.]

(d) 1391, Arnold the stonebreaker

I, Arnold the stonebreaker, of Hamburg, have decided to go on pilgrimage to comfort my soul. [Ibid., n. 105.]

(e) 1398, Wibe von Stelle

To Johann Lubbert's wife a pair of shoes, and also two pairs which

I had on the way to Aachen, and a pair which my son Werneke had. [Ibid., n. 116.]

4. Fourteenth-century London wills

(a) 1352, John de Holegh, hosier

To any one going on a pilgrimage to the Holy Sepulchre in Jerusalem, and to the tomb of St Katherine on Mount Synay, he leaves twenty pounds and to anyone making a pilgrimage to St James in Galis seven pounds; and if his executors be unable to find any one to undertake such pilgrimages, then one half of the said legacies to be distributed among the poor, and the other to be devoted to the repair of roads within twenty miles of London ... .[*Calendar of Wills proved and enrolled in the Court of Husting of London, AD 1258–AD 1688*, ed. R. Sharpe (2 vols, London 1889-90), 1, p. 657.]

(b) 1352, Thomas de Ware, fishmonger

Bequest of sixty shillings to any one making a pilgrimage in his name to St James, which sum of money is to be raised on the merchandise in the ship La Cristmasse, if she shall come safely to port, otherwise said bequest to be null and void. [Ibid., p. 664.]

(c) 1368, Hugh Peyntour

Bequest of twenty shillings to any one undertaking a pilgrimage with naked feet to the church of St Thomas in Canterbury and there offering at the high altar in his behalf one penny, at the tomb of St Thomas one penny, at St Mary 'under the vault' one penny, and at the shrines of St Augustine and St Stephen respectively one penny; and also to any making a pilgrimage on his behalf with naked feet to St Mary de Walsingham and there making certain offerings he leaves forty shillings. [Ibid., 2, p. 107.]

(d) 1373, John de Weston 'of St Ives', brewer

For a pilgrim to go to Santiago in Galicia on his behalf he leaves his best silver girdle and forty shillings. [Ibid., p. 168.]

(e) 1384, Peter Shepeye of Kent

Also for offering an image to the Blessed Mary of Southwark near Hampton, and for pilgrimages which he had promised to make thither; for a pilgrim to go on his behalf to St James in Galicia, in fulfilment of a vow which he had formerly made ... . [Ibid., p. 240.]

(f) 1385, Roger Crede, draper

Also if he happen not to go to Rome before he dies, he leaves ten marks for some honest man to go there on his behalf and there remain performing the stations and praying for his soul throughout an entire Lent. [Ibid., pp. 250-1.]

5. The Will of Queen Margrethe of Denmark, 1410

[Abbot Salomon of Esrom and Abbot Nicholas of Sora and their convents have agreed, whether the Queen lives or dies, to expend 3,000 Lübeck marks during the next two years, on her behalf, to support pilgrimages as follows:]

First, six men to Jerusalem and to Bethelehem and to the holy places thereabouts and to St Katherine's [Sinai].

Item, five men to Rome, to go around the churches there and visit the tombs of holy men there lie both apostles and others.

Item, three men to St James.

Item, three men to Saint Louis in France.

Item, three men to St Thomas of Canterbury in England.

Item, one man to St Magnus in Orkney.

Item, three men to the three Holy Kings in Cologne.

Item, three men to St Theobald [Iwold] in Thann in Alsace ['Thyestland']

and three men to St Francis in Assisi.

Item, one man thither where St Laurence lies [Rome?].

Item, one man thither where St Nicholas lies in Bari.

Item, one man thither where St George lies.

Item, one man thither where St Christopher lies.

Item, one man thither where St John Baptist lies [Amiens?], and one man thither where St John Evangelist lies.

Item, three men to St Matthias [Trier].

Item, one man thither where St Peter lies, and one man thither where St Paul lies, and one man thither where St Mary Magdalen lies [Aix-en-Provence], and one man thither where St Eskil lies [Eskilstuna, Sweden], and one man thither where St Dorothy lies [Rome?]

and one man thither where St Barbara lies [Venice?]

and one man thither where St Margaret lies [Montefiascone?]

Item, five men to the Holy Blood in Wilsnak.

Item, one man to St Vincent [Zaragoza?] and

one man to St Antony [Vienne?]

one man to Saints Fabian and Sebastian [Rome?].

Item, one man to St Gertrude [Nivelles] and
one man to St Severin in Cologne and
one man to St Brigid [Vadstena]
one man to St Olaf [Trondheim] and
one man to St Eric [Uppsala] and
one man to St Knut [Odensee].

Item, to the seven churches of Our Lady in the three kingdoms of Denmark, Sweden and Norway where Our Lady is most venerated, there shall go seven pilgrims and hold seven sung masses and seven processions.

Item, one man to St Mikkelsberg at Tönsberg [Norway].

Item, five pilgrims shall go to five cities, to the Holy Cross at Solna near Stockholm, the Holy Cross at Borre near Tönsberg, the Holy Cross in Hattula [Finland], the Holy Cross at Randers [Denmark] and the Holy Cross of St Hjaelper [Kliplev, Denmark]. And three men to the [sculpture of the] Deposition from the Cross at Stockholm, and there they shall sing three masses before the Deposition, one of the Holy Cross, one of the Resurrection of Our Lord and the third of the Holy Trinity.[15]

[*Kirkehistoriske Samlinger*, 3 (1880), pp. 377–9.]

6. Wills proved before Henry Chichele, archbishop of Canterbury

(a) 1415, Thomas earl of Arundel

Item, I ordain and will that William Ryman, or another in my name, go with all possible haste after my passage from this light on foot from London in pilgrimage to St Thomas of Canterbury and that two other pilgrimages be made by him, or by another, on foot from Arundel to St Richard of Chichester, on account of various vows which I promised personally to fulfil, offering to St Thomas twenty shillings and eight pence; and for the fulfilment of these pilgrimages I will that as much be expended for the labour and expenses of William or the other going in my name, and in alms-giving going and returning, as I would have spent if I had personally performed the aforesaid pilgrimages, at the discretion of my executors aforesaid. Item, I ordain and will that on account of a vow which I made to St John of Bridlington when I was there with the lord king that now is, when he was prince, that I would every year for the duration of my life either personally bring or send five marks to the said St John, ... by the said executors, together with the reasonable expenses of him who is to go there on the aforesaid business shall be paid and fulfilled and as quickly as possible. [*The Register of Henry Chichele archbishop of Canterbury 1414–1443, 2, Wills proved before the Archbishop or his Commisaries*, ed. E.F. Jacob (*CYS* 42) (Oxford 1937), p. 74.]

(b) 1429, Gerald Braybrooke, knight

I wol and ordeyn that thre priestes be hired to goo a pilgrimage for me, oon to Jerusalem, an other to Rome, the thriddere to Seynt James in Galice and to Seint Michelles Mount in England, for the whiche pilgrimage I assigne 1 li. and more yf hit needeth. And here charges sullen be that they saye her masses every day whanne thay be disposed and may have place, tyme and leyser to do it & to prey in special for my sowle, my fader and moder soules, my auncestres sowles and for al cristen sowles, and also to saye every day Placebo and Dirige and commendacioun, but the gretter nede lette hem. [Ibid., p. 411.]

(c) 1433, Benedict, minister of the church of St David's

Item, I leave to Master Henry Wells and to lord John Sutton ten pounds to visit in my name the places of St John [of] Bridlington and of St John of Beverley and also the place of St Mary of Walsingham, and I will that this sum be paid to them so that they can fulfil this commandment of mine with all possible haste after my decease. [Ibid., p. 485.]

(d) 1433, Thomas Polton, minister of the church of Worcester

Item, I leave 20 pounds sterling to find a good and worthy chaplain whom my executors will choose to send for me to Rome, to stay there in holy places according to their discretion, for my soul and the souls aforesaid, not given to any extraneous occupations or in any way distracted by them, for which purpose he shall give his corporal oath to my executors before his departure; also, that he should faithfully minister to poor recluses of both sexes and other poor persons in that city and really give to them in good money of those parts a hundred shillings, which I wish to be given to him, beside the twenty pounds aforesaid, for that purpose. [Ibid., p. 488.]

7. Will of Niccolò di Zambrino di Lozzano, citizen of Faenza, 1478

... Item, he has left and willed that at the expense of his estate, a good man be sent twice to visit the shrine of the blessed Virgin Mary of Loreto and there offer a candelabrum [*duplerium*] costing twenty good soldi.

Item, he has left and willed that at the expense of his estate a good man should be sent to visit the shrine of the blessed Antony of Vienne.

Item, he has bequeathed and willed that at the expense of his estate a good man should be sent to visit the shrines of the blessed Virgin Mary at the Annunziata of Florence, and there offer a *duplerium* costing twenty good soldi. And the same man who goes to visit the church of the Annunziata shall go to visit the church of the Blessed Virgin Mary at Prato and there offer a *duplerium* costing twenty good soldi. [*Chronica Breviora aliaque monumenta faventina*, ed. A. Messeri, *RIS* 28.iii, pp. 187–91.]

8. Wills from Sussex and Kent

(a) 1449, Walter Dolman of Merston, Sussex

Also I will that five persons go out of London on a pilgrimage: one a priest, to Rome, and sing, or do sing, there thirty masses at Scala Celi[16] if he may get as many thereof there as he may goodly, and the remainder at other devout places in Rome. And that person to have ten marks. And another person to go to Syon, founded in the honour of the Holy Saviour, at Lammas next after my passing out of this world, when pardon is used there to be had, and he to have five groats. The third pilgrim is to go unto our Lady of Walsingham at the day of the Assumption of our Lady, and he to have ten shillings. The fourth pilgrim, a priest, to go to Saint James in Hales [Galicia] and that he say or do say there five masses, and that priest to have five marks. And the fifth pilgrim to go unto Saint Thomas of Canterbury to be there upon St Thomas's day and he to have five shillings. And that every [one] of the said pilgrims to Syon, Walsingham and Canterbury hear five masses in the time of the said pilgrimages and to offer at everyone of the said places one penny. And that the said pilgrims do pray for my soul and all other[s] above specified. [*Transcripts of Sussex Wills*, 4 vols (*Sussex Record Society* 41–3, 45, 1937–41), pp. 210-11 (English modernised).]

(b) 1510, Robert Haryes of Ticehurst, Sussex

'I leave to Robert Hope and John Bele 26s and 8d to perform pilgrimages, namely, to Blessed Mary of Walsingham, St Thomas the Martyr of Canterbury, to the blood of Lord Jesus at Hayles and Magister John Schorne.'[17] [Ibid., 4, p. 244.]

(c) 1508, Edward Symond of Ashford, Kent

'Margaret my wife shall cause one to go to Henry the King of Wyndsor and to Master John Shorne for my soul.' [*Ashford Wills, AD 1461–1558*, ed. A. Hussey (Ashford–London 1938), p. 135.]

(d) 1504, William at Wood, Upchurch, Kent

'That William at Wood and Thomas Rider have promised to go pilgrimage for me – to our Lady of Walsingham, to the Rood of Reste, to the Rood of Grace of Boxley and to St Robert of Newenton [Newington] Parish, and they shall have for their labours 10s and four bushels of wheat.'[18] [*Testamenta Cantiana: East Kent*, ed. L. Duncan (London 1907), p. 348.]

(e) 1514, Simond Graunt, St Margaret at Cliffe, Kent

'That Richard Brown go to the Holy Blood of Hayles, and he to have a mare for his labour, or else 6s 8d with the mare.' [Ibid., p. 271.]

9. Some northern wills: from *Testamenta Eboracensia*

(a) 1400, Roger de Wandesford of Tireswell, Co. Notts

Item, I direct that my executors hire a man to go on pilgrimage to Beverley and Bridlington, to visit the glorious confessors there reposing, to whom I made a solemn vow when I was gravely threatened by the waves of the sea and almost drowned between Scotland and Norway. [1, (Surtees Society, 4, 1836), n. 187.]

(b) 1409, Master Thomas Walleworth, canon residentiary of York, prebendary of Langtoft in the same and rector of Hemingborough

Item, I leave to master John of Langtoft, my chaplain, for his long and good service, forty pounds and my little portable breviary (*portiforium*), with which I visited the sepulchre of our Lord Jesus Christ as a pilgrim. [Ibid., n. 258.]

(d) 1444, John Radcliff, citizen and merchant of York

Item, I leave ten pounds to be given to a chaplain to go on pilgrimage for me to the court of Rome and to celebrate in the Scala Coeli a trental of masses for my soul and [the souls] of my parents and for the souls of Katherine my wife, John my son, and Alice his wife, Nicholas my son and Agnes his wife, Hugh my brother and Agnes his wife, and Thomas my sons [and numerous others] and of all the faithful dead. [2 (Surtees Society, 30, 1855), n. 82.]

(e) 1465, Lady Margaret Aske

Item, I wish that a man be hired to go on pilgrimage to St Ninian in Scotland at my expense, to offer there on my behalf a ring with a diamond in it. Also I leave for a man to go to the blessed Thomas archbishop of Canterbury and there offer on my behalf one *salut*[19] of gold. [Ibid., n. 221.]

(f) 1466, Dominus William Boston of Newark, chaplain

Item, I leave 26s 8d to a priest to go on pilgrimage for me to Bridlington, Walsingham, Canterbury and Hailes. [Ibid., n. 228.]

(g) 1472, William Ecopp, rector of Hesleton

Item, I wish that a pilgrim, or pilgrims, shall be ordained, immediately after my burial, to [undertake] pilgrimage for me to the undermentioned saints, namely, the Crucifix by the north door of St Paul's London,[20] St Thomas of Canterbury, the blessed Mary of Walsingham, St Etheldreda of Ely, the Blessed Virgin Mary of Lincoln, the blessed Mary of Doncaster, St Thomas of Lancaster, St Saviour of Newburgh, the blessed Mary of Scarborough, St Botulph of Hackness, the Crucifix of Thorpbasset, the Blessed Mary of Guisborough, St John of Beverley, St John of Bridlington, St William of York, the Blessed Mary of Jesmount, the Blessed Mary of Carlisle, and St Ninian in the church of Candida Casa in Galway; and that the pilgrim, or pilgrims, should offer to each of the saints aforementioned four pence.[21] [3, (Surtees Society, 45, 1865), n. 57.]

(h) 1498, Lady Anne Scrope of Harling

To our Lady of Walsyngham, x of my grete beedes of goold lassed wt sylke crymmesyn & goold, wt a grete botton of goold, and tassellyd wt the same. To oure Lady of Pewe x of the same beedes. To Seint Edmond of Bury x of the same beedes. To Seint Thomas of

Counterbury x of the same beedes. [4, (Surtees Society, 53, 1868), n. 75.]

(i) 1516, Richard Peke of Wakefield

For pilgrimages not done, I bequeth to paviment in Northgatte in Wakefelde vi s. viij d; and iii s. iiij d. wher itt is moost nede, by the discrecion of Sir William Joys preste, to ament a fowl holle abowt the bridge. [5, (Surtees Society, 79, 1884), n. 63.]

(j) 1521, John Cowper, butcher of York

I will that Margaret, my wyff, or another, ride or goo pilgrimage for me, that is to say to oure Lady of Burgh, to oure Lady of Kirlell [Carlisle], to Kyng Henry of Wyndesour, and to the Roode of Dancastre at the brigge end, after my dethe, if I do it nott, nor cause it to be done before my dethe. [Ibid., n. 77.]

(k) 1520, Richard Wilflit, sailor, of Hull

Item, I gif and bequeath to the Holy Bloid of Welslayk [Wilsnack] iij. iiij d. Item, to our Lady of Walsyngham, iii s. iiij d. [Ibid., n. 92.]

(l) 1522, Thomas Strangeways, knight

Also I will that oon ride to Canturbury for me in pilgramage, and offer an noble into Sancte Thomas for me; and he that shall ride, for to go to our Lady of Walsyngham, and there for to offer unto that Blessed lady for me xx d. [Ibid., n. 129.]

CHAPTER 7
. . . .
Pilgrimage in One City: Pistoia

In 1144, according to legend, Bishop Atto of Pistoia obtained a relic of St James from Compostela itself. His letters seeking this boon were carried to Galicia, and the relic brought back, by Pistoiese pilgrims.[1] The apostle rapidly acquired his own chapel, hospital and office of works (*Opera*) and Pope Eugenius III granted indulgences for pilgrims to the shrine [1].[2] James henceforth enacted a dual role at Pistoia. On the one hand, he was the major civic patron, to whom officials, citizens and representatives of subject communities were obliged to make legally prescribed offerings at his shrine on the vigil of his major feast-day (25th July), a sort of compulsory pilgrimage.[3] Throughout Europe, clergy and people had for centuries attended on the patron saint of their church on his principal feast-day as a matter of obligation. In many places fairs, markets, games and other festivities improved the occasion; at Pistoia as elsewhere distinguished guests were invited to the celebrations, and other people from beyond the confines of the city's political obedience came too, doubtless as much to do a little business and enjoy the peripheral amusements as to pay homage to the saint and obtain the indulgences. Such people in all respects qualified as pilgrims. In July 1342 a *coup* was attempted at neighbouring Prato because so many of the inhabitants were absent at the Pistoiese *festa*.[4]

The saint was here performing the other half of his part, as the focus of the regional Jacobean pilgrimage which Eugenius III sought to encourage. In 1395 the *Opera* obtained a more extensive indulgence from the ever-generous Boniface IX and publicised it in the neighbouring dioceses [1,d)] That year, the officials recorded the handsome sum of £348 10s in offerings made to secure the indulgence ('Entrata di denari auti delle indulgentie & perdono si ebbe da misser lo papa'). In 1396 the figure fell to £143 10s and in 1397 to £106 8s, amounts still well worth having, but by 1403 the *Opera* received only £48 17s and in 1406 a mere £36 17s.[5] The clientele for the indulgence was probably always highly localised and became more so after the initial novelty and, perhaps, the initial effort put into publicity, subsided.

The *Opera* promoted pilgrimage to Santiago as well as hoping to encourage visitors to Pistoia itself. One of the beneficiaries of the saint's early miracles set off for Compostela on receiving his cure [1,c]. From the mid-fourteenth century the officials gave material assistance to pilgrims in the form of alms. Between *c.*1360 and *c.*1480 they recorded payments to about 3,000 pilgrims, by far the largest number going to Compostela.[6] They came not only from Pistoia, but in large numbers from its dependent territory (*contado*), from the neighbouring cities of Florence and Prato and their dependencies, and from further afield in Italy and even beyond. The numbers fluctuated greatly from year to year, and were in decline by the mid-fifteenth century. The clerks usually recorded the names of the pilgrims (and therefore their gender) and their places of origin, occasionally social status or occupation.

Most medieval pilgrims are, for us, nameless, but a source such as this for a moment takes us close to the common man in the act of pilgrimage. We get glimpses of family parties, and groups from small communities in Pistoia's countryside, setting out on the long road to Galicia, and we are able to identify several pilgrims who went twice or more. Many departed on or around the Feast of the Purification (2nd February). There was a regular ceremony in the sacristy of San Jacopo on that day (still recorded in a much-decayed fresco on the wall) at which intending pilgrims received candles and a blessing for their staffs and wallets. The accounts include payments for the wax expended for 'Candellatio', often mentioning the presence of pilgrims on the occasion [2,d,m].[7] The vast majority of these pilgrims were going to Compostela, but there were a few for other destinations, including Jerusalem, and also the shrine of St Antony in the Dauphiné. At least one fifteenth-century Pistoiese testator wanted pilgrimages both to St James and to St Antony carried out on his behalf [4,b]. There is some indication that inhabitants of communities in the city's dependent territory occupied their time and supplemented their income by carrying out vicarious pilgrimages [2,o].

The extracts translated here can only convey a flavour of a lengthy and repetitive record. They include some of the more colourful entries, mostly from before 1400. The period 1399–1406 (after which there is unfortunately an eleven-year gap in the record) saw the *Opera* handling large numbers of pilgrims, with over a hundred in each of the years 1399, 1401, 1404 and 1406. The approach of the turn of the century, and the ongoing anxieties caused by the Great Schism, probably heightened religious sentiment and sharpened the collective sense of the need for repentance. This certainly seems to be borne out by the phenomenon of the Bianchi, a devotional movement which swept over Italy in the summer of 1399,[8] for which the first chronicle of the Pistoiese notary Ser Luca Dominici is one of the principal sources [3].

Hordes of white-clad penitents processed between and within cities, in obedience, as they believed, to the command of the Virgin Mary, who had appeared in a vision to a peasant (exactly where was unclear) to say that only thus could the wrath of her Son against sinful mankind be deflected. The movement was, in a sense, a tissue of pilgrimages, physical and visual demonstrations of penitence in action. Wherever they went, the Bianchi were shown the choicest relics, including those whose exhibition was normally restricted, such as the Virgin's girdle at Prato [3,a,c]. The chronicle gives striking testimony to the determination of the faithful to converge on Rome as the year 1400 approached, even though no official Jubilee had been proclaimed; not all of them were *bianchi* [3,j,k]. At Rome too the most precious treasures were shown, including the Veronica, which Ser Luca invariably calls the *Sudario* [3,e,g,i]. Ser Luca himself went to Rome with a party from Pistoia at Easter 1400, and saw this and the other relics [3,l]. Compostela was also a focus. The chronicler related travellers' tales from returning Compostela pilgrims about the devotion in Italy and beyond [3,b,c)], and tells how a thief was released from prison on condition that he went on pilgrimage to Santiago [3,h]. This man in fact appears among the pilgrims recorded as receiving alms from the *Opera di San Jacopo*, which also gave alms to a family party of *bianchi*, perhaps from Germany, who departed for Galicia in December 1399 [3,o].

Together these sources bear witness to the ways in which pilgrimage impinged on the inhabitants of one Italian city, not one of the largest or most powerful, and untypical only perhaps because of its possession of a relic of the apostle and its consequent 'special relationship' with his major shrine. The chronicle of Ser Luca Dominici shows, in addition, how in 1399 the pilgrimage mode was locally employed to meet the requirements of an abnormal state of religious excitement.

DOCUMENTS

1. A regional pilgrimage

(a) 1145, November 22nd: Eugenius III to the bishops of Siena, Volterra, Florence, Lucca and Luni

We believe it has come to your notice what great miraculous signs the Lord, through the merits of the blessed apostle James, has at the present time vouchsafed to display at his holy altar in the church of Pistoia: whence the faithful people from various and distant parts of the earth, prompted by devotion, have begun to flock to that venerable place and seek remedies for their health. It therefore behoves faithful Christians, and especially those dwelling nearby, to give thanks to our Redeemer for so great a benefit bestowed, and faithfully to exhibit the due services of devotion to the blessed James, his apostle. Therefore we direct you, by apostolic writing, strictly to caution your people and parishioners, that they on no account interfere with men and women, wherever they may come from, who are by reason of devotion and prayer proceeding to so holy an oratory, or presume to inflict any harm or annoyance on them.

If they should presume to do so, you are publicly to proclaim them excommunicate as guilty of sacrilege and as violators of the truce of God, and to cause that sentence of excommunication to be firmly observed in your parishes until satisfaction shall have been made. [*AS*, July 6, pp. 27–8; *PL* 180 cols 102–3.]

(b) 1145, November 22nd: Eugenius III to all Christians

The unspeakable greatness of the divine mercy, which wishes all men to be saved and to come to the recognition of the truth, has demonstrated many and various notable miracles to stir the faithful, through the merits of the blessed apostle James, at his most sacred altar in the church of Pistoia. For as we have learned from our venerable brother Atto, the pious bishop of that city, and from other informants, the blind, the lame, the paralysed and those weakened by various other afflictions, have received their hoped-for remedy in that place, through the prayers and merits of blessed James, as we have said. We therefore, giving thanks to almighty God for so great a display of divine favour, have thought it fit that faithful Christians, who devoutly visit the aforesaid place out of piety, should receive some alleviation of their sins through us, and so, relying on the merits of Peter and Paul and also of James, the apostles of Christ, we decree by apostolic authority, that as often as they shall visit the said venerable oratory by reason of devotion and prayer, they may rejoice in receiving an indulgence of seven days of enjoined penance. [Ibid.]

(c) Two twelfth-century miracles of St James

A certain man of San Baronto, a monastery situated in the mountains eight miles from the city of Pistoia, had been suffering such affliction in his muscles for nearly two years that he could not move himself from any place unless he was dragged by someone. His legs were so swollen and full of evil humours that he could obtain no cure from any doctor; he had often spent much of what few resources he had to obtain relief, and nothing did him any good. When the fame of St James spread, because the Lord was performing many good things through his merits, the sick man hastened to the basilica of St Zeno, where the relics (*patrocinia*) of the apostle were bestowed, and there by his prayers received the remedy which previously, as I have said, he had sought from many physicians. So completely was he liberated from his affliction that he received his health immediately and set out on pilgrimage to Spain to the basilica of St James ...

The fame of the apostle grew in the city of Florence, which at that time was hostile to the city of Pistoia. A certain woman there, when she heard of this, arose joyfully and taking her son, who was paralysed and so hunchbacked that his head almost stuck to his knees, she put him on a cart and cheerfully began and performed the glorious journey; she entered the church of San Zeno and presented her son, whose whole body was bent double, to St James. A little later, in the sight of all who were present, his flesh began to stretch and expand, while the sound of cracking bones brought many others running; his body was stretched out and his head separated from his knees and raised up erect; admittedly the mark of a hump still remains on his back. This miracle was performed in the presence of many different people, that is Pistoiese, Florentines and Lucchese, and people from distant parts, who all together and with one accord blessed and praised the Lord with hands raised to heaven. The boy who had been cured returned with his mother to Florence on foot, having come from Florence to Pistoia in a basket in a cart, as you have heard. On his return, some believed and gave thanks to God, but others said that it was not he, as the Jews said of the man blind from birth whose sight Christ restored. Subsequently, however, the believers and unbelievers joined in agreement, for in that same city of Florence other miracles were superadded to this one, performed there by the Lord through the merits of the said apostle. The boy, who, as we have said, had been so curved over, came again with his mother to Pistoia to give proper thanks to God and the blessed James. I myself, thanks be to God, saw him with my own eyes; he had become active, ruddy and plump, showing no sign of his previous infirmity but for the slight hump which he retained. I saw him and spoke with him and asked him diligently about what had happened to him, and he told me what I had heard from all. I frequently saw the lord bishop give him alms. When the Florentines got to know the truth of this miracle, although they were at that time very hostile to the Pistoiese, many of them thenceforth began to come to St James with great reverence, barefoot and in woollen garments, especially women in compunction of heart, as if inspired from heaven. [*AS* July 6, pp. 63–4.]

(d) Publicising the Indulgence of 1395

We paid Jacopo the swordsman (*schermidore*) who stays at San Domenico for bearing letters to give notice of the indulgence to several cities and places, that is Florence and Bologna and Modena £8 10s.

To Agnolo di Arigho, the bishop's messenger, for similar cause £10 10s.

To Piero di Ser Agnolo for making letters to send to give notice of the said indulgence, £1.

To Ciatto, trumpeter, who was living at Prato, for proclaiming the indulgence (*perdono*) at Prato with his companions, £2. [Pistoia, Archivio di Stato, Archivio di San Jacopo, 759, fol. 329v.]

2. The *Opera di San Jacopo*: almsgiving to pilgrims

(a) 1362

Brother Baronto of the Servi on the 26th of January had for his needs one golden florin and when he went to Rome on the 19th of April one golden florin, in all two florins, value 6 pounds and 18 *soldi*.

To Ghina, [who is] extremely poor, because it has been imposed on her as a penance to go to Rome, … 20 *soldi*.

To eight pilgrims who went to St James of Galizia, citizens and *contadini*, on the 2nd of February, 40 *soldi*.

Giovanni di Jacopo Arrigoni on the day above-mentioned, he asked us for help to go to St James aforesaid, had 40 *soldi*.

To a poor 'apostle' who went to Rome, for a cloak [which] he bought from Pio, dealer in old clothes, 36 *soldi*.

To Giovanni di Vito, a poor man going to Rome, for a pair of shoes [which] he bought from Marco the shoemaker, on the 5th of February, Currado and Francesco know him, 20 *soldi*. [Ibid., 758, fol. 243v.]

(b) 1365

To Jacopo Berti and Giovanni Micheli, called Chiappa, who were going to the [Holy] Sepulchre, between them, £4.

To Giovanni di Coluccio from Buggiano, on the 6th of July, he was going to the Holy Sepulchre, £1.

To Niccolo della Melduccia of Perugia, to go to St Antony [of Vienne], £2.

To Monna Margherita, who stays in [the parish of] Sant'Andrea, she was going to St Francis [of Assisi] 10s.

To Monna Benina di Martino Mercati on the 24th of July, to go to St Francis 10s.

To Monna Giovanna of San Miniato, to go to St James 10s.

To Jacopo Bianchi of Prato who lives in Pistoia, to go to St James £1.

To Salvestro Ugholini for the same reason[9] £1. [Ibid., fol. 330v.]

(c) 1367

To Giovanni, a poor man living at the [Hospital of the] Ceppo, for a pair of shoes to go to Rome £1 4s.

To brother Baronto Grimaldi of the Servi to clothe Marco da Bologna, a poor pilgrim £12 3s 8d. [Ibid., fol. 395v.]

To a poor foreign pilgrim with his wife and five children, in alms 8s. [Ibid., fol. 401.]

(d) 1368

To Bartolomeo di Michele, apothecary, for two pounds of wax candles given to pilgrims going to St James of Galizia on the 2nd of February, £1. [Ibid., fol. 406v.]

(e) 1370

To a pilgrim who gave birth to a male child in the hospital of San Jacopo, £1 12s. [Ibid., 757, fol. 18v.]

(f) 1373

To Matteo di Meuccio, shearer, who went to St James on the 17th of April, £1.

To Michele di Vanni, called the Mouse, for the said reason, on the same day, £1.

To Francesco di Benuccio of Piuvica for the said reason on the same day, £1. [Ibid., fol. 82v.]

(g) 1376

Contro, porter, went to St James, in alms, £1.

Bianco, sawyer, went to St James, in alms, £1 ...

Monna Giovanna, laundress, went to St James, in alms £1 10s 0d ...

Ser Gilio di Maestro Picino of Assisi because of a favour which St James has done him, went to St James, in alms, £3. [Ibid., fols 168v–169.]

(h) 1379

To Giovanni Turini, simpleton (*mincione*), Jacopo di Commei, cobbler, Paolo Benedetti, and Giovanni Pacini who stays at the [hospital of the] Ceppo, £6. [Ibid., fol. 241.]

(i) 1382

To a poor man who said he had escaped from prison and was going to St James, 16th October, 10s. [Ibid., fol. 327v.]

(j) 1384

To four foreign ladies for the above-mentioned cause, £1 13s.

To Piero of Perugia, for the above-mentioned cause, 15s 6d.

To certain other good for nothings (*gallioffi*) who said they were going to St James, 11s.

To Lorenzo di Vita of Montecatini for the said cause £1 2s.

To an old man of Narni for the said cause 5s 6d.

To Antonio dello Scorcio from Pontassieve for the above-mentioned cause, 11s.

To Monna Menza and Monna Mattea of Prato for the above-mentioned cause, 11s.

To Simone di Gherardo of Agliana for the said cause £1 13s.

To Monna Giovanna, wife of Gherardo of Agliana, £1 13s.

To Paolo di Simone of Agliana for the said cause, £1 13s ... [Ibid., fol. 391v.]

(k) 1387

To a Jew who has turned Christian and wants to go to the [Holy] Sepulchre, £1. [Ibid., 759, fol. 71.]

To Brother Lippo of the city of Murcia (? *Muzia*) to go to the [Holy] Sepulchre, £1. [Ibid., fol. 71v.]

(l) 1392

Giovanni and Antonio from the region of Rome had 20 *soldi* to buy two staffs to go to St James of Galicia. [Ibid., fol. 217v.]

(m) 1395

We paid to these pilgrims who went to St James of Galicia, in alms and charity done to them, besides three candles of three ounces given to them after they had received staffs blessed in the chapel of St James on the morning of Santa Maria Candellatio when they went … . [Ibid., fol. 314.]

(n) 1396

To Cinto Benti of Luicciana, 2nd April, went to St James, made the Opera his heir in his will,[10] £4. [Ibid., fol. 346.]

(o) 1399

Jacopo di Nicolai of Vignole, for the said cause, £1 10s.

Donnino di Giovanni dal Pillone, poor man, for the said cause, £1 10s.

Andrea d'Agnolo, of the *capella* of San Paolo. He went on someone else's behalf (*ando per altrui*) 10s.

Andrea di Bartolo, *capella* of San Marco, for the said cause, £1.

Piero di Bene[11] of the said *capella* of San Marco for the said cause £1.

… To Andrea da Bonaccorso, Rofino di Vanuccio and Bindecto di Sigorino of Casale. For the said cause, 10s each, because they did not come to receive the staff with the other pilgrims in the chapel, altogether £1 10s. [Ibid., 756, fol. 50.]

To Niccolo di Niccolo of Germany [?][12] on the 16th day of December, he went to San Jacopo with his wife and two children, dressed in white, £1. [Ibid., fol. 52.]

(p) 1406

To Niccoloso di Bartolomeo of Germany (*della Magna*) pilgrim to St James, 4s.

To Marco di Bernardo of Germany, pilgrim to St Leonard [of Noblat?], he had £3.

To Giovanni di Puccio of Camerino, pilgrim to St James, very poor 10s.

To Monna Lorenza, wife of Luca di Ripolo of Perugia, pilgrim, she had 10s.

To Pierino di Migliore of the parish of San Lunardo because he was going to St James, had 20 *soldi*. [Ibid., fol. 325v.]

3. Ser Luca Dominici: the Bianchi, 1399

(a) *August 20th*

On this day the Girdle was shown at Prato, and many people dressed in white, especially from our *contado*, went to see it, and also from elsewhere, so that according to what I have heard there were more than 20,000 people in Prato. [*Cronache di Ser Luca Dominici*, ed. G.C. Gigliotti (2 vols, Pistoia 1933), 1, *Cronaca della Venuta dei Bianchi e della Moria 1399–1400*, p. 88.]

(b) *Late August*

They say that on the route to St James certain places have perished, and in particular Montpellier has been laid waste and another place half-burned down to the stones, because they did not want to admit the Bianchi; but I do not know this for certain. [Ibid., p. 110.]

(c) *Early September: Ser Luca describes the processions of Bianchi held at Pistoia and elsewhere*

Throughout the territory of Bologna, this was being done, and in all of Lombardy too; because certain people, who came from St James, said that as far as St James this was happening, and all along the route. And all night and all morning it was the same, inside and outside the city numerous companies were organised and went to Prato; and today at Prato they showed the Girdle and there were many people there. [Ibid., pp. 130–1.]

(d) *September 8th*

Also there came another company from Lucca, 30 of them. They were shown [the relics of] St Atto, with many lights and ceremony; and those who saw it held that it was a fine body of a saint (*uno bellissimo corpo di santo*) and similarly every company was shown the altar of St James uncovered. And in San Giovanni Ritondo there was bread and wine collected, and it was given to whomsoever wanted it, by the grace of God. [Ibid., pp. 134–5.]

(e) A letter from a factor of Gabriello di Bartolomeo Panciatichi at Rome, written on 10th September

In the evening it was proclaimed that the Sudario would be exhibited on Tuesday and so it was; and there was a great multitude of people there crying *misericordia*. ... On Tuesday evening it was proclaimed that *il Salvadore* [the *Sancta Sanctorum* at St John Lateran] would be opened this morning and the heads of St Peter and St Paul would be shown and all the relics of the saints that they possess would be put on the altar of St Peter; every notable thing would be shown, and so it was ... [Ibid., pp. 148–9.]

(f) September 13th

And on this day, around the hour of terce, our company from Pistoia with their crucifix entered Lucca in an orderly procession. They were more than 4,000 in number and they entered the chapel of the Holy Cross[13] and gave a silver cross with an inscription, most beautiful in form, to the *Opera*, it was regarded as a fine gift, and they saw St Zita[14] and at the Servi they each received from the commune of Lucca more abundant provisions than can be told. [Ibid., p. 140.]

(g) September 7th–15th

From the 7th of this month right through to the 15th, more than 200,000 *bianchi* entered Rome from different places and regions and especially from the whole Campagna, the subjects of count Dolce from as far as L'Aquila, and in infinite numbers from the Duchy [of Spoleto] and the Patrimony as far as the Romagna, according to certain eye-witnesses who have come from there and left on the 16th. And the Romans are doing likewise, and large numbers have gone forth from Rome, including members of the [papal] court. The Pope has shown the Sudario every day and given his blessing, and all the beautiful and precious things there are in Rome have been exhibited, and all the relics they can, even things that have not been shown for a hundred years past. And every day more people flock there, because the people I have mentioned encountered on their way back and between Rome and Todi more than 40,000 *bianchi* on their way to Rome, especially the company of Foligno, and they said they have emptied the communal prison; also the bishop of Città di Castello with 10,000 people and more and also other companies which they met *en route*, [with] more than 200 crucifixes; everyone was going to Rome, continually singing *Stabat Mater* and there were peace-makings and miracles and marvellous and beautiful things, Christ be praised. [Ibid., pp. 175–6.]

(h) September 14th

And it is a fact that Luca of Casore [in the *contado* of Pistoia] who was in prison for a theft of 22 florins which he committed from Giovanni Donati of Casore, was offered with the others and on Saturday 6th September the said Giovanni pardoned him entirely, and also for another twelve [florins] which he had had from him, without receiving a penny, on condition that he must go to St James of Galicia for the love of God. And this morning the said Luca, and Bino di Domenico, and someone from San Marco, who were both among the prisoners offered (they were in prison for life), set out for St James.[15] [Ibid., p. 159.]

(i) October 3rd

On this day, there arrived certain pilgrims, men and women, dressed in white with white staffs; they were going to St James. ... From Rome there was a letter that it was full of Bianchi to the extent that it couldn't hold them; there were great shortages, and the Pope showed the Sudario every day. [Ibid., pp 180–1.]

(j) October 30th

On Thursday the 30th there came a company of Bianchi from Germany: they numbered 16 people, very respectable, and they had a lady with them. Before them was one who carried on top of a pole a square banner, one a half *bracci* wide and long, with the Virgin Mary depicted on it, who had under her mantle Bianchi shown as they go about, and on one side St Peter and on the other St Paul and two little angels above, and the sun and the moon, and olive above, and they had caps lined with white linen cloth and they sang *Stabat Mater* and other songs of praise most devoutly and well, and they were going to Rome, and they sang in San Jacopo very well. [Ibid., p. 208.]

(k) November 10th

This day more than 200 pilgrims from Paris arrived, and they were going to Rome on foot and on horseback, mostly on horseback, men, women and people of good standing, they were not dressed in white, and among them there were men and women well dressed and well mounted and very honourable. [Ibid., p. 210.]

(l) April 1400

Note that on the 4th of April we went to Rome; we departed early on Sunday morning, the day of St Lazarus; there were more than thirty of us, and we stayed there from Palm Sunday to Good Friday. We received the papal benediction three times, and we saw the Sudario three times and the heads of Sts Peter and Paul twice, and all the fine things of Rome, and we entered by the Porta Santa sixteen times. The Thursday after Easter, on the 22nd of April, we arrived here safe and sound, stopped at the crucifix [of Santa Maria Ripalta in Pistoia] and then parted and went to our homes. Never have so many people been seen as there were there and all along the way. [Ibid., p. 233.]

4. Testamentary pilgrimages

(a) 1380

To Giovanni di Guglielmo of Serravalle, called Pagharino, on 16th December, so as to go to St James of Galicia for the soul of Jacopo di Mone who lived in the *borgo* of Melano, parish of San Prospero, who left a vineyard of four *staia* or thereabouts, outside the *borgo* in the place called Notricieto, on condition that we should send someone to St James. Therefore we have sold the said vineyard and from that money give the said Giovanni fifteen gold florins on condition that he must go to St James without begging on the way except in case of necessity. ... [Marginal note] Note that in place of the said Giovanni Jacopo Domenichi went because the said Giovanni was ill. [Archivio di San Jacopo, 757, fol. 283v.]

(b) 1438–39

This is to certify that, by virtue of the will of Giachino of the parish of Sant'Andrea, Monna Sandra his wife sent Giovanni di Vita of Brandeglio to Sant'Antonio of Vienne and the said Giovanni brought back the testimonial (*fede*) sealed by the chief governor of that place on 18th March 1438. The said Monna Sandra has the said testimonial.

Item, on behalf of the said Giachino, she sent the said Giovanni di Vita to St James of Galicia[16] and he brought back the testimonial, sealed on 20th April 1439. The said Monna Sandra has the said testimonial. [Archivio di San Jacopo, 6, fol. 161v.]

. . . .

PART THREE

Pilgrimage in One Country: England

CHAPTER 8

Englishmen Abroad

Two chapters of the *Treatise on the Laws and Customs of England*, composed around 1189, consider situations created by the absence of suitors and defendants on overseas pilgrimage (including, at first indistinguishably, 'crusade'). The first explains the essoin (a legal excuse for absence from court proceedings). If the pilgrim had received the legal summons before he departed, the court proceedings would take their course. If he had not, he would be granted a delay of at least a year (if he had gone to Jerusalem) or of a period, at the discretion of the king or his justices, appropriate to the length of the journey. The possibility of death abroad on pilgrimage was recognised in the provision of a variant version of the standard writ of *Mort d'ancestor*, which was used if there was dispute over the succession to a free tenancy. Normally, the sheriff was instructed to impanel a jury whose members were to pronounce on issues of fact: whether the father of the plaintiff had been in legitimate possession of the land on the day of his death, whether his death had occurred within the time limit covered by the action, and whether the plaintiff was the true heir. If, however, 'the ancestor ... seised in the manner stated above, has set out on a pilgrimage', the jury was to be asked whether 'the ancestor' had been in legitimate possession on the day of his departure (to Jerusalem or to St James), 'on which journey he died'.[1] The fact or otherwise of the death might be disputed, as court records show: the plaintiff might have to produce witnesses to prove it.

Other rights as well as inheritance could be affected by a death on pilgrimage. A woman might have to sue for her dowry, which she was only legally entitled to recover if her husband was in fact dead [1,a]. Other problems could arise from pilgrimage as from any other kind of travel: if a pilgrim came back to find that his property had been misappropriated, the writ of *novel disseisin* was available to him.

The thirteenth-century lawbook known as 'Bracton' gives a lengthy discussion of essoins as they applied to pilgrims.[2] By this time the courts were distinguishing between absence on a 'simple pilgrimage' to Jerusalem, in which case the party was granted an essoin of a year and a day, with scope for further delays at the discretion of the court, or participation in a full crusading expedition, a 'general passage', in which case the action was to be adjourned *sine die*, 'until it be known for a certainty concerning his death or his return, on account of the privilege of those who are signed with the cross'. If the summons had been received before departure, the pilgrim should appoint an attorney or remain undefended. If a pilgrimage were elsewhere than to the Holy Land, 'as to St James or elsewhere', the basic essoin of absence 'beyond the sea' was granted.

It should be noted that the lowly and unfree, who had no such legal rights to protect, also participated in pilgrimage abroad. In the year 1275–76 a serf on a Wiltshire estate fined for the freedom to sell his chattels so that he could go the Holy Land; a hundred years later, John of Gaunt gave permission for Agnes Snell of Knowsthorpe, who exercised the office of reeve, to absent herself to go to Rome, where she would pray for him and her other benefactors.[3] The vast bulk of the evidence, however, concerns the law-worthy. The appointment of attorneys by intending pilgrims ('crusaders' and others) is frequently registered in the Patent Rolls, especially after the mid-thirteenth century, as are English royal safe-conducts and permissions to travel. This is why pilgrimage abroad leaves a much bigger mark on the record than domestic pilgrimage. For much of the thirteenth century, the rapidly deteriorating situation in the Holy Land, papal efforts to arouse a military response, and, in the reign of Edward I, the king's own crusading pedigree and interests, ensured that the records contain numerous references to persons departing to 'Jerusalem', who are sometimes described as 'pilgrims', sometimes not.

Alongside Holy Land pilgrims in the Patent Rolls are the names of many pilgrims to Compostela, and others who are described simply as going 'beyond seas' on pilgrimage. This was the usage of the courts and did not mean *outre mer*, the Holy Land: the English were already mentally settling in behind their watery walls, and with perfect logic calling everywhere else *ultra mare*. On 27th January 1316, John de Bryanjoun, 'going on pilgrimage beyond the sea', was granted protection until Michaelmas; three days later he received a safe-conduct which specified that he was going to Santiago to fulfil a vow. In December 1318 John de Weston was described as going 'beyond seas' on a pilgrimage to Cologne.[4] Even when we do not now know where he or she was going, the pilgrim seems normally to have been distinguished in the Patent Rolls from others who are described simply as setting out *ultra mare* or 'out of the realm', by the use of a qualifying phrase like *peregrinaturus*, which signalled his good intentions and privileged status.

Shrines other than Jerusalem and Santiago are mentioned relatively rarely. There are occasional references to the shrine of the Three Kings at Cologne, and also to an old-established favourite, St Gilles in Provence. In the mid-thirteenth century, the canonisation of Edmund of Abingdon, late archbishop of Canterbury, promoted a flurry of English pilgrimage to the Cistercian abbey of Pontigny. Edmund died at Soissy in France on 16th November 1240, and was buried, according to his own wish, at Pontigny. His canonisation was proclaimed on 11th January 1247 and the Patent Rolls mention English pilgrims to Pontigny well into the fourteenth century. Henry III himself vowed to undertake the pilgrimage during an illness and in 1252 sought safe-conduct to go in person to Pontigny, promising he would go no further,[5] and one witness at an *Inquisition Post Mortem* remembered that the heir's father had been to Pontigny and vowed to call his son Edmund [2,c].

There is no apparent reflection in these records of English pilgrimage to Rome for the Jubilee of 1300, although one or two witnesses at *Inquisitions Post Mortem* later remember it [2,d]. The contrast with what happened fifty years later is marked [4,a]. When in 1343 he proclaimed the 1350 Jubilee, Clement VI knew all about the state of war between England and France, although he did not perhaps foresee its long continuance or the victory at Crécy in 1346 which encouraged English hopes of substantial gains. Nor can he have foreseen the devastating outbreak of plague which would begin to afflict western Europe late in 1347 and was not everywhere entirely at an end when the Jubilee year began. From the point of view of Edward III's government, a flood of requests from English subjects for permission to leave the kingdom on pilgrimage, taking with them horses and substantial amounts of money, was an unwelcome development. Attempts to control such movements were not new, and had recently been strengthened. On 9th February 1344, the sheriff of Kent and others were ordered to prevent 'any baron, soldier, knight or other man at arms, or religious, or pilgrim, going beyond the realm to foreign parts without our special licence', and on the 12th the export of 'sterling, silver in the lump, and gold and silver vessels' was forbidden.[6] It must have been at about this time that William de Clinton, earl of Huntingdon, petitioned the pope for bulls to the king that he might leave the realm to go on pilgrimage (*sainte vouage*) in penance for his sins, and not be molested in body or goods, by the king or his ministers or restrained from the said pilgrimage, a petition that Clement granted on 23rd April 1344.[7]

Now these attempted restrictions were being reaffirmed, and the damage done to manpower by the plague (it was claimed) merely aggravated the situation. From the pope's point of view, apart from his desire to make the Jubilee profitable for the Roman church and the citizens of Rome alike, the troubles of the times made it all the more urgent for men to seek forgiveness of their sins. The hostilities between the kings, just as they had obstructed and continued to obstruct plans for a crusade, now threatened the success of the Jubilee and could be represented as an impediment to the spiritual well-being of the Christians under their rule, a view expressed in a number of papal letters to both kings. Edward nonetheless eventually acceded to the requests of a number of his subjects for permission to go to obtain the benefits of the Jubilee. His instructions to the constable of Dover Castle to permit their passage frequently specified the numbers in the party and the horses they were taking with them. In all, over 250 pilgrims were named, to whom their anonymous servants and grooms have to be added; most departures were in or after September. That the recorded figures do not represent the total of English pilgrims to Rome in 1350 is indicated by the grant of royal pardons to unlicensed pilgrims, of which one survives in the Patent Rolls [4,c,vi], as well as by the evidence for pilgrimage by members of religious orders without the permission of their superiors. Such cases were among the business which the pope had to tidy up after the Jubilee year ended.[8]

In the later fourteenth century, the Patent Rolls include numerous licences to ship-owners and ship-masters to transport stated numbers of pilgrims to Santiago. These licences continued to be issued in the fifteenth century, attaining significant numbers, it has been noted, in Santiago holy years such as 1428, 1434 and 1445.[9] Their interest is not only that they give at least an approximate order of magnitude for this sector of English pilgrimage, but that they reflect governmental concerns. The terms on which the licences are granted vary, but many specify that the pilgrims conveyed should be laity (this in an effort to prevent clergy from entering into illicit communication and benefice-hunting at the papal court); that they should not include persons of rank; that they should take with them no significant quantities of coin or bullion; or that they should all have to take an oath to the keeper of the port from which they departed. Most of the ports involved were, predictably, in the west country, but east- and south-coast shipmen also participated in the traffic: the author of a versified lament on the horrors of sea-borne pilgrimage envisaged pilgrims departing from Sandwich, Winchelsea or Bristol, and John Paston in 1473 was intending to embark from Yarmouth.[10] The pilgrims were not supposed to be magnates, but the ship-owner might be. Peter de Courtenay, 'the king's kinsman', was licensed in May 1395 to take 200 pilgrims to Santiago in his (unnamed) barge. This remained a family business: Edward Courtenay, earl of Devon, received licence in February 1413 to take forty pilgrims in his barge *La Marie* of Kingswere and in May to ship fifty pilgrims in *la Margarete* of Plymouth.[11]

It is clear that the overseas entanglements of the English kings had a continuing impact on their attitude to pilgrimage overseas by their subjects and indeed by would-be pilgrims to England. Although most of the sources quoted here concern English pilgrims, a few have been included which show the king in his capacity as lord of extensive French territories, granting safe-conduct to pilgrims, for example from Brittany, who wanted to traverse those territories. A clause of the truce negotiated with Charles VII by William de la Pole in 1444 provided that 'true pilgrims may visit the ancient shrines of saints as pilgrims were used to do, in companies great or small, and it shall be sufficient for them to ask leave of the porters to enter towns, castles etc.'[12]

DOCUMENTS

1. The Reigns of John and Henry III

(a) 1200, Staffordshire

Matilda, widow of William of Wolvesey, claims her dower from Ralph of Hintes. He claims that her busband is still alive 'and she counterclaims that he had died on his pilgrimage to St James. And it was ruled that she should produce sufficient witness that he had died within three weeks after the feast of St Hilary; and she then produced Reginald de Morton; and Ulric of Scropton, who said that they were there when he died and were witnesses of his burial.' [*Curia Regis Rolls*, 1, p. 151.]

(b) Taking refuge in pilgrimage

(i) *1218–19, York* William, the son of Lecia, was found drowned, and his mother Lecia was the first to find him. But it is said that she is dead, and the jurors say that she went to Jerusalem and the village of Walton has recognised this. ... No one is suspected. Judgement: Misadventure. [*Rolls of the Justices in Eyre for Yorkshire 1218–19*, ed. D.M. Stenton (Selden Society 56, 1937), n. 431, p. 183.]

(ii) *1221, Worcester* Howel le Marchis, a certain wandering robber, and his associates attacked a certain carter and wanted to rob him, so that the carter killed Howel and defended himself against the others and got away from them. Since it was attested that Howel was a robber, let the carter be quit. Be it known that he is in the lands of Jerusalem, but he may safely return, quit of that death. [*Rolls of the Justices in Eyre for Lincolnshire 1218–19 and Worcestershire 1221*, ed. D.M. Stenton (Selden Society 53, 1934), p. 593.]

(c) 1223, May 6th

The Abbot of St Augustine's of Canterbury, who by the royal licence has gone on pilgrimage to Cologne, has letters patent of protection, to last until the feast of St Michael [29th September], in the seventh year of the king's reign. [*CPR H III*, 1, p. 372.]

(d) 1232, March 21st, at Bordeaux

The King concedes to Richard Gray that if by chance he meet the common fate of humanity on the journey which he has undertaken to St James for the purpose of prayer, the will which he made before his return from England and before he departed on this journey, concerning the crops then sown on his lands and his other possessions and chattels, shall be upheld and unaltered, so far as concerns the King, in respect of the crops, possessions and chattels aforesaid. [*CPR H III*, 2, p. 467.]

(e) 1233, November 27th

To the official of the archdeacon of Canterbury: 'Our beloved and faithful John of Newmarket has laid it before us that while he was on his pilgrimage to St James, on which journey a certain chaplain was accompanying him, the said chaplain robbed him of his jewels; which chaplain, so John says, you are holding in prison on account of the money and aforesaid jewels which were found on him.' [The official is to establish ownership of the goods and restore them to John.] [*CCR H III*, 1, p. 344.]

(f) 1235, April

Licence to Simon Whystlegray to carry pilgrims to Jerusalem, Santiago or elsewhere in his ship *Gladyghyne*.[13] [*CPR H III*, 3, p. 98.]

(g) 1236, January 9th

Licence to the master and brethren of the Hospital of St Nicholas, Portsmouth to receive a house granted by the king to Philip the Clerk, a leper, for his upkeep; they are to minister to him or find him the wherewithal to go to the Holy Land. [Ibid., p. 134.]

(h) 1237, April 1st

Confirmation of the will of Henry de Bohun, earl of Hereford, made before starting for Santiago in Lent. [Ibid., p. 178.]

(i) 1248, October 6th

Protection for Walter bishop of Norwich, going to St Gilles, until the Purification [2nd February]. [Ibid., 4, p. 28.]

(j) 1254, May 2nd

Protection for Amicia, countess of Devon, going to Pontigny.[14] [*CPR H III*, 4, p. 408.]

(k) 1256, November 8th

Mandate to Philip Lovel, treasurer, that he provide for the king three of the most precious cloths of gold that he can find in London and delive them to Drogo de Barentyn, to offer in the king's name at the tomb of the Three Kings, buried at Cologne, as a gift of the king. [*CCR H III*, 10, p. 5.]

(l) 1261, December 28th

Geoffrey de Lucy and Nicholas Segrave have gone to Pontigny and are granted protection along with many others, including many servants of the Lord Edward. [*CPR H III*, 5, p. 181.]

2. The Reigns of Edward I and Edward II

(a) 1278

Carlisle: proof of age of Patrick Bouche, taken 7th December 1300. Thomas de Kempeley, aged 60, his godfather, remembers that in the year of his birth (6 Edward I) he came from Santiago, 22 years ago on Friday in Passion Week last. [*CIPM 3*, n. 618.]

(b) 1281

Dorset: proof of Age of Alice de Windsor, taken 1297. William Denebaud of Henton, aged 37, says that Hamo his father, on the feast of SS Peter and Paul [June 29th] after the said Alice's birth, took his journey for the Holy Land and died on the Feast of St Thomas the Apostle [December 21st] at Nijuns [Nyons, Drôme] on his way home, 16 years ago. [Ibid., n. 484.]

(c) 1287

Lincoln: Proof of Age of Edmund de Coleville, taken February 14th 1309. Thomas de Santo Laudo, knight, aged 40, says the said Edmund was born at Castlebithan on January 25th 1288 and baptised in the church of St James there. Robert de Coleville and William de Bergh lifted him from the sacred font and named him Edmund in devotion to St Edmund of Pontigny, because his father, travelling there, vowed to name his son Edmund. [Ibid., 5, n. 157.]

(d) Remembering the Jubilee

(i) *1297* Thweng, East Riding: proof of age of Robert de Foxoles, taken May 24th 1319. Marmaduke Garton aged 60, attests to his birth in 1297 'because Richard his [own] brother crossed the seas and stayed three years and returned with the pilgrims coming from the court [of Rome] in the year of Jubilee'. [Ibid., 6, n. 202.]

(ii) *1300* Chichester: proof of age of John de Bohun, taken April 14th 1321. S. de Stedeham attests to his birth in 1300, saying 'that year was the year of Jubilee, and immediately after the said John was born, he took his journey for the Roman court to obtain the indulgences'. [Ibid., n. 433.]

(e) 1306, September 20th

To the king of Castile. Commending Reginald le Lumbard, whom the king is sending to make his offering at Santiago. He [Edward] has been ill and has now recovered. He asks the king of Castile to aid

Reginald with his counsel so that his offering may be well made, and asks for safe-conduct etc. [*CCR Ed I*, 5, p. 458.]

(f) 1307

Kent: proof of age of John de Kyriel, taken August 16th 1329. Thomas Elys, aged over 60, took his journey to Santiago on the Feast of the Purification [February 2nd][15] after John's birth, the Monday after St Michael [September 29th]. [*CIPM* 7, n. 249.]

(g) 1308, June 5th

Safe-conduct until Michaelmas for Gerald Donum, king's yeoman, going on pilgrimage to the church of St Mary Rocamadour in fulfilment of a vow, made at sea when in danger of shipwreck between England and Ireland, that he would not suffer his beard to be cut until he had accomplished his pilgrimage to that church. [*CPR Ed II*, 1, p. 76.]

(h) Controlling the Straits

(i) 1308, August 12th To Robert de Kendale, constable of Dover Castle and Warden of the Cinque Ports. To allow Payn de Turberville, who is going to Jerusalem on pilgrimage, to take with him 300 marks sterling, notwithstanding prohibitions. [*CCR Ed II*, 1, p. 122.]

(ii) 1308, October 4th To the same: ordering him to stop any knights, esquires or men of arms from crossing the sea, without the king's especial licence, for pilgrimages or other purposes, or from taking horses and arms with them. [Ibid., p. 124.]

(i) 1310, February

Wiltshire: proof of age of John Mauduit, taken 1332, 5th May. Born Feast of the Purification, 1310. Robert Swetyng accompanied John Strug, knight, John's godfather, and the next day started for Santiago. [*CIPM* 7, n. 479.]

(j) 1311, February 17th

'Since our beloved servant Peter Auger, the bearer of these presents, recently vowed that he would not shave his beard until he had completed a pilgrimage in certain regions overseas, and the said Peter fears that some people, because of his abundant beard, may accuse him of having been a Templar and cause him difficulties for that reason, we, wishing to bear testimony to the truth, inform you by the tenor of these presents that the aforesaid Peter is a gentleman of our bedchamber and has never been a Templar, but has allowed his beard to grow long for the reason noted above.'[16] [*Foedera*, 3, p. 250.]

(k) 1313

Essex: proof of age of Bartholomew de Bryanson, taken August 11th 1334. Born July 29th 1313: Richard Sole, aged over 45, says his father went to the Holy Land the same year, and died there. [*CIPM* 7, n. 634.]

(l) 1313, April 29th

Notification to the prior general of the Order of the Carmelites and to the provincial prior of that order in England, that John de Bonkil, of their order, is going on a pilgrimage for the well-being of the king and his people to the Holy Land. Request to them to grant to him a licence to set out, and enquiry if they would care to provide him with a fellow of their order who could go on pilgrimage with him, and also to command all friars of their order to receive the said John and his fellow on the journey. [*CPR Ed II*, 1, p. 566.]

(m) 1314, July 26th

Protection until All Saints [1st November] for Richard Lovel, going on pilgrimage to Cologne. [Ibid., 2, p. 161.]

(n) 1315, April 8th

The king approves the chancellor's action in sending a knight to Boston to investigate the arrest of a ship there. He understands from the chancellor 'that the people of the marches of Wales and Scotland are going in great numbers on pilgrimage to Santiago and taking much with them'. Mandate to command the constable of Dover and the keepers of the passage there not to suffer any pilgrim to pass out of the realm until further orders are received from the king and council. [*Calendar of Chancery Warrants*, 1, p. 413.]

(o) 1315, May

Essex: proof of Age of Edward de Wodeham, taken May 19th 1336. Born October 20th 1314. John Ivot, aged 50 years, on Monday in Whitsun week next after the birth of the said Edward took his journey for Santiago, and made his will on the same day, which he has in his possession and by its date he well remembers the age of the said Edward. [*CIPM* 8, n. 37.]

(p) Miscellaneous permissions, 1315–18

(i) 1315, November 1st Edmund de Somerville, going to Pontigny, nominates attorneys until Easter. [*CPR Ed II*, 2, p. 365.]

(ii) 1317, March 24th Protection until the Nativity of the Virgin (8th September) for John Blankpayn, going on pilgrimage to Rome. [Ibid., p. 641.]

(iii) 1317, April 28th Protection until Michaelmas for John de Luk, clerk, going on pilgimage to St Gilles. [Ibid., 2, p. 642.]

(iv) 1318, December 28th Protection for John de Weston, going 'beyond seas' on pilgrimage to Cologne. [Ibid., 3, p. 261.]

(q) 1320, April 20th

The archbishop of Dublin commissioned to absolve Edmund le Boutillier, knight, his wife, and James their son, from their vow of pilgrimage to Compostela, impossible because of the Anglo-Irish wars. The expense of the journey to be calculated and paid to the Holy Land subsidy. [*CEPR* 2, p. 196.]

(r) 1322, December 26th

William de Boudon, clerk, is going to Santiago to fulfil a vow made by Queen Isabella and receives simple protection and safe-conduct until Michaelmas. [*CPR Ed II*, 4, p. 229.]

(s) 1323, April 3rd

Richard Baldewyn, Carmelite & *familiaris noster*, is going to St Mary the Virgin of Toulouse, St James and St Mary Magdalen [Provence], in fulfilment of a vow: request that he be received favourably by all Carmelites. [Ibid., 4, p. 271.]

3. The Reign of Edward III to 1348

(a) 1329, September 30th

Edmund earl of Kent and Margaret his Countess are permitted *permutatio* of vows taken by them, 'twice by him, that is to say on the death of Margaret, queen of England, his mother, to fulfil a similar vow made by her and not fulfilled, and subsequently when he was gravely ill; and once by Margaret his wife, namely when the said Edmund was ill, to visit in person the shrine of the blessed apostle James; they are within three years to give to the church of the apostle whose shrine they were bound to visit as much as they would have expended in going and returning; in place of the bodily effort of the pilgrimage they shall accept a salutary penance from their confessor; it being noted that when they had set out on the said pilgrimage and reached the region of Gascony, they could proceed no further without grave personal danger because of plots (*insidiae*) laid against them in Spain'.[17] [John XXII, 9, n. 46768.]

(b) 1330, April 11th

To Matilda de Brionie of the diocese of London, who, on her way to visit the Holy Sepulchre, Santiago and Assisi, was, after leaving Valence, upset out of a boat on the Rhone, when some of her fellow pilgrims were drowned, and her money lost so that she could not prosecute her pilgrimage. Dispensation to enter some convent instead of fulfilling her purpose. [*CEPR* 3, p. 318.]

(c) Licences for temporary non-residence granted to priests

(i) *1330, November 3rd* To Sir Ralph [Kerneyghe], rector of St Erme, until the Purification, 'to visit the shrine of the blessed Apostle James in Galicia, and the Roman court, to expedite business there, within the stated term; then, without further delay, to return to the said church'. [Grandisson 1, p. 589.]

(ii) *1331, March 18th* To Sir Thomas de Dolecote, until St John the Baptist (June 24th) ' in order to visit the shrine of blessed Edmund of Pontigny'. [Ibid., p. 603.]

(iii) *1334, September 24th* To Master John Knight, 'licence to visit the shrine of blessed Thomas archbishop of Canterbury and of blessed Mary Magdalen in Provence, near Avignon, until Christmas'. [Ibid., 2, p. 765.]

(c) 1331, May 20th

To Elias, grand master of the Order of St John of Jerusalem. Commending to his friendship brother Adam de Colesham, knight of that order, who is going by the king's licence to the Holy Land to fulfil the vow that he made for the health of the soul of the late king out of the affection that he bore to the said king, and requesting him to aid Adam with his counsel and assistance. [*CCR Ed III*, 2, p. 315.]

(d) John Amory, a pilgrim from Leicestershire

(i) *1332, January 22nd* Protection and registration of attorneys, until Midsummer, for John Amory, going to Santiago. [*CPR Ed III*, 2, p. 232.]

(ii) 1353, June Leicester: proof of Age of John Amory, taken June 1353. Born November 6th 1331. John son of Robert, aged 60 years, and Peter son of Robert, aged 54 years, say that on the Feast of St Hilary following the said John's birth, John, the said John's father, enfeoffed John de Leycester and William de Dunton, chaplains of his manor of Frollesworth, to hold under a certain form and condition, before he started on his way to Santiago, and the said John and Peter were then named witnesses of the charter made for that purpose.

Robert son of Alan, aged 60 years and more, says that the said John was born at Frollesworth, co. Leicester, and baptised in the church of St Nicholas there on November 6th 5 Edward III [1331]; and this he knows because on the day of the Purification following the birth of the said John, John Amory, the said John's father, started on his way to Santiago. [*CIPM* 10, n. 124.]

(e) 1332, June

Gloucester: proof of age of John Dunne, taken November 24th 1355. John was born at the feast of St Barnabas (June 11th) 1332. Richard le Sumpter, aged 62 years, says that in the week in which the said John was born, John Canty of Coubrug [Cowbridge] and many other pilgrims were drowned at Dunster as they were going to Santiago. [Ibid., n. 265.]

(f) 1333, June

Hertford: proof of Age of John de Noers, taken July 3rd 1355. John was born on the eve of St Margaret (July 20th) 1333. Andrew Plaitour, aged 56 years, says that on Sunday, the feast of Holy Trinity, 1333, he was coming to St Albans from his pilgrimage to Santiago on his way to his own house at Aldebury, and at St Albans there came to him many of his neighbours from Aldebury, and on the following eve of St Margaret he was a godfather of the said John. [Ibid., n. 274.]

(g) 1333, July 29th

Mandate to the bishop of Lichfield, at the king's request, to commute the vow to visit Jerusalem, made by Peter de Thornton, knight, when his wife Lucy was sick, he being now infirm and unable to travel. He is to give to the Holy Land subsidy as much as his journey would have cost, and is to fast or perform some work of piety. [*CEPR* 2, p. 382.]

(h) 1334

Lincoln: proof of Age of Robert Bate of Hacunby, taken May 3rd 1354. Robert was 21 on the feast of St Nicholas (December 6th) last. Robert Bagot, aged 60 years and more, had a boy called William born on the same feast, who at the Purification last set out on his 'journey' to the Holy Land. Robert son of John Walgot, aged 60 and more, began his journey to Santiago at the Epiphany following, and 20 years have elapsed since his return. Thomas de Blaunkeney of Dunesbury, aged 40 years and more, says that he was present at the baptism, serving in the office of clerk, and at Easter following he began a yearly pilgrimage to Canterbury, and since then 21 years have elapsed. [*CIPM* 10, n. 194.]

(i) 1334, November

Surrey: proof of age of Katharine de Wyke. Inquest held February 24th 1351. She was 16 on the feast of St Edmund the King (20th November) last. William atte Gate, aged 40 years, says that on Sunday after the said Katharine's birth his staff and wallet (*compera*) were blessed in the church of Asshe, and he started for Santiago on the Monday following; and he remembers it well because on the same Sunday he enfeoffed for life John de Wythewell, chaplain, of all his lands in Asshe by his charter dated Sunday after St Edmund the King, 8 Edward III [1334]. [Ibid., 9, n. 670.]

(j) 1337, March 20th: Edward III petitions the pope

Our beloved and faithful Bartholomew de Burghersh, brother of the venerable father the lord bishop of Lincoln, in a time of joyful peace in our kingdom, desiring to fight for God rather than in the world, without the licence or knowledge of us, his temporal lord (to whom he is bound by his oath to render obedience), vowed that he would not put on nor bear arms until he had visited the Lord's Sepulchre and the shrine of St James, or had in person fought with the enemies of the Cross of Christ. It is now necessary that the said Bartholomew, by our command and on the decision of our Parliament, should set out with our other lieges to Gascony to defend our people and our inheritance; and since, because of his vigour and prudence his services are extremely desirable to us, especially at this time, and he cannot safely proceed unarmed because of the dangers which, unless God avert them, it is to be feared are likely to arise, we devoutly petition Your Clemency (which we ever trust to be favourable to our request) that mercifully considering the imminent and urgent necessity of defending both our inheritance there and elsewhere, and the people entrusted to us, against the perils raised up against us, it will please you in this perplexity to consider both the conscience and the safety of the said Bartholomew, mercifully committing to some prelate of our kingdom, in whom you have confidence, the power to absolve him by apostolic authority of this vow (from which, according to the judgement of some authorities, the authority of the superior to whom he had previously sworn, is excepted), or otherwise profitably to commute the said vow because of the stated reasons, so that he may be able to bear arms in our service against our enemies.[18] [*Foedera*, 4, pp. 738–9.]

(k) A royal clerk goes to Jerusalem

(i) *1343, March 14th* To Martinus 'de Castro' (Martino di Zaccaria). 'We have often been told that among all the Christian inhabitants in eastern parts you have from your youth faithfully and strenuously laboured for the honour of Christ and the Cross against the blasphemers of the Cross, Saracens and Turks; and that in addition you have seen and treated in a friendly manner our subjects and people of our nation in the said eastern parts. Although we have never seen you, these two things (although one would be enough) give us reasonable cause to love you. We wish you to know, that, as debtors, we desire nothing more than to lay down our life for Christ there where Christ laid down his life for us; for which purpose we hope, when the time comes, to have you as friend and ally, to your own honour and benefit. Since, although we have never previously written to you, you have been useful and benevolent to our people, we think it enough to tell you, without beseeching, that the bearer of these presents, William de Kildesby, our beloved secretary, coming to the region of the holy city of Jerusalem, is and has been our faithful and beloved Secretary, so that going and coming he may enjoy your assistance and be guided by appropriate favours, in consideration of us.'[19] [*Foedera*, 5, p. 160.]

(ii) *1343, April 21st* Indult to William de Kildesby, canon of London, at the king's request, to visit with six persons the Lord's Sepulchre and that of St Catherine who was buried by angels, he having a great devotion to that virgin martyr. They are not to take anything with them which may be of service to the enemies of the Christian faith. [*CEPR* 2, p. 546.]

(l) 1341, February 2nd

Essex: proof of age of John de Markeshale, taken July 13th 1362. Born February 2nd 1341. Edmund Boteler testifies to the date 'because at the said Feast of the Purification on which the said John was born he started for Compostela, and so the age of the said John runs in his memory'. [*CIPM* 11, n. 388.]

(m) 1342

Canterbury: proof of age of Katherine and Joan Gower, taken May 1st 1357. Katherine was born on 25th November 1340. Philip Pykehare remembers his own daughter being born on the same day, while on the day Joan was born (the Saturday before John the Baptist, 16 Ed. III. i.e. June 22nd 1342) he set out on his journey to the court of Rome'. Robert Westbech says 'that on the Sunday Katherine was born he went on pilgrimage to Santiago and the Holy Land; and on the quinzaine of St John the Baptist after the Saturday on which Joan was born, he returned home. [Ibid., 10, n. 395.]

(n) 1343

Elizabeth de Burgh, lady of Clare, petitions the pope that she may choose a confessor to 'transmute' the vow she made in her husband's lifetime to visit the Holy Land and Santiago, 'which, being forty, she cannot hope to fulfil'. [*CEPR*, Petitions, pp. 22–3.] (The petition was granted on October 22nd [*CEPR* 1, p. 112].)

(o) 1343, February

Lincoln: proof of age of Joan de Salfletby, taken April 26th 1359. She was 16 on the 6th February last. Robert de Alford, aged 33 years and more, agrees and says that on the Monday after the birth of the said Alice, his father, Ralph de Alford, started on his journey to Santiago on pilgrimage whereof he had made a vow on account of a danger in which he had been in the water of Humber. [*CIPM* 10, n. 475.]

(p) 1343, August

Canterbury: proof of age of William Sepvans, taken September 18th 1364. Born August 28th 1343. Henry Bolle, aged 40 years, and Michael Seymakers, aged 50 years say that they started on a journey to Santiago for the amendment of their lives on the morrow of St Augustine, 17 Edward III [August 29th, 1343]. [Ibid., 11, n. 611.]

(q) 1343, September

Ewelme, Oxon: proof of age of John de Burgherssh, taken November 14th 1366. Born Feast of St Michael [September 29th] 1343. Eustace Roser, aged 50 years, William Wayte, aged 56 years, Philip Greenefeld, aged 53 years, Walter Fairman, aged 54 years, William Motte, aged 50 years, Richard Syth, aged 56 years, and Henry Houstwey, aged 56 years, agree and say that on the day of the birth they started with other neighbours of the country for Santiago, and the day on which they started is enrolled in the missal of the same church [Ewelme] and it is now 23 years ago. [Ibid., 12, n. 88.]

(r) 1344, July 30th

To the mayor and bailiffs of Dover: since the venerable father Benedict, bishop of Cardica [Kardhitsa, in Thessaly] is with our licence about to go to parts overseas to perform certain pilgrimages to holy places in the name of Philippa queen of England, our dearest consort, we command that you permit the aforesaid bishop, with his horses and a reasonable household and expenses in gold, to cross from the port of Dover without any impediment. [*Foedera*, 6, pp. 418–19.]

(s) 1345, July 16th

Order to the sheriffs of London to arrest all merchants of 'Pisa and of Luk [Lucca] which is in the power of Pisa' and to confiscate their goods, 'so that the merchants of Pisa be not released by mainprise or otherwise, though the merchants of Luk may be so released, as Robert son of Thomas de Bradestan, John de Sancto Philiberto, and William Dachet, going on pilgrimage to the Holy Land, have been arrested unjustly at Pisa'.[20] [*CCR Ed III*, 7, p. 639.]

(t) John Rivers, knight, pilgrim and Dominican friar

(i) 1346, June 20th Licence, at his instant request and in fulfilment of a vow for the saving of his soul uttered by him at another time to go to the Holy Land, for John Rivers to go to that land as soon as he can conveniently set out. [*CPR Ed III*, 7, p. 128.]

(ii) 1346, August 16th Papal indult to John Rivers, knight of the diocese of Worcester, to visit the Holy Sepulchre with John de Noble priest, and John Wayfor, donzel, members of his household.[21] (*CEPR* 3, p. 28.)

(iii) 1364, October 15th: Pope Urban V to the bishops of Worcester and London and the abbot of Gloucester John Rivers, brother of the Order

of Preachers, originating from the diocese of Worcester, as a soldier at one time accompanied Edward king of England on active service and was involved in many battles in which homicides were committed, although he does not remember that he killed or mutilated anyone; and the aforesaid king appointed him as a judge in a case involving the penalty of blood, although John never condemned anyone to that penalty; subsequently, his wife died and he visited the Lord's Sepulchre and the oratories of the Holy Land and at last took the habit of the brethren of the Order of Preachers. If, taking all the relevant circumstances into account, it seems [to the addressees] that the war in which John was involved on the king's behalf was a just one, or if they entertain a reasonable doubt as to its justice or injustice, and the said John did not appoint a lieutenant in the case deputed to him,[22] they may dispense him to receive all orders including priesthood, at the appropriate times, any apostolic constitutions or statutes of the aforesaid Order notwithstanding. [Urban V, *Secrètes*, n. 11871.]

(u) 1347

Woodford by Thrapston, Northants: proof of age of Henry Boson, taken October 28th 1368; born Sunday after Michaelmas, 1347. Richard le Wryght, aged 50 and more, says that in the year Henry was born his brother Roger started for the Holy Land and appointed him his executor, which Roger died there. [*CIPM* 12, n. 261.]

(v) 1348, March 22nd

To the constable of Dover etc.: order to permit Elizabeth, late the wife of Robert de Assheton, who is about to set out to the Holy Land on pilgrimage, by the king's licence, to cross from the port with a chaplain and two yeomen, to the said parts. [*CCR Ed III*, 8, p. 501.]

(w) 1348, July 23rd

Protection for one year for John Bret, 'going on pilgrimage to divers places beyond seas in fulfilment of vows made in very great peril of the sea on his way back to England after the taking of Calais'. [*CPR Ed III*, 8, p. 132.]

4. The Reign of Edward III, 1349–72

(a) War and Jubilee

(i) 1349, September 6th Grant that the confessor of Thomas de Wale, knight, may commute his vow of staying in Rome during the whole of the Jubilee year for other works of piety, provided that he stay there 15 days. [*CEPR* 3, p. 331.]

(ii) 1349, November 21st: Clement VI to Edward III The pope has received from Edward's envoy an explanation of why at All Saints last (November 1st) he did not send envoys to treat of peace with Philip of France. ... The pope is grieved at the destruction of his hopes, and entreats Edward to consider the motives which there are for peace and how the absence of it hinders many from gaining the indulgence of the Jubilee by visiting the basilicas of Sts Peter and Paul and the church of St John Lateran. He asks for envoys to be sent to him on February 2nd and for a prorogation of the truce, now nearly expired.[23] [*CEPR* 3, p. 42.]

(iii) A chronicler's account of exchanges between Pope and King about the Jubilee In the year of grace 1349 a general absolution began at Rome and many made ready to go to Rome; but the king forbade their passage because of the French war. Wherefore the pope sent envoys to the king of England primarily because of the journey (*passagium*). First that the king should not obstruct the holy passage of those wishing to visit the holy places of the apostles. Secondly that he should grant a truce, so that the earl of Lancaster should not campaign in Aquitaine to the disturbance of those wishing to go on pilgrimage (*loca sancta adire*). Similarly, that the king should not prevent, or permit to be prevented persons promoted by the curia by bull from receiving their benefices as incumbents. On the first article the reply was that the king was engaged in war and therefore he lacked resources and it was also necessary for him to consider the treasure of his kingdom, lest, to the detriment of himself and his people, it should be taken out of the kingdom while the war lasted. And in addition the king proclaimed that all Englishmen, whether at Rome or elsewhere overseas, should make haste to return, on pain of forfeiture of life and property. [Henry Knighton, *Chronicon* (2 vols, RS 92), 2, pp. 65–6.]

(iv) 1349, December 1st: To the mayor and bailiffs of Sandwich 'Since no small part of the people of our realm of England has died in the present pestilence, and the treasury of the kingdom is largely exhausted, and since, as we understand, many persons of this our realm

are going abroad, and plan to go abroad, with money which they could have kept in the kingdom; we, noting that, if these departures are tolerated, the kingdom will within a short space of time be destitute of both men and treasure, and that grave peril could arise to us and to the said kingdom from this cause, unless an appropriate remedy is rapidly applied, [prohibit the movement abroad of] men at arms, or pilgrims, or any others of the said kingdom, or elsewhere, of whatever status or condition he be, unless he be known to be a merchant, notary or envoy.' [*Foedera*, 5, p. 668.]

(v) 1350, September 8th To all admirals etc. 'Since we have granted to our beloved and faithful Adam Brabazon, citizen of London, that he may with certain men of his own household go on pilgrimage to great Rome to obtain the absolution of his soul there [*ad Magnam Romam, pro absolutione animae ibidem optinenda, peregre valeat proficisci*], we direct you that you permit Adam and his men aforesaid, together with three or four horses, and his reasonable expenses in gold, going and coming, when they arrive at the ports or places under your command, to cross freely and without impediment to parts overseas (on condition however that they take nothing more in gold or silver beyond their expenses aforesaid), notwithstanding any ordinance, proclamation or mandate to you to the contrary.[24] [Ibid., p. 681.]

(vi) 1350, November 30th Pardon to Richard Spicer of Bristol for going on pilgrimage to the city of Rome without licence, contrary to the proclamations and prohibitions lately made by the king and council. [*CPR Ed III*, 9, p. 19.]

(vii) 1350, December 1st Papal mandate to the chapter of St Peter's to exhibit the Veronica to Margaret [countess] Marshall, kinswoman of king Edward. [*CEPR* 3, p. 48.]

(viii) 1350, December 30th Provision mandate in favour of John de Wilton, a clerk of Salisbury, of a canonry and prebend in St Laurence, Salisbury, void by reason that John of Salisbury, alias Pictoris, who had come to Rome in order to obtain the plenary remission of the year of Jubilee, died on his return at Piacenza. [Ibid., p. 361.]

(b) 1354, February 10th

Order to the sheriffs of London, 'upon sight of these presents, to cause proclamation to be made that no pilgrim shall cross from England to parts beyond without the king's special order, upon pain of forfeiture, and if they find any doing so after the proclamation they shall arrest them with their goods and chattels and keep them safely until further order, certifying the king in chancery from time to time of the names of those so arrested and of the nature and value of the goods and chattels found with them, and they shall not omit this on pain of forfeiture.' [*CCR Ed III*, 10, p. 67.]

(c) 1355, January 29th

Petition of Andrew Luttrell, knight,[25] John Newmarche and John de Rythur, esquires of Henry of Lancaster, for licence to visit the Holy Sepulchre, each with twelve horsemen and attendants. [*CEPR, Petitions* 1, p. 272.]

(d) 1355, March 17th

Petition of Joan de Bar le Duc, countess of Warenne. At sea between England and France she vowed not to return to England until she had visited Santiago; afterwards hearing of her husband's death she returned to England to look after his property, and prays for the prorogation of her vow for three years. Granted for a year and a half, or the vow may be commuted by the Great Penitentiary. [Ibid., p. 287.]

(e) 1356, February

Ipswich: proof of age of Thomas de Londham, taken November 3rd 1376. Born October 12th 1355. John Schereman, 60 and more, went to Santiago at the Feast of the Purification following. Robert Berdevale, 48 and more, 'says that at the Purification after the birth he departed beyond seas to great Rome'. [*CIPM* 14, n. 303.]

(f) 1357, April 1st

'To the collectors of the petty custom in the port of London and to the king's inspector in that port. Order, upon pain of forfeiture, not to permit any pilgrims to pass to parts beyond from that port without the king's special licence until further order, and to make scrutiny of all merchants and others who may henceforward pass to the said parts and come to England, arresting all letters, instruments and other things found prejudicial to the king and his people, together with the persons with whom they were found, and to send such letters etc. to chancery from time to time under seal, and to keep the persons so arrested in prison until further order, as although the king lately ordered the collectors and inspector not to permit any pilgrims to cross from the port of that city to parts beyond, and to make scrutiny of all crossing from that port whether they carried letters, etc. prejudicial to the king, yet they have permitted great numbers of pilgrims and others to cross with letters and other prejudicial things without making such scrutiny.' [*CCR Ed III*, 10, p. 396.]

(g) 1358, January 17th

Thomas Roper, son and heir of Robert Hamound, citizen and roper (*coriarius*) of London, going to Santiago on pilgrimage, nominates William le Bakere, a fishmonger, as his attorney until Whitsun. [*CPR Ed III*, 10, p. 645.]

(h) 1358, April 16th.

Protection and safe-conduct until Michaelmas 'for Peter Juayns of Mondate, and some fellows of his, merchants of Spain, who lately when coming with a ship laden with wine by Calais, being in peril of the sea, uttered unanimously vows that if delivered from the peril they would visit the shrine of St Mary of Rocamadour on pilgrimage and who have sold their wine at the said town and received the price, now passing to the said place in fulfilment of the vow'. [Ibid., 11, p. 45.]

(i) 1358

Inquest held at Little Perndon, Essex, on January 29th 1359, to establish the death of John de Benstede. Thomas, chamberlain of the deceased, who was with him at his death at the tomb of St Katherine [on Mount Sinai] says that he died there about the feast of St Margaret [20th July] last. [*CIPM* 10, n. 468.]

(j) 1361, March 30th

Licence for Richard Baddyng and Paul de Portesmutha to take pilgrims to Santiago in a ship of theirs called *la Nicholas* of La Rye, from the port of La Rye, notwithstanding any mandate or proclamation to the contrary; provided that the pilgrims do not take with them 'sterlynges', silver, armour or horses. [*CPR Ed III*, 11, p. 586.]

(k) 1361, June 2nd

To Robert de Herle, constable of Dover Castle etc. Order to take an oath of John Gybourn that he will not entertain any carpenters, masons or other craftsmen, workmen or men fit to bear arms in the ship which he has caused to be new made intending to send her to Santiago with pilgrims on her first voyage, for that voyage or otherwise, and to suffer the said ship to pass thither from this time with as many other persons as would sail in her, any command to the contary notwithstanding; as the king of his favour has given the said John licence to take pilgrims in the said ship to Santiago with the above exceptions. [*CCR Ed III*, 11, p. 270.]

(l) 1361, May

March of Wales: proof of age of John de Cherleton, taken July 9th 1382; born 25th April 1361. Griffith ap Jevan, David ap Jevan and Wyllym ap Jor', 48 and more, 'say that on Monday after the feast of St Augustine, apostle of the English [26th May], they set out together for Santiago, and they were in the church of La Pole to take leave of their neighbours when they saw the said heir baptised'. [*CIPM* 15, n. 659.]

(m) 1361, July 25th

Order to the mayor and bailiffs of Dartmouth or Plymouth, to make 'a sufficient ship, of those not arrested for the passage of Robert de Stafford, seneschal of Gascony, to be delivered to Andrew Luterell and Elizabeth his wife for their passage and the passage of 24 persons, men and women, and 24 horses of their company, in either of the ports named where Andrew shall choose to cross the sea, any arrests of ships for the king's service (the passage of the said steward excepted) and any commands or commissions to the contrary notwithstanding; as the said Andrew and Elizabeth and their company are sailing for Santiago with the king's licence'. [*CCR Ed III*, 11, p. 197.]

(n) 1362, January 26th

Admission of guardians in England, Wales and Ireland of Humphrey de Bohun, earl of Hereford, the king's ward, who is going beyond the seas on pilgrimage 'during his nonage'; should he attain full age during his absence they shall become his attorneys. [*CPR Ed III*, 12, p. 173.]

(o) 1366, January 15th

Protection during pleasure for the men, lands, rents and possessions of Edmund le Morteyn, who with the king's licence lately set out on pilgrimage to the Holy Land and whom his attorneys believe to be in good health; on their petition showing that certain persons asserting that he has died in the said land are planning to invade and destroy his lands and possessons. [*CPR Ed III*, 13, p. 193.]

(p) 1366, January 15th

Petition from Isolda Parewastel of Bridgwater, that 'for three years she has daily visited the Lord's Sepulchre and other holy places of the Holy Land, and has there been stripped and placed head downwards on a rack, and beaten; then, half dead, she miraculously escaped from the Saracens and now proposes to build a chapel at Bridgewater in honour of the Blessed Virgin, and for her soul's health and those of her ancestors, and to endow it with one priest with a yearly rent of 36 florins. She therefore prays for licence to found and endow the same and reserve the right of patronage to herself and her heirs. [*CEPR, Petitions* 1, pp. 512–13.]

(q) 1366, February 6th

Licence for William abbot of Evesham to go on pilgrimage beyond seas with certain household servants, to visit the head of St John the Baptist at Amiens,[26] the bodies of the Three Kings at Cologne, the shrine of St Francis of Assisi and Santiago in Galicia, provided that he turn not aside elsewhere, but return as soon as he conveniently can, that he send no messenger, letters, money or any thing in writing or otherwise into any other parts on any other account, and that do not sue or procure to the king's prejudice, as he has promised by oath in the presence of Simon bishop of Ely, the chancellor. [*CPR Ed III*, 13, p. 217.]

(r) 1367, October

York: proof of age of Margaret Chaumont, taken November 10th 1382. Born October 11th 1367. William de Sutton, aged 52 and more, says that his brother William started on a pilgrimage 'to the Roman court' that day and has not yet returned(!). [*CIPM* 15, n. 893.]

(s) 1367, November 22nd

Adam de Sancto Ivone permitted to cross on a pilgrimage from Dover with 2 yeomen, 3 hackneys each under 40s, and 40 pounds expenses, provided he taken no [other] sum of money or letters or anything in writing or otherwise which could turn to the prejudice of the king, the realm or any of the king's subjects, and that none of the king's hostages from France cross out of the realm by virtue of this mandate. He is to cross once only and that within a month, or the licence will be null. [Ibid., p. 70.]

(t) Licences to ship pilgrims to Santiago

(i) *1368, February 15th* William Derby of Bristol is licensed 'to load a ship of his, newly made, with pilgrims of middling condition with no great estate, who wish to go on a pilgrimage to Santiago, and to take them to the place where such pilgrimage is to be made, all clerks, knights, esquires and other nobles being excepted'. [*CPR Ed III*, 14, pp. 134–5.]

(ii) *1368, March 23rd* Also to Walter de Derby of Bristol 'to take from Bristol and neighbouring ports to the parts of La Groyne [Corunna] in Spain, in his newly built ship called *la Gracedieu* of Bristol, as many pilgrims as the ship can conveniently carry, and bring back from there victuals and other merchandise, provided that the ship be not arrested for the king's service and that horses, gold or silver, bows, arrows or other armour or anything prejudicial to the King and Crown pass over in the ship'. [Ibid., p. 226.]

(iii) *1368, March 26th* John Sloo, William Sommwell and John Dodyng are similarly licensed for *la cog Thomas*, in lieu of a licence to Sloo for *la saintemarie cog*, now arrested to take men to Gascony for Edward prince of Aquitaine and Wales. [Ibid., p. 228.]

(u) 1369, April 3rd

Thomas Lamb of Appelee is pardoned in respect of the suit and any outlawry consequent on his being indicted, while a pilgrim to the Holy Land, for stealing 13 house rafters from the prior of Bokyngton. [*CPR Ed III*, 14, p. 228.]

(v) 1369, May 10th

Joan wife of Thomas Burton of London has made humble petition for the restitution of £43 10s, arrested by 'the searcher of the king's forfeitures in the river Thames' at Gravesend, also the ship of Flanders in which it was found and the master thereof, 'showing that to fulfil his vows her husband departed from the city of London on a pilgrimage towards the Holy Land and other thresholds of the saints, and that on his journey he was in the parts overseas taken and imprisoned and put to ransom and is yet there detained'. Joan sold all her goods and chattels and, knowing nothing of the ordinance against taking money out of the realm without licence, set out 'to sail to foreign parts for delivering of her husband' and was thus apprehended. [*CCR Ed III*, 12, pp. 27–8.]

(x) 1373

Inquest taken at Sturminster Marshall, Dorset, June 10th 1376. Wenteliana, sister and heir of John son of John de Keynes, knight, died on July 29th 1375. Her aunt Elizabeth de Keynes would have been her heir, 'but in Christmas week, 47 Edward III [1373] the said Elizabeth with some neighbours of hers set out for the Holy Land, and the neighbours returned a year ago and said very truly that she was dead, as the jurors also say'. [*CIPM* 14, n. 234.]

5. The Reign of Richard II

(a) Permissions to go to Rome, 1378

(i) June 20th [To the keepers of the passage at Dover etc. on behalf of] William Sallon of Bolton, chaplain, 'going to to the court of Rome for his soul's health'.

John Swan, vicar of St Paul Malmesbury, 'going to the court of Rome for conscience sake and taking 40s'.

John de Stebbyng, clerk, 'going thither with one yeoman on pilgrimage and for futherance of other his business there and taking 20s'. [*CCR R II*, 1, p. 528.]

(ii) September 28th Ralph Flesshewer of Chesterfield, Sara his wife and Henry his son, Agnes Spicer, Agnes Innocent, Agnes Leche, Joan Brette, Maude Porter and Anabilla de Wakefield, going to the court of Rome. [Ibid., p. 530.]

(b) 1380, January

Tamworth: proof of age of William Hethill, taken at Tamworth, March 10th 1401. Born at Baginton and baptised there January 25th 1380. Robert atte Grene, 51 or more, John atte Mersh, 48 and more, Richard atte Byrches, 44 and more, Henry Barkere of Tamworth, 49 or more, and John Notehurst, 53 or more, began a pilgrimage to the court of Rome on the day that William was born and baptised. [*CIPM* 18, n. 529.]

(c) 1381, February 22nd

To Humphrey Passour, the king's searcher in the port of Plymouth. Order upon petition made on behalf of brother Hugh Leye of the order of Friars Preachers in the city of London, of the king's alms to restore to him certain books and 5 marks 11 shillings in money, although forfeit, if arrested for the cause stated and none other; as it is shown the king that with licence of his provincial he was minded to pass in that port on pilgrimage to Santiago, and that the searcher arrested the said books and money as forfeit for that he had not with him the king's passport. [*CCR R II*, 1, p. 439.]

(d) 1383, July 13th

Protection and safe-conduct for a year for Geoffrey de Poulglou, knight, and Master Roger Brocherioul, clerk, of Brittany, and a certain lady and two maidens of their party, going on pilgrimage through the dominion and power of the king, both by sea and land, to the blessed Virgin Mary of Rocamadour and St James of Galicia, and elsewhere as it shall please them. [*Foedera*, 7, p. 405.]

(e) 1384, May 4th

'Considering the great devotion which our beloved and faithful Thomas de Roos of Hamelake has to go on pilgrimage to Jerusalem, which pilgrimage he vowed a long time ago, and the great gnawing of conscience which he therefore has that he should fulfil the aforesaid vow, we grant him that he may go on pilgrimage to the parts aforesaid, without impediment from us or any of our heirs whomsoever.' [Ibid., p. 426.]

(b) Restrictions on overseas traffic, 1389

(i) 1389: *Statutes of the Realm, 12 Richard II, c. 20* 'The King wills and commands by the Assent of the Lords in this Parliament, that all Pilgrims and other People, except notorious and known merchants, & also Soldiers & Men of Arms that will pass by the Sea out of the Realm, shall pass at the Ports of Dover and Plymouth and not elsewhere, without special licence of the King himself; but they that shall pass toward Ireland shall pass at Liverpool, Chester, Bristol or elsewhere that shall please them.

(ii) 1389, June 15th To the keeper of the passage in the port of London and in the River Thames. Order under pain of forfeiture to suffer no lieges in that port and river to pass to any foreign parts save known merchants, any previous command of the king notwithstanding; as the pope has excommunicated all them of Spain, who are the king's enemies and notorious schismatics, and all others who repair to them or have communication with them; and a great number of the king's lieges are minded to go on pilgrimage or for other cause to Santiago in Spain, and other foreign parts, taking with them divers sums of money in the lump, in plate and in coin contrary to the king's order and prohibition. (*CCR R II*, 3, p. 592.)

(g) Permissions to go to Rome, 1390

(i) *January 10th* Ralph Bellaworth may 'go on pilgrimage to the Roman court and obtain a benefice there'.[27] [*CPR R II*, 4, p. 171.]

(ii) *February 20th* The king's liege Thomas Bradwell is permitted to leave from Dover, Sandwich or elsewhere on pilgrimage to the Roman court with his companion John Rede, with one horse and 200 marks for expenses, 'on condition that neither of them attempt aught in that court prejudicial to the Crown or laws and customs of England'. [Ibid., 4, p. 200.]

(h) 1390, September 20th

The bishop of Derry is mandated to absolve and dispense John de Wyom, Cistercian monk of Kirkstead, 'who not as an apostate but as a pilgrim came to Rome without licence of his superior to get the indulgence granted by Urban VI and at times on the way put off his habit and assumed a secular dress which he still wears, and now desires to return to his monastery'. [*CEPR* 4, p. 328.]

(i) 1390, November 18th

William de Botreaux the elder, knight, may cross from Dover to the Roman court and on pilgrimage to Jerusalem with five servants, 6 horses and other 'harness', to perform his vow.[28] [*CPR R II*, 4, p. 324.]

(j) 1391, March 25th

Thomas Norton may before Michaelmas ship in the *George* of Bristol as many pilgrims as he pleases, one voyage only, to Corunna, 'whereof he may make proclamation in every part of the realm, but the pilgrims must be of the king's allegiance and amity, and must not carry gold or silver, in bullion or money, contrary to statute'. [Ibid., p. 387.]

(k) 1391, September 18th

Mandate to the bishop of London to commute into other works of piety the vow of Margaret, wife of George Frungg, knight, dwelling in London, who, when wife of the late Thomas de Naunton, knight, vowed, at his command and with his consent, to visit Santiago de Compostela, but who, on account of her age and the number of her children, and because the said George does not consent, is unable to fulfil her vows. The bishop is to impose a salutary penance and cause her to assign for the repair of the churches of Rome, to the collector deputed in the Roman court for the purpose by the Pope, a sum equal to the expenses of the journey and the offerings which she would have made to the church of Santiago. [*CEPR* 4, pp. 388–9.]

(l) 1393, December 16th

To Francis Vinceguerre, a Lombard dwelling in London, to pay 48 marks to Walter Yonge, John Waselyn and William Killum and to five women who are journeying on pilgrimage to the Holy Land in their company, namely 6 marks apiece. [*CCR R II*, 5, p. 523.]

(m) 1399, May 13th

Indult to Catherine Kelsey, of the diocese of London, to leave the place near St Peter's, Rome, where she is now and has been for some time enclosed, and accompanied by a woman of her own tongue, to go on pilgrimage or visit her relatives and friends and return, and to use her goods; her vow to remain the same place for life and to live on alms only notwithstanding. [*CEPR* 5, p. 249.]

6. The Fifteenth Century

(a) 1400, December 13th

To Thomas Kyrkeby, clerk of the diocese of Carlisle. Power to visit by deputy the Holy Sepulchre and the shrine of St James, it being inconvenient for him to fulfil the vow, made by him when grievously sick, to do so in person; provided that he send the same offerings which he would have made. The corporal labours [of pilgrimage] are to be commuted into other labours and works of piety. [Ibid., p. 378.]

(b) 1403, March 14th

Licence for Agnes Bardolf, lady of Wormegey, late the wife of Thomas Mortymer knight, to go on pilgrimage to the cities of Rome and Cologne and other foreign parts from any part of the realm with twelve men and twelve horses in her company and her goods and harness, and to pay £300 for her expenses to merchants of Genoa and other persons in the realm who will pay to her letters of exchange to their fellows in foreign parts. [*CPR H IV*, 1, p. 214.]

(c) 1409, May 20th

Exemplification, at the request of Thomas Swinburne, knight, mayor of Bordeaux, of letters patent of Charles king of France, dated at Tours, 4 January 1408–9, granting safe-conduct for one year to the said Thomas, coming to the marches of Bordeaux and the county of Guyenne to keep the truce for the King of England, and afterwards going on pilgrimage to 'Seint Jacques' in Galicia, and his company to the number of thirty persons. [Ibid., 4, p. 82.]

(d) 1409, October 8th

Grant to the king's esquire Henry Fowler, serjeant of the office of the larder, who for the convalescence and health of the king's person and for the safety of his own soul has vowed to go on pilgrimage on foot to the Holy Land, of all fees, wages and Christmas and Easter gifts pertaining to his office during the time that he is thus on pilgrimage. [Ibid., 4, p. 113.]

(e) 1411, March 18th

Licence to John Kennynghale, Benedictine of Bury St Edmund's, 'after asking, even though he do not obtain his superior's leave, to visit Rome as a pilgrim'. [CEPR 6, p. 276.]

(f) 1412, April 20th

Indult to John Bebe, priest of the diocese of Lincoln, that the confessor of his choice may commute his vow to visit the Lord's Sepulchre etc., he being unable to fulfil it by reason of the leprosy with which he has since been smitten and his poverty. [Ibid., p. 305.]

(g) 1412, August 13th

Licence to the abbot of St Augustine's Canterbury to go out of the realm to the Holy City of Jerusalem to fulfil a vow. [CPR H IV, 4, p. 409.]

(h) 1414, March 4th

To Edmund bishop of Exeter. Absolution *ad cautelam* from the vow he took in or about his twenty-fifth year, and before he became bishop, to go to Santiago if his sister recovered from illness. Peter bishop of Dax, papal nuncio, asserted his power (which some have doubted) to commute the vow into other works of piety. He has performed the works and has sent many offerings to shrines by pilgrims. He is to give a chalice of pure silver of the weight of 2 marks sterling. [*CEPR* 6, p. 439.]

(i) 1426, March 4th

To Jean archbishop of Rouen. Louis bishop of Therouanne, chancellor of France and lieutenant of John duke of Bedford, and the members of the royal council at Paris, have set forth to the pope that Thomas Montacute, earl of Salisbury, when formerly on his way back to England from a visit to the Lord's Sepulchre, fell grievously ill, and made a vow to revisit, if cured, the said Sepulchre, without saying when; that, afterwards, when restored to health, and being in a certain battle, he confirmed and repeated this said vow; that although he made two attempts to fulfil this vow, nevertheless, being a vassal of Henry king of England, he has been prevented by authority of the said king; and that when recently he made a third attempt to fulfil his said vows, and rejecting the persuasions of the said chancellor and other members of the said great council, would have set out, they repeated to him the oaths of fealty which he had taken to the said king, asserting that he could and ought not to absent himself from the service of the king, without the king's express leave, the pope therefore grants faculty to the above archbishop to commute the said oaths into other works of piety. [Ibid., 7, pp. 438–9.]

(j) 1428, May 19th

Commission to John Newton, mayor of Bristol, John Sharp, sheriff of the same, Richard Newton and John Burton, and to any three of them including the said mayor and sheriff, to enquire as to the owners and masters of the ships and vessels who are stated to have shipped at Bristol, and in the waters of Severn, a greater number of pilgrims for Santiago, and conveyed them thither, than the king's licence allowed, to the king's prejudice and the deception of the court of his Chancery. [*CPR H VI*, 1, p. 493.]

(k) 1433, July 25th

Appointment of Thomas Haseley to be collector of the two pence from each noble put in exchange by pilgrims and others about to proceed to the Roman court, the Holy Land, or other Holy Places: he to account for the same yearly at the Exchequer and to receive such payments as may be agreed upon between him and the Treasurer of England. [Ibid., 2, p. 282.]

(l) 1434, February 16th

Commission to Thomas Stawell, knight, John Warre esq., John Hody, Alexander Hody and the sheriff of Somerset, and to two or more of them, to enquire on oath of the said county as to the number of ships which have sailed from any port of the county without the king's licence for Santiago. [Ibid., p. 471.]

(m) 1436, October 9th

'Be it known that we have learned from the account of our dearest and faithful councillor, John Lord Scrope, of the distinguished treatment, honour, generosity and favour that the most powerful and illustrious prince, our dearest kinsman the marquis of Mantua recently bestowed upon him when he traversed his lands and dominions on his way to the Lord's Sepulchre and when he returned thence.' [The king reciprocates by granting the marquis the power to bestow the royal livery on fifty persons of his choice, provided they be of noble blood and standing.] [*Foedera*, 10, p. 655.]

(n) 1440, November 7th

Absolution of Robert de Wylby, baron of the diocese of Lincoln, from the vow he formerly made to visit the Lord's Sepulchre and divers other pious places; his recent petition containing that he lately set out, but has been captured with his household in 'Almain' by certain enemies of the realm of England, and imprisoned and despoiled of his goods and held to so much ransom that he fears he will not recover his liberty without very great and almost irrecoverable loss; his petition adding that even if he recovers his liberty, he might incur greater and perhaps intolerable losses and perils if he began to carry out his vow anew. [*CEPR* 9, p. 84.]

(o) 1446, December 10th

Licence for Reginald West, knight, 'who proposes soon to set out for the court of Rome and other foreign parts, and thence for the Holy Land, there, God willing, to fulfil his vows', provided that he take with him nothing prejudicial to us or our kingdom of England, whether silver or gold in bullion or in coin, other than his reasonable expenses, with one or two silver and gilded cups for use on the aforesaid journey, beyond our town of Calais. [*Foedera*, 11, pp. 148–9.]

(p) 1448, March 3rd

Be it known that in consideration of the good and laudable military service which our faithful knight Lord Scales[29] has performed for us and our late father, for the space of thirty years, and wishes to perform in future, and because it has pleased the Almighty throughout that time to preserve him unhurt from all the harms and perils of war, he has vowed to visit the Holy Land as a pilgrim, and with our licence proposes to set out thither, and as he says not to use arms, unless in our presence, until he has completed his pilgrimage; considering the foregoing, we have conceded and granted licence to our aforesaid Knight that he may go on pilgrimage to the said land, and return thence, without any impediment, vexation or annoyance from us, or any of our heirs, officials, subjects or servants whatsoever; any statute, act or ordinance to the contrary notwithstanding. [Ibid., pp. 197–8.]

(q) The 1450 Jubilee

(i) *1450, April 13th* Robert Rodes, layman of the diocese of Durham set out to obtain the Jubilee indulgence but fell ill at Basel and could not proceed. If he gives four gold florins to the *camera* of the poor he shall gain all the indulgences granted to those who visit the four churches of the City [Rome] as if he had visited them during the prescribed time. [*CEPR* 10, p. 66.]

(ii) *1451, September 38th* Grant to Richard Tunstall, esquire of Henry VI, at his recent petition (containing that in the year of Jubilee he made up his mind, but not under the form of a vow, to visit the shrine of the Apostles Peter and Paul, but that he was so much occupied with arduous business in the service of king Henry that he could not go to Rome without the indignation of the said king, wherefore the king had petitioned the pope to make him a sharer in the indulgence of the said year of Jubilee). He shall, being contrite and having confessed, after visiting on three successive days the churches of St Paul, London, and St Peter's, Westminster, saying on each day seven times the Lord's Prayer and Hail Mary, and giving on the said days 10d sterling to the poor, gain the plenary indulgence of the Jubilee as if he had visited Rome and the appointed basilicas and churches thereof. [Ibid., pp. 102–3.]

(iii) *1450, June 17th* To Sybil, widow of Roger Boys of the diocese of Norwich. The confessor of her choice may absolve her from all her sins 'and also (seeing that she, who is about eighty years old, vowed to visit the shrines of SS Peter and Paul and that on account of a certain hindrance and old age she cannot do so, and has sent at her expense a certain religious and a servant to visit the said shrines) may absolve her from the said vow, enjoining penance. [Ibid., p. 525.]

(r) Anthony Woodville, the King's brother-in-law

(i) *1471* 'Although long before this time, our dearest kinsman Antony Woodville[30], Earl Rivers, lord of Scales, Nucelles and the Isle of Wight, valiant knight of our Order of the Garter, and brother of our dearest consort Elizabeth queen of England, vowed to go in person in arms against the unbelievers and ferocious foes of the Christian faith, to resist their onslaught on the true worshippers of God, and also resolved, for the salvation of his soul, to visit various far-flung parts of the world, by way of devotion and pilgrimage, the internal wars of our kingdom have prevented him from fulfilling his vows. ...' [Now that Edward has peaceful possession of the Crown, he willingly grants his brother-in-law permission to perform his pilgrimage.] [*Foedera*, 11, pp. 727–8.]

(ii) *1476, March 1st* The pope offers pardon to any guilty person or persons who within a fortnight shall reveal the whole or part of the theft of valuables 'which has recently been committed at Bracciano in the diocese of Sutri, against Anthony Wydeville, earl Rivers, brother of queen Elizabeth, who had gone to visit the churches of Rome in order to gain the Jubilee indulgence'. [*CEPR* 13, p. 221.]

(s) 1477, October 16th

[Sixtus IV issues a monition on behalf of Richard Heron, merchant of the Staple of Calais, who has protested to the Pope against the seizure of his goods and his own subsequent imprisonment at Calais] ' ... trusting in the said society [of the Staple] and its ordinances, and also trusting that all good Christians who come to visit the shrines of the Apostles at Rome are, with all their goods, in the safe-guard and protection of the holy apostolic see, the said Richard, about eighteen years ago, with the intention of visiting the said shrines in order to gain the indulgences granted to those who visited them and other churches of Rome, caused to be brought from England to the said town, in order to make the said pilgrimage, and also to pay his debts, five hundred great bales of wool of England, there called 'sarplers', which, with a great quantity of wools of England which he had already in the said staple, were of the value of 24,000 marks of silver and more, and arranged that the proceeds thereof should be deposited with William fitzJohan, a merchant of the said society, and prepared to depart from Calais and make his pilgrimage ... .[31] [*CEPR* 14, pp. 229–30.]

(t) 1478, October 24th

Licence and faculty for William Lucas, priest of the diocese of London (who is an anchorite and has voluntarily enclosed himself in a certain enclosure near the church of All Hallows, London, and has lived laudably therein for several years, and who on account of his singular devotion to SS Peter and Paul desires before he departs this life to visit their shrines at Rome and divers other holy places), to leave the said enclosure, without other licence, and visit the said shrines etc. and remain without the said enclosure for fifteen months from the day of setting out. [Ibid., p. 625.]

CHAPTER 9

Pilgrimage in England

The kings of England were professionally interested in the shrines of their kingdom. They were frequently pilgrims themselves, and so too were their queens, who sometimes embarked on pilgrimage tours of the country [2,9]. They were also careful to send conspicuous gifts, often on an annual basis, to prominent shrines such as Canterbury or Walsingham or, of course, the royal foundation of Westminster, and, like their subjects, they left instructions for offerings in their wills. Henry III sent a silver-gilt image of himself to Bromholm in Norfolk, in honour of the Holy Rood, in 1234,[1] while Henry VII directed in his will that an image of himself with an inscription reading 'St Thomas, intercede for me' be set up as close as possible to the saint's shrine at Canterbury; a similar image had already been set up at Walsingham.[2]

The pilgrimages performed by the king's subjects within his kingdom, however, normally attracted governmental attention only when disorders arose.[3] From time to time, the king tried to quash cults of political significance, for example those which came into being after the deaths of Simon de Montfort in 1265 and Archbishop Scrope of York in 1405.[4] After the execution of Thomas of Lancaster in 1320, not only he but some of his adherents were credited with miracles.[5] Subsequently the same saintly merits which some attributed to Thomas were attributed to his enemy Edward II, but Thomas was the bigger gainer from Edward III's succession, although the new king's petitions to the pope for his canonisation bore no fruit. The king claimed that the people were flocking not only to Thomas's tomb but to the place of his passion (or execution) and that cures were occurring. Walsingham recorded that in 1359 blood flowed from the tomb at Pontefract and that in 1390 Thomas was 'canonized'.[6]

Concerns with domestic order were considerably aggravated by the Peasants' Revolt and the spread of Lollardy. In these circumstances, the suspicion (never entirely absent from the minds of the authorities lay and ecclesiastical) that pilgrimage might be used as a cover for vagabondage and even subversion became more overt [31]. For their part, many Lollards were outspoken opponents of pilgrimage, which was bound up in their eyes with idolatry and with profiteering on the part of the clergy.[7] By contrast, many witnessess at *Inquisitions Post Mortem* seem simply to have accepted pilgrimage as a part of their lives, remembering both foreign and domestic pilgrimages and their attendant circumstances, for example being injured on the way back from Canterbury [14]. They sometimes also reveal how extremely localised pilgrimage could be: a group of Wiltshiremen described their visit to the parish church of Box on the feast of the Assumption as a pilgrimage, and a Somerset witness remembered setting out 'on pilgrimage' to Our Lady of Cleeve in the same county [20, 39]. Margery Kempe, whose foreign pilgrimages were more extensive than most, was one day 'asked if she would go two mile from where she dwelled on pilgrimage' to an isolated church of St Michael (identified as St Michael's Mintling, near Lynn).[8] The contest for the presumably modest offerings that were attracted by such local pilgrimages could even raise echoes in the papal court [3]. References to pilgrimage occur sporadically in episcopal registers.[9] Bishops granted minor indulgences to local churches, while the popes made full use of their unique powers to grant greater ones, and a host of minor English churches and chapels benefited accordingly.

It was not solely for the sake of pilgrims that the king was concerned with the state of the road between London and Dover, but they were among those affected. In 1343 an inquest established the responsibility for the maintenance of Rochester Bridge: it was divided between many Kentish communities, the master and brethren of the hospital of St Mary in Strood, and the king himself, who 'makes the barbican and the drawbridge'.[10] In 1366 the state of the roads in Strood, on the approach to the bridge from London, was a matter of concern [26], and in 1396 a royal proclamation sought to regulate the hire of horses on the road, establishing rates: ' from Southwark to Rochester 12d, from Rochester to Canterbury 12d, and from Canterbury to Dover 6d, and from town to town according to that rate of 12d and the number of miles'.[11]

The Paston Letters contain several references to pilgrimage [38]. The family was itself closely associated with a pilgrimage church, the Cluniac priory of Bromholm. The scope of the pilgrimages undertaken in the family's immediate circle was mostly limited to Norwich and Ipswich, and Canterbury probably represented the effective limit of the ambitions of the local population: in November 1466 Sir James Gloys told Sir John Paston that he had not been able to gather in much rent at Snailwell because most of the tenants were absent at Canterbury or elsewhere.[12] The Pastons also received news of actual or intended pilgrimages by the great (including Edward IV) to Walsingham. Not all of the pilgrimage noticed in the letters was entirely routine. The year 1471 was a troubled one, with not only pitched battles (Tewkesbury and Barnet) and executions, but a plague epidemic; this accumulation of misfortunes clearly did nothing to keep pilgrims off the roads.

DOCUMENTS

1. 1236, July 19th

The king to the officials of gaol delivery at Lincoln. 'Since we have heard that John son of Baldry and Henry son of Toly and Agnes his wife are detained in our prison at Lincoln on the accusation of a certain woman who accuses them of the death of Laurence son of Baldry, her husband; and no decision was made about them when they were produced before our beloved and faithful William of York and his associates, the last itinerant justices in the county of Lincoln, because it was then attested that the aforesaid Laurence had gone on pilgrimage to Bromholm and it did not appear that he had ever died; we direct you that you do nothing about them at present, but release them on the bail of twelve law-worthy men until the coming of the justices for the next assize in those parts, so that it can be discovered in the meantime whether this Laurence has been killed or not, and whether they are guilty of his death or not.' [CCR H III, 3, p. 368.]

2. 1243, April 25th: Pope Innocent IV to the queen of England

Yielding to your devout prayers, we concede to you by the present authority that since from time to time it happens, by reason of devotion, that you come to many monasteries, of Cistercians and others, of the kingdom of England, you are permitted, with ten good and honest women, to enter their churches and cloisters for the purpose of prayer; any custom or statute confirmed by the Apostolic see or other authority notwithstanding.[13] [Foedera, 1, p. 417.]

3. 1252, October 14th: Pope Innocent IV to the archbishop of Canterbury

Our beloved son Robert Anketil, rector of the church of St Peter at Saltwood and of the chapels of the village of Hythe dependent upon it, in your diocese, has complained to us that a certain cross with holy relics enclosed in it was once given to one of these chapels, that is St Leonard's in that village. Out of devotion to this cross many pilgrims and others came to the chapel, and made devout oblations and gifts there. The parishioners of the said chapel, taking advantage, so it is said, of the fact that the donor of the cross made the gift in his last will on the condition that the offerings or legacies or other goods arising out of veneration of the cross should in no wise come into the hands of the rector or of the chaplains or of the ministers of the chapel, nor be ceded to their use, nor to others by their disposition, but instead should be disposed of by the men of the village as they thought fit, have for some time at will received these offerings, legacies and goods, and still do so, treating the cross and relics as if they were clergy. They have spent [the offerings etc.] not just on the work necessary to that chapel but according to their wishes and as lavishly as possible. They have also for some time converted and [still] convert [them] to their own use, giving and exchanging them at will and improperly consuming [them], to the not inconsiderable prejudice and disadvantage of the rector of the said chapel. Since therefore laymen, however religious, have no power to dispose of ecclesiastical persons or property, and having regard to the fact that there is danger here to the souls of the parishioners themselves, and out of zealous concern for their salvation not wishing this to pass unnoticed, we command that, if the case is as stated, you direct the aforesaid parishioners to permit the rector to take peaceful possession of the offerings and other things which come to the oft-mentioned chapel, whether on account of the cross or otherwise, and to make proper satisfaction for what they have hitherto received and expended, unprofitably and to the prejudice of the said rector, compelling them if necessary by means of ecclesiastical censure, without right of appeal. [Innocent IV, n. 6094, 3, p. 131.]

4. 1261, February 11th

John de Cave is commissioned to find out by inquest the truth behind a petition by John le Champeneys that when he and his mother were on pilgrimage to Walsingham he was badly beaten during a quarrel between Roger le Worth of Binetre, in whose house he was lodged, and others, and accidentally killed him in self-defence, since when he has been forced to abjure the realm. [*CPR H III*, 5, p. 182.]

5. 1285, November 5th

Pardon to William de Faccumbe, detained in the prison of Canterbury, for the death of Peter de Cumpton; while with the king on pilgrimage to the shrine of St Thomas the Martyr, he killed him by misadventure. [*CPR Ed I*, 2, p. 198.]

6. 1309, 13th May

To the Warden of the Cinque Ports and two others: commission of oyer and terminer on complaint by William Blakeman, Robert Brembel, Thomas Laverant, Walter Oystreman and Robert Pyn of Faversham, that being on a pilgrimage to St Thomas the Martyr, Clement le Ampuller and Reginald le Deghers, the bailiffs, and Walter Bette, John Haket, John Dalham and Roger de Horton, citizens of Canterbury, assaulted them on their arrival in that city, maimed Robert Brembel, and imprisoned them, and when they, the complainants, obtained in the chancery a writ of replevin, the said Clement, Reginald, Walter, John, Jon and Roger and others, with the assent of the commonalty of the city conspiring to deprive the writ of its due effect and to detain them in prison, alleged that they had approached the city with evil intent and had assaulted and maimed the said Roger de Horton, one of the city bailiffs, who had come to arrest them ... [*CPR Ed II*, 1 p. 117.]

7. c.1312

Essex: proof of age of Margaret de Bovill, taken April 12th 1328. Thomas Baynard, knight, aged 60, says that at the time of the birth, 16 or more years ago, he was of the household of Sir Hugh de Neville, who at that time was making a pilgrimage to St Thomas of Hereford[14] and was in his suite. [*CIPM* 7, n. 169.]

8. 1316, June

Stafford: proof of age of John de More, taken 16th April 1336. Born on the feast of St Barnabas [June 11th] 9 Edward II. John le Clerc, aged 46, testifies to this 'because on Monday next after the said feast he took his way for St Thomas the Martyr and in returning fell into a sickness, on account of which he made his will, which he has still in his possession, and by its date he well remember the aforesaid John's age'. [Ibid., 8, n. 60.]

9. 1322, December 23rd

The queen, Isabella, is going on pilgrimage to divers places within the realm; mandate to sheriffs and other bailiffs to provide upon request for her goods and harness and necessaries for her household, at her cost: until Michaelmas. [*CPR Ed II*, 4, p. 227.]

10. 1332, April

Stratford upon Avon: proof of age of Walter Botereaux, taken 10th October 1353. 21 on 12th March last. Hugh le Harpour, aged 46 years, John le Clerk, aged 53 years, and Adam la Notte, aged 46 years and more, say that in Easter week following the said Walter's birth they began their journey together to St Thomas of Canterbury and in going thither they fell among thieves on 'la Bleo'[15] and were there robbed and badly wounded. [*CIPM* 10, n. 119, p. 113.]

11. 1333, April

Leicester: proof of age of William de Ferrariis, taken 10th March 1354. Born and baptised 28th February, 7 Edward III. William Levere, aged 50 or more, says that in Easter week after the said William's birth he started on a pilgrimage to St Thomas of Lancaster at Ponte-fract and in going thither his brother Geoffrey died suddenly. [Ibid., n. 195.]

12. 1335, May

Lincoln: proof of Age of John de Cracroft, taken April 6th 1358. Born and baptised March 13th 9 Edward III. Philip de Thoresthorp, aged 46 and more, & Richard de Bilesby, aged 36 years and more, say that at Ascensiontide after the birth of the said John, the said Philip, and Eude de Billesby, father of the said Richard, went on pilgrimage to Canterbury, in the company of Robert de Cracroft, father of the aforesaid John, in fulfilment of a vow on account of danger in coming from the assizes at Lincoln in thunder and lightning, from which they were in fear of death. [Ibid., n. 479.]

13. 1335, December 14th

Protection until Michaelmas for William de Nesham, *peregrinus*, lately come from the Holy Land and now returning thither, who is collecting alms.[16] [*CPR Ed III*, 3, p. 188.]

14. 1336

York: proof of age of Robert Crook, taken August 3rd 1361. Born Friday after the Purification [February 8th], 10 Edward III. John Cause, aged 45, says that in the month of the birth he went on pilgrimage to Canterbury and in coming back he broke his left arm. William de Hyllung, aged 42, says that at Easter after the birth he went on pilgrimage to Canterbury with his father, and in returning by accident fell from his horse and broke his right leg, more than 23 years ago. [*CIPM* 11, n. 133.]

15. 1336, March/April

York: Liberty of Holderness: proof of age of William de Ros, taken March 7th 1358. Born February 14th 10 Edward III. John de Sprotte, aged 60 or more, says that at Easter after the birth of the said William he began his journey to Canterbury on pilgrimage by reason of his devotion to St Thomas the Martyr, having made a vow on the occasion of an illness. [Ibid., 10, n. 456.]

16. 1337, June

Lincoln: proof of age of Walter de Bermyngham, taken December 1360. Born and baptised June 24th 11 Edward III. Roger de Holbeche, aged 40 years and more, Hubert del Feld, aged 44 years and more, say that on Monday after the birth of the said heir they started on their journey to Canterbury on pilgrimage to St Thomas the Martyr, in which journey, returning from Canterbury, Roger was taken ill at London and lay there a fortnight. [Ibid., n. 533.]

17. 1339, April

Northampton: proof of age of Adam de Wolverton, taken April 18th 1361. Born March 30th 1339. John de Mersh, aged 48 years and more, William de Bosenko, aged 50 years, and Thomas de Twyford, aged 46 years and more, say that on the Monday after the birth they started together on their way to Walsingham on pilgrimage. [Ibid., 11, n. 123.]

18. 1341, November 6th

Order to the Treasurer and Barons of the Exchequer to supersede any demands for subsidy made of the Master and brethren of the Eastbridge hospital at Canterbury, 'founded for the maintenance of poor pilgrims and other infirm persons resorting thither to remain until they are healed of their infirmities'.[17] [*CCR Ed III*, 6, pp. 305–6.]

19. 1347, November 13th

Commission of oyez and terminez on 'a complaint by master Richard de Brayleigh, dean of the church of St Peter Exeter, and parson of the church of Coleton,[18] that Peter de Ralegh, knight, Benedict Sparke, Henry Batyn, John Wygor and others, confederate together, coming armed contrary to the statutes of the peace to the chapel of St Theobald, Coleton, and by grievous threats demanding, nay extorting, toll and other unwonted customs fom men coming to his chapel for the cause of pilgrimage and devotion and veneration to St Theobald, to do oblations and other works of devotion, and from others selling victuals in the cemetery and sanctuary of the chapel and in the fee of the church of Coleton, have by force prevented those and others who would have come as pilgrims from doing their oblations and other pious works, and have carried away his goods and assaulted his men and servants, whereby he has lost the profit and emolument of the said oblations and the service of his men and servants for a great time.' [*CPR Ed III*, 7, pp. 464–5.]

20. 1349, August

Malmesbury: proof of age of Walter fitz Waryn, taken September 19th 1347. Born August 15th 1349. John Brimylham, Richard Parget, William Kaynesham, Thomas Mowle, Henry Umfrey, William Heyr, Peter Davy, Robert Cliverden and Thomas Clyve, say that the heir was born at Boxe and baptized in the church there on the feast of the Assumption, 23 Edward III. This they know because the church is dedicated to the honour of the Assumption, and they were there on that day in one company as pilgrims, and saw how Walter de Paveley, the heir's godfather, lifted him from the sacred font. [*CIPM*, 13, n. 288.]

21. 1351, February

Bedford: proof of age of Thomas de Ardres, taken May 22nd 1372; born February 9th 1351. John Curteys went barefoot to Beverley the Thursday following. [Ibid., n. 231.]

22. 1351, March 14th

Walter de Mauny is licensed to endow a chapel he has built in 'the cemetery near London, which he bought at the time of the great mortality in England, for the burial of poor men and strangers, and to erect therein a college of twelve or more chaplains'. Simultaneously, an indulgence of 1 year and 40 days is granted to those who visit the chapel and cemetery 'founded for the burial of poor and pilgrims' on the principal feasts of the BVM. [*CEPR* 3, p. 395.]

23. 1358, May 9th

Protection and safe-conduct for William de Colysburn, 'who for the salvation of his soul proposes to make divers pilgrimages as well in England, Ireland and Wales as in foreign parts'. [*CPR Ed III*, 11, p. 39.]

24. 1363, November 20th

Relaxation, for ten years, of a year and forty days of enjoined penance to penitents who on the principal feasts of the year visit the chapel of St Mary the Virgin, in the poor hospital of Canterbury called 'Estbrugge', founded by St Thomas the Martyr, for the poor, for *Romipetae*,[19] for others coming to Canterbury and needing shelter, and for lying-in women. [*CEPR* 4, p. 36.]

25. 1364, March 22nd

For ten years, relaxation of 1 year and 40 days of enjoined penance 'to penitents who on the principal feasts of the year visit and give alms to the chapel of St Mary the Virgin, built between the two gates of the Cistercian monastery of Kingswood (Gloucs.), in which chapel, as it is asserted, miracles are done by her intercession, and to which many blind and lame come from England, Wales, Ireland and Scotland'. [Ibid., p. 38.]

26. 1366, June 6th

Commission to the sheriff of Kent and Nicholas Heryng, reciting that the town of Strode [Strood] by Rochester, through which is the common passage of magnates, pilgrims and others visiting the shrine of St Thomas of Canterbury and returning therefrom, for lack of paving and through the negligence of the inhabitants is now so deep and heavy for horse and foot that great peril may arise therefrom; and appointing them to assemble all the inhabitants of the town and charge each of them with the paving of the part opposite their tenements, so that the whole be paved before St Peter's Chains [August 1st] next, and to coerce all contrariants by distraints, amercement or otherwise. [*CPR Ed III*, 13, p. 256.]

27. 1367, February 5th

Whereas John Holdernesse of Dannebury, co. Essex, in returning from a pilgrimage to the Lord's Sepulchre, which grievously threatened him on a stormy sea, vowed to visit in pilgrimage all the shrines of the saints in the king's realm, which vow he intends to fulfil as devotedly as possible, as he says, God willing, and himself praying the king to fortify him with his special protection in making this pilgrimage; the king, approving of his devotion in this matter, has taken him and his goods into his protection for one year in going to the said places, staying there, and returning. [Ibid., p. 375.]

28. 1371, April

Luton, Beds: proof of age of William de Ferrariis, taken April 22nd 1394. Born April 25th 1371. John Spayne, aged 59 years and more, John Rytton, aged 56 and more, and William Stratle, aged 60 years and more, say that they remember because at that time they were journeying on pilgrimage to St Thomas of Canterbury and during their pilgrimage they were told in London of the birth of the said heir by Robert de Hoo, the heir's godfather. [*CIPM*, 17, n. 429.]

29. 1378, February

Dunster, Somerset: proof of age of Thomas Bratton, taken June 30th 1399. Born February 1st 1378. William Hamelyn and John Huwyssh, each aged 60 years or more, and John Ryvers, aged 50 years or more, know this because they were starting on a journey towards St Thomas of Canterbury on pilgrimage when Thomas Stratton, godfather of the said Thomas, announced the birth to them at Dunster. [Ibid., 17, n. 1317.]

30. 1381, June

Houghton Conquest, Beds: proof of age of John Conquest, taken May 18th 1402. Born Thursday June 30th 1379 [*recte* 1381]. Richard Doucesson, William Catesson, William Straunge and Thomas Querndon, on 10th June 1381 set out on a pilgrimage to Canterbury, and when they returned to Houghton Conquest six days later they found all their houses and barns in Chapel End there accidentally burnt down. [Ibid., 18, n. 665.]

31. 1381–82 Statutes of the Realm, 12 Richard II

c. 3 That no Servant or Labourer, be he man or woman, shall depart at the end of his Term out of the Hundred, Rape or Wapentake where he is dwelling, to serve or dwell elsewhere, or by colour to go from thence on Pilgrimage, unless be bring a Letter Patent containing the cause of his going, and the Time of his Return, if he ought to return, under the king's seal.

c. 7 Item, it is accorded and assented, that of every Person that goeth begging, and is able to serve and labour, it shall be done of him that departeth out of the Hundred and other places aforesaid without Letter testimonial as afore is said, except people of Religion and Hermits [approved], having letters testimonial of their Ordinaries. And that the Beggars impotent to serve shall abide in the Cities and Towns where they be dwelling at the time of the proclamation of this statute; and if the people of Cities and other Towns will not or may not suffice to find them, that the said Beggars shall draw them to other Towns within the Hundred, Rape or Wapentake, or to the Towns where they were born, within forty days after the proclamation made, and there shall continually abide during their lives. And that all of them that go in Pilgrimage as Beggars, and be able to travail, it shall be done as of the said Servants and Labourers, if they have no Letters testimonial of their Pilgrimage under the said Seals. And that the scholars of the Universities that go begging have letters testimonial of their Chancellor upon the same pain.[20]

32. 1382, October

Caxton, Cambs: proof of age of Fulk de Grey, taken July 22nd 1405. Born October 28th 1382. Edward Brond, aged 62, was on a pilgrimage to Canterbury with Fulk's father when his mother was pregnant and gave birth. John Gelyn, 54, set off for Santiago on the 2nd February following. [*CIPM* 18, n. 1180.]

33. 1401, August 19th

To the prior and convent of Bromholm, Norfolk; indult that fit priests appointed by them may 'hear the confessions of and grant absolution to, except in cases reserved to the apostolic see, the multitude who resort from afar to the church on account of a certain notable piece of the true wood of the Cross; it sometimes happening that some, their sins, it is presumed, being the cause, are unable perfectly to look upon the said piece, thereby sometimes incurring infirmities of divers sorts'. [*CEPR* 5, p. 432.]

34. 1401, November 16th

Indult to Emma Schermann of the diocese of York, who formerly took the vow of a recluse and had herself for many years enclosed in a cell in the place of Pontefract, with a little garden contiguous thereto for the sake of taking fresh air; on account of the tumults and clamours of the people in the said place, to tranfer herself to another cell with a little garden and to leave her cell yearly for the purpose of visiting churches and other pious places and of gaining the indulgences granted there without requiring licence of the diocesan or other. [Ibid., p. 471.]

35. 1405, April 24th

Indulgence, for 10 years, of 5 years and 5 quarantines on a number of major feast days and their octaves, and the six days of Whitsun, to visitors and almsgivers 'for the conservation of the chapel of St Tinotus near Chepstow, in the diocese of Hereford, to which, situated on the River Severn between England and Wales, resorts a multitude both of English and Welsh'. [Ibid., 6, p. 24.]

36. 1414, March 3rd

Grant of indulgence of 7 years and 7 quarantines to those who on numerous named major feast days 'visit the chapel without the west door of the church of the Cistercian monastery of St Mary the Virgin, Tintern, in the diocese of Llandaff, and give alms for the repair and decoration of its buildings and ornaments, in which chapel an image of St Mary the Virgin has been fairly and honourably and devoutly placed, and although the attempt has been made, has been unable to be placed elsewhere, on account of which miracle, and because mass is said daily by the monks at the altar of the said chapel, a very great multitude resorts to the chapel'. [Ibid., 6, p. 452.]

37. 1436, March 10th

Commission to William Fulthorp knight, Alexander Nevill esq., and Robert Rudstane esq. to arrest brother John Nyghtyngale, monk of the Benedictine house of Whitby, who has forged the seal of Thomas, bishop of Durham, to certain counterfeit letters executory upon letters apostolic obtained upon pretence the vow of pilgrimage to the apostolic see, and committed other offences against his order, and who is a vagabond in secular garb, and to deliver him, when taken, to his abbot. [*CPR H VI*, 2, p. 607.]

38. Pilgrimage in the Paston Letters

(a) 1443, September 28th: Margery Paston to John Paston 'Right worshipful husband, I recommend me to you, desiring heartily to hear of your welfare, thanking God of your amending of the great disease that ye have had; and I thank you for the letter that ye sent me, for by my troth my mother and I were never in heart's ease from the time that we knew of your sickness, till we knew truly of your amending. My mother behested another image of wax of the weight of you to our Lady of Walsingham, and she sent four nobles to the four Orders of Friars at Norwich to pray for you, and I have behested to go on pilgrimage to Walsingham and to St Leonard's [Norwich] for you ... ' [*Paston Letters* 2, p. 55 (slightly modernised).]

(b) *1450, March 11th: Agnes Paston to John Paston* 'Richard Lynsted came this day from Paston, and let me know that on Saturday last past Dravale, half brother to Waryn Harman, was taken with enemies walking by the seaside, and had him forth with them; and they took two pilgrims, a man and a woman, and they robbed the woman, and let her go, and led the man to the sea, and when they knew he was a pilgrim, they gave him money and set him again on the land.'[21] [Ibid., p. 135.]

(c) *1455, January 9th: Edmund Clere to John Paston* Blessed be God, the King [Henry VI] is well amended, and hath been since Christmas Day, and on St John's Day commanded his almoner to ride to Canterbury with his offering, and commanded the secretary to offer at St Edward's. [Ibid., 3, p. 13.]

(d) *1456, November 18th: Sir John Fastolf to John Paston* My Lord of Norfolk is removed from Framlingham on foot to go to Walsingham, and daily I wait that he would come hither. [Ibid., 3, p. 112.]

(e) *1461, October 11th: Clement Paston to John Paston* The King [Edward IV] is this day at Greenwich, and there will be still till the Parliament begins. Some say he will go to Walsingham, but Mr Sotyll said in the hall in the Temple that he had not word of any such pilgrimage. [Ibid., p. 314.]

(f) *1469, May 22nd: James Hawte to Sir John Paston* ... as for the King, as I understand, he departed to Walsingham upon Friday come sevennight, and the Queen also if God send her good health. [Ibid., 5, p. 28.]

(g) *1470, June 22nd: John Paston to Sir John Paston* 'I propose to go to Canterbury on foot this next week, with God's grace and so to come to London from thence.' [Ibid., p. 74.]

(h) *1471, 15th September: Sir John Paston to John Paston* I heard yesterday, that a worsted man of Norfolk, that sold worsteds at Winchester, said that my Lord of Norfolk and my Lady were on pilgrimage at our Lady [of Walsingham] on foot, and so they went to Caster. ... Item, I pray you send me word if any of our friends or wellwillers be dede, for I fear that there is great death in Norwich, and in other Borough towns in Norfolk, for I ensure you it is the most universal death that ever I wist in England; for by my troth, I cannot hear by pilgrims that pass the country, nor no other man that rideth or goeth any country, that any Borough town in England is free from that sickness ... [Ibid., pp. 109–10.]

28th September: As for tidings, the King, and the Queen and much other people, are ridden and gone to Canterbury, never so much people seen in pilgrimage heretofore at once, as men say ... [Ibid., p. 112.]

39. 1467, November 16th

Somerset: proof of age of Richard Warre, taken June 20th, 1491. Born Feast of St Edmund, 7 Edward IV. Richard Houper began a pilgrimage to the chapel of Our Lady of 'Clyve' [Cleeve Abbey]. [*CIPM H VII*, 1, n. 616.]

40. 1473, May 17th

Forasmuch as this day many persons being strong of body to service in husbandry and other labours feign them to be sick and feeble and some ... in going on pilgrimages, and not of power to perform it without alms of the people, and some also feign to be clerks in universities using study and not of power to continue it without help of the people, by means of which feignings, divers fall into the said beggings in cities, boroughs and other places, and so living idly will not do service but wander about from town to town in vagabondage, sowing seditious languages whereby the country people be put in great fear and jeopardy of their lives and losses of their goods, and many other inconveniences follow by occasion of the same, as murders, robberies and riots, mischievous to the disturb-ance of the people and contrary to the king's law and peace. Our sovereign lord ... straitly chargeth and commandeth that no person able to labour or do service live idly, but serve in husbandry and other businesses according to his laws; and that no person go in pilgrimage not able to perform it without begging, unless he have letters testimonal under the great seal ordained for the same, testify-ing the cause of his going and the places whence he came and whither he shall go ... [*CCR Ed IV*, 1, pp. 298–9.]

41. 1481, April

Norfolk: proof of age of Thomas Grey, taken June 12th 1502.

Born and baptised April 20th 21 years previously. Nicholas Markaunt the elder, aged 44 and more, says that he went on pilgrimage to St David's (*iter peregrinationis arripuit versus Meneviam*). [*CIPM Henry VII*, 2, n. 543.]

42. 1481, October

Norfolk: proof of age of Richard Colvyle, taken October 22nd 1502. Born and baptised 21 years ago on October 20th. William Gatisend, aged 60 and more, began a pilgrimage to St David's in Wales. [Ibid., 2, n. 637.]

43. 1482, January

Cambridge: proof of age of Thomas Pygot, taken 18th February 1503. Born and baptised 21 years previously on 18th January. Henry Aylmere, aged 46 or more, began a pilgrimage to St Michael's Mount in Cornwall. [Ibid., 2, n. 563.]

44. 1487, April 11th

Indult to the abbot and convent of the monastery of St Mary, Hailes, of the Cistercian Order, diocese of Worcester, at their supplication. John XXII, having learned that in the church of the above monastery were preserved some drops of the most precious blood of Jesus Christ, and that for this reason many faithful of those parts frequented the church on pilgrimage, granted that the abbot of the same and his successors might depute two suitable priests, secular or religious, as confessors or penitentiaries, to hear the confessions of pilgrims, and, except in cases reserved to the apostolic see, absolve them and impose a penance. In view of the continuing pilgrimages to that church and at the petition of the above abbot and convent, the pope hereby grants an indult that the said abbot and his successors may in person or through two similar priests, deputed by them for this purpose, minister the Eucharist to all pilgrims in the Church, as often as shall be expedient, and even at Easter, without prejudice to anyone and saving always the right of the parish church and any other, and may bless the beads of such pilgrims as touch them against the place where the blood is preserved. [*CEPR* 15, p. 37.]

. . . .

CHAPTER 10

Pilgrimage to and from Scotland

There is no question here of giving an adequate account of Scottish medieval pilgrimage. Still less is it intended to imply (despite the best efforts of Edward I and Edward III) that Scotland was (or is) in any sense part of England. The focus is on the English evidence for Scottish pilgrimage, which is important especially for Scots pilgrims coming to or passing through England *en route* to their shrine of choice. I have paid very brief attention to Scottish sources to amplify one or two points, but I have not attempted to describe, for example, the devotions paid by the fifteenth-century kings of Scots to Scottish shrines, above all St Ninian at Whithorn and St Duthac at Tain.[1]

Rymer included in his *Foedera* numerous safe-conducts issued to Scots by the English kings between 1291 and about 1500, drawn from the *Rotuli Scotorum*, which (published in the early nineteenth century) contain many more than he used. Unsurprisingly, there are few between the 1290s, when Edward I's aggressive intentions towards Scotland became manifest, and the late 1350s. (Examples earlier than 1290 are to be found among the Close Rolls and Patent Rolls.) Of these safe-conducts only some concerned pilgrimage. A large number were permissions to merchants to do business, some were for students at the English universities, and a great many were for Scots involved in the endless diplomatic exchanges which marked the tortuous course of Anglo-Scottish relations. Some, particularly in the fifteenth century when those relations were less fraught, did not specify the nature of the beneficiary's business at all. It may be noted that several of the names of those who received licence to traverse England on pilgrimage recur elsewhere, not merely (in the case of noblemen lay and ecclesiastical) as diplomats, but as merchants, like Robert Hog burgess of Edinburgh [11], or the brothers Thomas and Gilbert Macolagh.[2]

Several other individuals, lay and ecclesiastical, made repeated pilgrimages, or at least received safe-conduct to do so, as well as frequent visits on other business. These included the bishops of St Andrew's, the Dunbar earls of March and many of the Douglas family, to name only a few. The volume of safe-conducts, however, can give only part of the total picture. They were issued principally to persons of substance, travelling with a considerable equipage (or marketable goods), whose movements were therefore interesting both to robbers and to the English authorities. The pilgrims from Aberdeen who experienced a miracle at Canterbury in 1445 [27] do not appear among those who received safe-conducts, any more than do the individual names of the sometimes very numerous servants who accompanied bishops, abbots and lords.

A few Scottish pilgrims were officially permitted to traverse England during the reign of Edward II. One small party, in 1320, was assigned an escort for the duration of its crossing of the kingdom and directed not to deviate from the 'high road' [8]. Early in the next reign a rather romantic and chivalrous exception was made to the rule that the resistant Scots were *personae non gratae*. On 1st September 1329 James lord of Douglas received protection and safe-conduct for seven years; he was taking the heart of Robert Bruce to the Holy Land and also, it was noted, venturing 'in the aid of Christians against the Saracens'. Douglas did not live to complete his mission or to avail himself of the return half of his safe-conduct, for he died fighting the Moors on a Spanish battlefield, and was eviscerated for the journey back to his homeland; the Bruce's heart was interred at Melrose.[3] The silence of the English records does not mean that no other pilgrims left Scotland for foreign parts in this period, only that they probably went by sea. In 1438 a clause of the nine-year truce agreed with James II safeguarded the goods of any subjects, including merchants, fishermen and pilgrims, who were forced by bad weather to land at a port belonging to the other party.[4] It is strongly implied in the elaborately worded safe-conduct issued by Edward IV in 1476 for James III, who was purposing to visit Amiens, that the king of Scots was prone to sea-sickness and for this reason preferred to go overland through England [34].

In 1357 the Treaty of Berwick ushered in a long period of relative peace punctuated by outbursts of skirmishing, tension, hostage-taking and phoney war. It also re-opened the doors to Scottish pilgrims to, and passing through, England. Fairly large numbers of safe-conducts for this purpose were issued throughout the 1360s, tailing off to a low point in the later 1370s and then running at a modest level with gaps, for example between 1412 and 1425, and again between 1428 and 1439. In 1451 and 1452 substantial parties came to Canterbury, and in 1453 several passed through *en route* to Rome.

Of the recorded pilgrims, many wished simply to visit St Thomas of Canterbury, whose popularity in Scotland initially owed something to his resistance to an English king who had threatened Scots independence; the great abbey of Arbroath was dedicated to Becket, and in 1358 the abbot sought a relic of him from Canterbury.[5] Sometimes other English shrines, most often Walsingham, were on the proposed itinerary, but these were usually left unspecified in a general permission to the pilgrim to go where he would within a stated period of time. David Bruce and his wife frequently received safe-conducts for visits to Canterbury and occasionally for Walsingham.[6] Hailes is mentioned once by name; interestingly the pilgrims in question intended first to visit another relic of the Holy Blood, at Wilsnack in northern Germany [29]. Several pilgrims were simply passing through England or combined a tour of English shrines with journeys further afield. Their destinations included not only Compostela, Rome and the Holy Land, but the shrine of John the Baptist at Amiens. Both the great saints John had a flourishing cult in Scotland; the name of Perth's professional soccer club, St Johnstone, recalls to this day that this was the city of the Baptist, 'St John's Toun'. The largest observable contingent for Amiens departed in 1366 [18,b], while a few Scots also headed to the quintessentially French shrine of St Denis [15].

There is some evidence of pilgrimage from England to St Andrew's in the thirteenth century [3, 5]. It seems that William earl Marshal was intending such a pilgrimage in 1226 when word reached him that the king (young as he was) suspected that he was up to no good and he called the journey off, to Henry's expressed displeasure.[7] An early and one may suppose highly political English pilgrim to the shrine of St Ninian at Whithorn in Galloway was the future Edward II. On 21st September 1301 Edward I was informed that certain Scots of Galloway, hearing of the proposed pilgrimage of 'my lord your son', had tried to remove the image of the saint to the New Abbey, only to find that it had miraculously removed itself back to Whithorn (thus presumably signifying the saint's approval of the English visitation).[8] Other evidence for English pilgrimage to a shrine much favoured by the late medieval Scots monarchy is much later and somewhat localised. St Ninian is remembered in mid-fifteenth century Yorkshire wills, and one witness at a Yorkshire *Inquisition Post Mortem* recalled a pilgrimage there performed in 1482 [35].[9] The Scottish Treasurer's Accounts include a few, still later, payments to English pilgrims to the shrine [36]. Only the safe-conduct granted in 1459 to the bishop of Brechin, who proposed a pilgrimage to St Cuthbert at Durham, affords evidence of reciprocating Scottish pilgrimage to a saint of northern England [32].

Of English pilgrimage to Scotland, or of 'foreign' pilgrims crossing England to Scotland, there is otherwise only slight evidence in these sources. A Fleming who received a safe-conduct from Edward II in 1325 had made a vow to go to St Andrew's [9]. This is the only Scottish shrine to appear on the lists of destinations for penitential pilgrims compiled by the Flemish cities, but it appears in virtually all of them.[10] If St Andrew's attracted a clientele from the Low Countries, it is likely that it was transported by ship rather than overland and left little mark on English records.

For the most part these sources, like their counterparts for English pilgrims in the Patent Rolls and Close Rolls, are uninformative except as to the fact, or the intention, of pilgrimage. Like them also, however, they occasionally give interesting detail about an itinerary, or such matters as the efforts to reclaim a sum of money deposited in Venice by a Holy Land pilgrim who had died before returning [12]. Occasionally correlation not only between entries but with different sources is possible. Thus it is that we know that one substantial knightly party set out from Scotland for the Holy Land late in 1381; that one member of it died on the island of Candia the following year; and that some of its other members, seemingly depleted in numbers, were making their way back through England in February–March of 1383 [20].[11]

DOCUMENTS

1. *1222, August 12th*

Alexander king of Scots has letters of safe-conduct, without term, on his coming on pilgrimage to Canterbury and to the Lord King to speak with him, during his stay and on his return. [*Foedera*, 1, p. 256.]

2. 1260, October 3rd

The king, at the instance of A[lexander III] king of Scotland, grants Walter Lindsay, who with the king's licence is going on pilgrimage to St James, adjournment of his knighting from the next feast of St Edward [18th March] until the following Easter. [*CCR H III*, 11, p. 216.]

3. 1273, August 23rd

Safe-conduct until Michaelmas for Richard son of Philip, Laurence Scot and Nicholas de Wygennale, going to Scotland to visit St Andrew's. [*CPR Ed I*, 1, p. 28.]

4. 1276, February 24th

Safe-conduct until Midsummer for Mary, mother of the king of Scotland, coming to St Thomas.[12] [Ibid., p. 136.]

5. 1285, November

Cambridge: proof of Age of John le Hauckere, taken June 10th 1308. Born on the day of St Clement the Pope [23rd November], 13 Edward I [1285]. Robert de la Brok of Elesworth, William Frankeleyn of Bokesworth, William Morel of Fendrayton, John Pint and William de la Grave of Suavesheye, each 50 or more, agree, pretending their knowledge of the lapse of so much time because on the day the said John was baptized in the same church, they caused their staves and purses to be consecrated and all together took their journey for St Andrew's in Scotland. [*CIPM* 5, n. 67, p. 36.]

6. 1291, December 30th

To the *custodes* of the kingdom in favour of John earl of Atholl, 'who has set forth on pilgrimage to St James with our licence'. [*Rot. Scot*, 1, p. 6.]

7. 1314, December 22nd

Safe-conduct at the instance of Ralph of Montermer for Duncan of Fife and his entourage, going overseas on pilgrimage. [*Foedera*, 3, p. 505.]

8. 1320, April 25th

'Be it known that since we have conceded to James Cunningham and Reginald More, men of Scotland, that they, with an appropriate escort, may proceed through our kingdom to parts overseas on pilgrimage, we have assigned our beloved Richard Trot to escort them to the aforesaid parts overseas; with the proviso that they enter the kingdom by the high road and do not deviate from it to any other part; and therefore we direct you that you give aid and counsel to the aforesaid Richard in this matter, as often as you shall be advised thereof by Richard.' [Ibid., p. 829.]

9. 1325, May 1st

Safe-conduct until Christmas for John Host of Flanders, coming on pilgrimage to St Andrew's in Scotland in fulfilment of a vow, and returning home. [*CPR Ed II*, 5, p. 124.]

10. 1358, May 14th

Safe-conduct for Alienora countess of Carrick, 'coming on pilgrimage into our kingdom of England to visit the shrines of the saints'.[13] [*Rot. Scot.*, 1, p. 824.]

11. 1362, January 21st

Safe-conduct for Roger Hog[14] and his wife Margaret, 'coming on pilgrimage to St James through our kingdom of England and elsewhere through our dominions both beyond the sea and this side of the sea (*& alibi per potestatem dominiam nostram tam in partibus transmarinis quam cismarinis*).' [Ibid., pp. 869–60.]

12. 1363, December 11th

Be it known that William, clerk and *familiaris* of the nobleman William, earl of Douglas, and proctor of William de Winton, son and heir of Alan de Winton, who died on his pilgrimage to Mount Sinai to visit the shrine of St Katherine there, has in our presence constituted as his attorneys and substitutes Adam Wymondham, citizen of our city of London, and Niccolò Negrebon, citizen of the city of Venice, [to act] jointly or separately as his special messengers and proctors to obtain restitution of forty gold ducats which the aforesaid Alan deposited in the hand and custody of Niccolò Zucull, citizen of the said city of Venice, from Niccolò if he is present or in his absence from Costantino, Giovanni and Marco, the sons of Niccolò Zucull, and to make letters of quittance or any security which may be appropriate and anything else which may be necessary in this case ... [Ibid., p. 879.]

13. 1364, November 4th

Safe-conduct for William de Rossy of the Order of St Francis in Scotland, for England and thence 'to the regions of Lombardy to the general chapter of the said order' and also 'to parts overseas as far as St James'. [Ibid., p. 885.]

14. 1364, November 4th

Safe-conduct for Laurence Govan, coming on pilgrimage into our kingdom of England and elsewhere and thence to parts overseas as far as St John of Amiens and other holy places. [Ibid., p. 886.]

15. 1365, May 20th

Safe-conduct for David Fleming and John Balygirnach, coming into England on pilgrimage and thence overseas as far as St Denis. [Ibid., p. 893.]

16. 1365, 20th May

Safe-conduct for William bishop of St Andrew's who 'proposes to visit the shrines of the saints in England as well in overseas parts on pilgrimage'. [Ibid., p. 893.]

17. 1366, March 20th

Safe-conduct for Adam of Tyningham, dean of Aberdeen, coming on pilgrimage to England and elsewhere and 'to parts abroad as far as St John of Amiens'. [Ibid., p. 901.]

18. October 1366: multiple safe-conducts

(a) *14th October* Safe-conducts *without* the clause 'to parts abroad ... ' for Adam Paren of Wanfrey, John de Lestalrrey, knight, Hector Lawler knight, Thomas Bisset knight. [Ibid.]

(b) *15th October* Safe-conducts as above for Richard Cumyn knight, and William Marchale.

Safe-conducts as above *and* for St John of Amiens for John de Hawyck chaplain, John Edmonston knight, John Tonaygarth chaplain, Walter Wardlaw archdeacon of Laudon, Hugh Barclay *scutifer*, Thomas Somerville knight, John de Cragy, John Inyot, Master Thomas Tode canon of Glasgow.

Safe-conducts as above *and* for St James for James Seneschal and Alexander Skrymchur of Arbroath, and for William of Fallington.

Safe-conduct for the Holy Land, for Walter Monynge and Laurence Gelybrand.

Safe-conduct for John Inglis, coming on pilgrimage into England. [Ibid.]

19. 1374, April 16th

'Jacobus Ponche' of Florence has royal letters of safe-conduct at the request of the noble earl of Douglas in Scotland; [he is] coming with five companions and six horses through the domains and power of the king and thence to Rome and St James on pilgrimage, to last for a year. [Ibid., p. 963.]

20. The mixed fortunes of a party

(a) *1381, December 4th* Safe-conduct for Alexander Lindsay, knight, 'who is setting out on pilgrimage to the Holy Land, as it is said, with a company of 12 men and 12 horses'.

Also, for Patrick de Hebborn, knight, with 12 men and 12 horses.

Also for John de Abernethy, knight, with 6 men and 6 horses.

Also for John de Edmonston and John de Tours, with 16 men and 16 horses. [*Rot. Scot.*, 2, p. 40.]

(b) *1382* This year died Alexander Lindsay, a pilgrim to Jerusalem, on the island of Candia. [Walter Bower, *Scotichronicon*, ed. D.E.R. Watt (10 vols, Aberdeen 1993–96), 7 p. 388.]

(c) *1383, February 27th* Safe-conduct for John Joneson, knight, 'who is about to enter the kingdom of England from parts overseas with six mounted men in his company, staying there and going to what places he pleases within that kingdom on pilgrimage and thence returning to Scotland'.

Similarly for John Tours, knight, for Patrick Heybourne and for John Edmonston, each with six mounted men. [*Rot. Scot.*, 2, pp. 48–9.]

21. 1383, January 16th

Safe-conduct for James Lindsay, knight of Scotland, 'coming into the kingdom of the king of England, for various pilgrimages there, to St Thomas of Canterbury, Walsingham, and wherever else he chooses', with 100 persons and horses and impedimenta. [Ibid., p. 346.]

22. 1390, March 9th

Safe-conduct for Henry de Preston, knight, 'who proposes to enter our kingdom of England and there visit the tomb of the glorious martyr St Thomas of Canterbury, because of the great devotion which he is known to have to that martyr'. [Ibid., p. 103.]

23. 1395, October 23rd

Safe-conduct for John Sinclair coming into the kingdom of England and proceeding towards overseas parts, and going on pilgrimage both by way of fortified towns and elsewhere. He must show these letters to the officials at his entrance to any town. [Ibid., p. 130.]

24. 1406, July 6th

Safe-conduct for John Gray and John Tomson, *familiares* of Robert duke of Albany, 'who are setting out on pilgrimage for St James of Galicia to fulfil their vows, as the king hears, from the city of London towards the aforesaid place'. [Ibid., pp. 178–9.]

25. 1411, January 29th

Safe-conduct for John Hathyngton, Scot, who has vowed to go on pilgrimage to St James in foreign parts for the salvation of his soul. [Ibid., p. 195.]

26. 1440, June 12th

Safe-conduct for Walter abbot of Arbroath, 'entering the kingdom of England to perform certain pilgrimages which he has previously promised to perform'. [Ibid., p. 316.]

27. 1445, July 25th: The Prior and Chapter of Canterbury announce a miracle

'... Alexander Stephenson, born at Aberdeen in Scotland, twenty-four years old, suffered severely from contracted feet, with vile worms lurking in them. ... After making a vow at a place of pilgrimage of the Virgin called *Sequt*[15] he made his way to the shrine of the holy martyr Thomas ... and there, in the full view of men, the glorious athlete of God, first wringing horrible shrieks from him, restored his feet to him on the second day of May last before the date of this present letter, and on the third day immediately following permitted the said Alexander, with the aid of God's mercy stepping easily on the earth, to depart hence joyfully, safe and sound. We have received the fullest proof of this event, since the said Alexander then went with the grace of God on pilgrimage to the Holy Blood of Wilsnack, in fulfilment of his vow, and then returned to the shrine of the holy martyr Thomas, by the favour of that martyr, successfully and on foot. We therefore, wishing not to hide the glory of the martyr Thomas in the shadows of ignorance, but rather that it should shine on the candelabrum of the faith in the sight of all Christians, to the praise of the divine majesty, have solemnly caused to be published in our holy church of Canterbury, according to the demands of the law, those things which are legally required for the proof of a miracle. We had previously, under the guidance of the divine clemency, taken the oaths of the aforesaid Alexander, of Alexander Arat, gentleman, of Robert Davidson, and John Thomson, of the aforementioned town in Scotland, immediately they appeared in our presence on the aforesaid first day of May ... [*LC*, 3, pp. 191–2.]

28. 1446, March 18th

Safe-conduct for James bishop of St Andrew's with 30 persons, and also for Master John Legat,[16] Master William Mudy and John Fleming, going 'to the city of Rome and other holy places'. [*Rot. Scot.*, 2, p. 328.]

29. 1451, June 9th

'Be it known that James Hunter and Henry Herward, chaplains of Scotland, have made vows to go on pilgrimage, with the help of God's grace, to the holy places of Wilsnack, Canterbury, Walsingham and Hailes. So that they may be enabled to fulfil their vows in greater tranquillity we have taken under our safe-conduct and special protection the aforesaid James and Henry, who are at present in our kingdom of England, both together and separately, wherever they may go, by land and sea, on horseback or on foot, with two servants in their company and all other permitted property and harness; passing for the aforesaid reason to the said place of Wilsnack and returning into our kingdom and there staying and fulfilling their aforesaid vows and thence returning to their own place freely and without impediment.' [Ibid., p. 347.]

30. 1452, January 22nd

Safe-conducts for: the bishops of Glasgow, Moray, and Dunblane; the abbots of Melrose, Dunfermline and Paisley; William earl of Douglas and James his brother; Alexander Montgomery; James lord Hamilton; Andrew lord Gray; Master Andrew Duresder, dean of Dunkeld; Patrick Young, dean of Aberdeen; John Methven, doctor of canon law; John Arous archdeacon of Glasgow, with 120 persons, coming 'to the royal presence ... and also to our royal city of Canterbury by reason of pilgrimage'.[17] [Ibid., pp. 354–5.]

31. 1453

May 22nd Safe-conducts for James earl of Douglas, lord of Galway; Archibald Douglas, earl of Moray; Hugh Douglas earl of Ormonde; John Douglas lord of Balvany; Master John Clerk, rector of Kilbride; John Shaw; Mark Haliburton, John Freseli, John Uchre, chaplains; Master William Heris, rector of Kilpatrick; Dom. James Douglas, provost of Dalkeith; David Forde, James Doddes, John Doddes, Louis de Carieth, with a hundred persons, 'Scots wishing to visit the shrines of the apostles on pilgrimage'.

Also, for James Hamilton, James lord Livingstone, Archibald Dundas, Dom. Gavin Hamilton provost of Bothville, John Hamilton, master James Inglis*, Master Robert Hamilton chaplain, David Spalding of Dundee, David Fleming, Robert Hamilton, William Bonley, Master William Bane, Patrick Weddale, William Banere, Adam Cosour*, Thomas Frest, with twelve persons. [Ibid., p. 362.]

[*These names reappear in batches of safe-conducts issued a few days later for Rome.]

May 30th The venerable father Thomas abbot of Paisley, George Falowe, burgess of Edinburgh; Master Walter Stewart of Dalswinton, Master James Inglis* canon of Glasgow, Lord Thomas Forsyth vicar of 'Legeharwode', with seven persons; Master James Lindsay provost of Linclowden, George Fawlo, William de Carrebris, Adam Cosur* burgess of Stirling, with 20 persons. [Ibid., p. 363.]

32. 1458, November 16th

To Thomas Clerk, clerk of the diocese of Glasgow. Containing that, upon the late William Songale, layman, of the diocese of Glasgow, who had married a sister of his, attacking him with offensive arms, Thomas accidentally killed him, and adding that he has as far as possible made satisfaction to the kin and friends of the said layman and has for the soul of the defunct visited as a pilgrim the shrines of the apostles and the apostolic see, caused masses to be celebrated for the purpose in the chapel called the *Scala Celi* without the walls of Rome, and done other works of charity for the welfare of the soul of the same defunct, and has at length been absolved from the guilt of homicide by one of the pope's minor penitentiaries in Rome, who has enjoined upon him a salutary penance. Dispensation to be promoted to minor orders, minister therein and receive a retain a benefice of office without cure etc. [*CEPR* 12, pp. 2–3.]

32. 1459, July 13th

Safe-conduct for the venerable father George bishop of Brechin, coming into the kingdom of England on pilgrimage to the royal city of Durham with forty servants ... [Ibid., p. 390.]

33. 1464, June 14th

Safe-conducts for Alexander Forstar, lord of Corstophine, John Lauder of Hawton, knight, Henry Leverton of Sawny, John Wardlaw of Recardton, Gilbert Forster, 'Scots setting out on pilgrimage in the kingdom of England to the holy martyr Thomas of Canterbury and to St John of Amiens in the parts of Picardy, with thirty servants of theirs, Scots'.[18] [Ibid., p. 414.]

34. 1476, 15th May

'We understand that the most excellent and illustrious prince James, king of Scotland, our dearly beloved brother and kinsman, for devotion and pilgrimage and the fulfilment of a vow made by him wishes to cross to foreign parts and especially to the city of Amiens, and fears that the sea crossing would be in no small measure damaging to his disposition and bodily health. Wherefore he has sent his ambassadors to us to request safe-conduct through our realm and dominions.' [Ibid., p. 453.]

35. 1482

York: proof of age of Ralph Westthorp, taken March 20th 1503. 21 years old on 24th January last. Richard Scheperd, aged 50 and more, began a pilgrimage to St Ninian in Scotland; Richard Walker aged 48 or more, began a pilgrimage to St Thomas in Kent. [*CIPM Henry VII*, 2, n. 640, p. 403.]

36. 1506, 1st May

.... to ane pilgryme of Ingland that Sanct Niniane kythit [did] miracle for xviij s.

... Item, to certaine Inglis pilgrimes in Wigtoun, be the Kingys comand xiij s [*Accounts of the Lord High Treasurer of Scotland*, ed. T. Dickson (11 vols, Edinburgh 1877–1916), 4, p. 193.]

CHAPTER II

European Visitors

The majority of European pilgrims who visited England almost certainly did so to venerate Thomas Becket. In 1394 Richard II congratulated the archbishop of Canterbury on a miracle which had lately occurred at the shrine. No particulars are given, but the king remarked that there was special reason to thank God 'who has deigned to work this miracle in our days, and upon a foreigner, as though for the purpose of spreading to strange and distant countries the glorious fame of his very martyr abovesaid'.[1] If pilgrims were of lowly social standing, they were unlikely to leave their mark on the royal records, at least if they were only travelling in small groups. In March 1236, however, Henry III instructed the constable of Dover not to permit 'any magnate or other man of rank (*Magnas vel alius Potens*) of the power of the king of France' to land in England without the king's special mandate or licence, as the count of Eu had just done.[2] The safe-conducts from time to time recorded in the Patent Rolls or elsewhere were for persons of rank.

Canterbury was included among the 'greater pilgrimages' to which repentant heretics were sentenced by the inquisition of southern France,[3] and a number of other British destinations were included in the lists kept by the Flemish cities which employed pilgrimage as a punishment for crime. This of course is no guide to how frequently they were in fact used. The following table shows which shrines were listed by which Flemish cities.[4] It seems clear, first, that substantial borrowing and imitation went to the making of these lists, and secondly that (leaving aside the special celebrity of Canterbury) the strong bias towards the eastern side of England, with the inclusion of such destinations as Lincoln, Peterborough, Yarmouth and Louth, reveals the regional knowledge and commercial affiliations of the compilers. The strong links of Flanders with Scotland are attested by

Shrine	Flemish city
Canterbury	Ghent, Aalst, Dendermonde, Oudenaarde, Leuven, Antwerp, Tournai, Lier
St Andrew's	Ghent, Aalst, Dendermonde, Oudenaarde, Ypres, Lier, Bruges, Antwerp, Courtrai
Salisbury (Our Lady)	Ghent, Aalst, Dendermonde, Oudenaarde
Walsingham	Ghent, Aalst, Dendermonde
St Nicholas (Yarmouth)	Ghent, Aalst, Dendermonde
St Peter (Peterborough)	Ghent, Aalst, Dendermonde
St John of Beverley	Ghent, Aalst, Dendermonde
St Catherine (Lincoln)	Ghent, Aalst, Dendermonde
Our Lady of Lincoln	Ghent, Aalst, Dendermonde
St Giles (Dover)	Ghent, Aalst, Dendermonde
St Thomas of Hereford	Ghent, Aalst, Dendermonde
Bury St Edmund's	Ghent, Aalst, Tournai
St Peter's, York	Aalst, Dendermonde
Our Lady of Oxford	Antwerp
St Patrick's Purgatory	Antwerp
St Peter's, Louth	Ghent

the fact that St Andrew's features in nine lists, one more than Canterbury.

In his capacity as lord of Ireland, the king of England occasionally took cognisance of pilgrims to St Patrick's Purgatory. The most interesting document is perhaps the certificate issued in 1358 on behalf of Malatesta 'Ungaro' of Rimini and his companion Niccolò Beccaria of Ferrara, who had successfully completed the ordeal of a day and a night's enclosure in the cave on an island in Lough Derg which was the goal of the pilgrimage [11]. Malatesta Ungaro (so-called because he was knighted by king Louis of Hungary) shared not only in his family's collective activities as military captains and papal vicars in north-eastern Italy, but in their predilections for the Franciscan Order and for pilgrimage. His journey to Lough Derg was remembered in Italian literary tradition and can be seen, Franco Cardini has suggested, as expressing a 'chivalric' ethos in which long-distance pilgrimage, with its rigours and dangers, constituted an appropriate adventure, both physical and spiritual, for the military man.[5] Another pilgrim to the Purgatory, the Hungarian nobleman Laurence of Páztho, seems to have come into the same category [17]. Although the supposedly obligatory fifteen-day fast which should have preceded his entry to the cave was considerably modified, the emphasis of the account is on his knightly fortitude and fixity of purpose.[6]

DOCUMENTS

1. *1228*

This year there came into England a certain archbishop from Greater Armenia, to visit on pilgrimage the relics of the saints of this region and the holy places, as he had done in other kingdoms. He showed letters of the pope commending his person to religious and ecclesiastical prelates, so he was received by them with due reverence and honourably treated. [Roger of Wendover, *Flores Historiarum*, ed. H. Coxe (4 vols + appendix, London 1842), 4, p. 176.]

2. *1233, August 18th*

Safe-conduct until All Saints [1st November] for Stephen de Samer, knight of the power of Louis king of France, coming to the shrine of St Thomas. [*CPR H III*, 3, p. 23.]

3. *1233, September 13th*

Safe-conduct until Martinmas [11th November] for Marie countess of Ponthieu and her entourage coming on pilgrimage to England. [Ibid., p. 25.]

4. *1235, June 22nd*

The duke of Norway has letters of safe-conduct to come into England, by reason of pilgrimage to the Holy Land, to stay there and cross from there towards and to return from the Holy Land. [Ibid., p. 109.]

5. *1252, May 26th*

'Be it known that we have granted to our beloved Alphonse count of Eu safe-conduct in his coming to Canterbury by reason of pilgrimage and returning thence to his own place; and therefore you are commanded neither to inflict, nor permit to be inflicted, any damage or annoyance on the aforesaid Count or on the household he brings with him, during his journey to perform the aforesaid pilgrimage.' [*Foedera*, 1, p. 473.]

6. 1255, December 2nd

Safe-conduct etc., for 'the noble Arnaut, count of Guînes, [who] has sought our licence to come to England to perform certain pilgrimages which he has vowed there'. [*CPR H III*, 4, p. 452.]

7. 1258, July 28th

'The king to the distinguished prince, and most dear to himself, Thomas [*recte* Theobald] illustrious king of Navarre and count Palatine of Champagne and Brie, greeting and sincere affection. We have derived great joy and pleasure from what you have notified to us by your letters, that you and the noble count of Nevers, your kinsman, together with certain other nobles, wish to come on pilgrimage to the venerable relics of the blessed Thomas the Martyr at Canterbury and to have our safe-conduct for the purpose. We have decided most willingly to grant the safe-conduct. Because at the time of receiving your letters we were in the midst of our journey north, at the furthest extremity of our kingdom, which we have had to undertake because of difficult business touching the state of our kingdom, and we desire by all means to see you in person and to converse with you on your arrival in our kingdom, we affectionately request your serenity that you so arrange your arrival in England that you are at Canterbury in the octave of St Michael [29th September] next, and can thence come to London to us, to spend some time with us, when, God willing, we propose to be there to meet you.' [*CCR H III*, 10, p. 321.]

8. 1339, May 1st

Protection until Midsummer for Werner de Erchenges of Strasbourg in Aleman who with royal protection has performed certain pilgrimages 'at the city of London' and is returning to his own parts. [*CPR Ed III*, 3, p. 246.]

9. 1355, August 16th

Protection and safe-conduct until the Nativity of the Virgin Mary (September 8th) for Arnold de Semalles, called 'the Archpriest', coming with one fellow from France to the shrine of St Thomas, with the king's licence. [Ibid., 10, p. 277.]

10. 1357, June 6th

Protection etc., until St Peter's Chains (August 1st) for William Delby and Thomas Hedgeuil, knights of France, coming to the *limina* of St Thomas, each with three knights, grooms, harness, goods and other things. [Ibid., p. 561.]

11. 1358, October 24th

'The noble Malatesta de'Ungariis of Rimini, knight, has in our presence fully related how he, recently come from his homeland, with much bodily effort visited on pilgrimage the Purgatory of St Patrick, situated in our land of Ireland, and as is the custom remained enclosed therein one whole day and night; urgently praying us that we grant him royal letters in corroboration of the above. We, considering the hazards of the pilgrimage, although we accept the claim of so great a noble in this matter, are also informed by letters from Aumary de St Amand, knight, our Justiciar of Ireland, and also from the Prior and Convent of the said Purgatory and other men of great authority, that the aforesaid noble performed his pilgrimage correctly and indeed courageously. We therefore judge it proper to add the testimony of our authority to these, and so that the truth of the aforesaid, unhampered by any doubt, may be more clearly manifested to all, have granted to him these our letters sealed with the royal seal. Given in our Palace of Westminster, on the twenty-fourth day of October.

The like for Nicholas de Beccariis of Ferrara, *donzel*, a Lombard by nation.' [*Foedera* 6, p. 108.]

12. 1361, March 3rd

'Pay from our Treasury to our beloved and faithful kinsman John duke of Brittany nine pounds, for his expenses in going on pilgrimage to Walsingham and thence returning, to have as our gift.' [Ibid., p. 315.]

13. 1363, June 17th

To Guy, count of St Pol. 'Desiring your bodily health, we hereby give you leave to betake yourself out of the city [London] where you are obliged to remain hostage for the fulfilment of the terms of the peace made between us and our dearest brother of France, to Our Lady of Walsingham, within fifteen days from the date of these presents, as long as you present yourself to us and to our Council, in the said city of London, at the end of the said fifteen days, to remain there hostage in the manner and form by which you are obliged and have again promised by your faith and oath.' [Ibid., p. 419.]

14. 1364, February 7th

'The religious men, brother Nerses, abbot of the monastery of St George in Lesser Armenia, and Jacobus his fellow monk, have come to us to petition that (since the kingdom of Armenia, in which the Christian faith used to flourish entire and devout, has been overrun by the hateful madness of the Saracens, who, profaning the sanctuary of God, have put the said monastery, among other churches, to the flame, and daily destroy and overturn altars, and, which is worse, kill all the Christians that they seize, having inflicted various outrages on them, not sparing order, sex or age; and thus the Christian religion is outlawed there, and faithful Christians, put to flight for fear, lead their lives in misery, begging throughout the world) we would be willing to grant licence to them, abbot and monk, thus exiled and leading a wandering life (*vitam ducentibus peregrinam*) that they may stay for some time in our kingdom of England, under the wings of our protection, to visit the shrines of the saints. We, mindful of the Supreme King, who wishes to be honoured in the persons of pilgrims and guests, and wishing to show favour to the aforesaid abbot and monk, have decided to concede that licence to them ...' [Ibid., pp. 432–3.]

15. 1367, January 14th

To the collectors of the petty custom and the king's controller and searcher in the Port of London. Order, upon the petition of Hermann de Mulyk of Almain, attorney of Bernard Usterfeld merchant, after payment of the customs thereupon due, to deliver to the said Herman a mail filed with goods called 'ermyns' to make his advantage thereof; as the petitioner has shown that he delivered the said mail in the port of Caleys to John de Hatfield merchant of Almayn to be taken over to the city of London with goods of the said John in a ship called 'la Laurence' of Wale by Calais, and that the same was put ashore in the port of London among other the merchandise of the said John, by a servant of his in whose keeping the same was, in the absence of the said Hermann and without his knowledge, while he was at Canterbury upon his pilgrimage, wherefore it was by the searcher arrested as forfeit to the king, and is kept under arrest for that it was found not cocketed or customed, praying restitution therefore seeing that no fault is found in him. [*CCR Ed III*, 11, p. 363.]

16. 1397, September 6th

Be it known that the noble man Raymond vicomte de Perilleux [Ramon de Perellós], knight of Rhodes, chamberlain of our dearest father of France, is coming to our kingdom of England and proposes to pass through that kingdom and proceed to our land of Ireland, to see and visit the Purgatory of St Patrick, with twenty men and thirty horses in his escort.[7] [*Foedera* 8, pp. 14–15.]

17. 1411–12: The pilgrimage of Laurence of Páztho, Hungarian nobleman, to St Patrick's Purgatory

(a) *From the safe-conduct of the Emperor Sigismund* '... The magnificent Laurence Rathold of Páztho brought up and well-known from childhood in our royal court, proved faithful in good times and bad, inflamed by the spirit of devotion proposes to visit the shrine of the blessed James in Compostela and the Purgatory of St Patrick in Ireland, and led by the fineness of his mind intends to traverse different parts of the world in the pursuit of military exercise and improvement ...' [Delehaye, p. 46.]

(b) *He arrives in Ireland* When the aforesaid knight arrived in the presence of the primate [Nicholas archbishop of Armagh] and showed him the royal letters, also sagaciously explaining in his own words the reason of his coming, he was received by the primate with fitting honour. As is the custom of pilgrims, having obtained testimonial letters from the primate on his character as a knight, he made pilgrimage to the city of Dublin, which contains the translated relics of saints Patrick, Columba and Brigid, and stayed there for several days in devout observance of prayers and fasts for the profitable completion of his journey. One day, while he was resting on his bed, the future events of his pilgrimage were divinely relayed to him by St Patrick, in whom he was fixing the spiritual anchor of his intent. [Ibid., pp. 46–7.]

(c) *He enters the Purgatory* Because he had established his knightly heart on a firm rock, the prior permitted the knight his vow. Then the knight stripped off his clothes and shoes, and was clad by the prior in three white albs of the canons and a new pair of drawers, as is the custom of Irish pilgrims, and bowing his knees prostrated himself on the ground. Then the prior with a canon performed the office of the dead, with the exequies, over him. When he had completed the exequies as far as the responsory 'Free me, O Lord, from death eternal on that fearful day when heaven and earth shall be moved' the prior raised the knight up and, singing the responsory, led him four paces between east and north from the chapel, to a cave walled and vaulted with stone; its opening is the entry to the Purgatory. ... The prior and the canon, singing the verse of the responsory, 'That day, that day of wrath, calamity and misery' opened the locked door of the cave, sprinkling the knight with holy water and saying farewell; he then entered the cave. The prior refastened the door securely, and the knight remained there alone. [Ibid., pp. 49–50.]

18. Decrees of the Venetian Senate

(a) *1402, August 3rd* 'That leave be conceded to Ser Lorenzo Contarini, captain of the Flanders galleys, while at Sandwich, to visit St Thomas of Canterbury in fulfilment of his vow, appointing as his lieutenant the master of the galley in which he is. He is to go and return in one day, not being allowed to sleep out of the galley. [*Calendar of State Papers and Manuscripts Relating to English Affairs existing in the Archives and Collections of Venice and other Libraries of Northern Italy, 1202–1509,* ed. Rawdon Brown (1864), n. 144.]

(b) *May 1429* Decree of the Senate permitting the captain of the Flanders Galleys, Stefano Contarini, when on the homeward voyage, to go from Sandwich to Canterbury. [Ibid., n. 241.]

. . . .

PART FOUR

Verdicts on Pilgrimage

. . . .
Criticism and Evaluation of Pilgrimage

In theory, the genuine pilgrim had an unimpeachable justification for his travels which is often not conceded to 'travellers' in modern British society or to nomadic peoples trying to make space for themselves within or alongside settled societies. Yet even when genuine he was not universally accepted, let alone welcomed. This is suggested by the *topos* met with in miracle collections and saints' lives, in which an innkeeper or alewife refuses free hospitality or refreshment to a pilgrim and has to be taught the error of his or her ways. The ill-advised wife of a knight, somewhere near Abingdon, was brewing when five pilgrims to Canterbury came by and asked for a drink for love of the martyr: she replied intemperately, 'No saint, no Thomas. No one demands anything today, not for the sake the Lord, or of the blessed Virgin Mary. Be off, *trutanni!*' The abusive term *trutannus*, meaning beggar or impostor, probably expresses the view of at least lower-class pilgrims entertained by many respectable householders.[1]

A current of criticism of Christian pilgrimage flowed from early times.[2] Christianity was a religion of the spirit; God was no more present in one place than in another; the journey was a distraction from the interior quest. The perception that pilgrimage could easily be made an excuse for a mere holiday lies behind the phrasing of a sixth-century model letter on behalf of a pilgrim. The bearer is to be commended because he is braving arduous journeys for the love of God, 'not, as is the common custom, for the sake of diversion (*vacandi causa*)'.[3] This suspicion persisted, for very good reasons. Through long centuries in which the vast majority of people had restricted opportunities for legitimate mobility, pilgrimage offered such an opportunity, and if Honorius *Augustodunensis* is any guide, the pilgrim whose primary purpose was to see the sights was not unknown early in the twelfth century [1]. This was bad, if not as bad as using ill-gotten money to pay for one's travels, a possibility noted by Honorius as it had been noted by the authors of canon 43 of the Council of Châlons four centuries earlier. The notion that the money – and the effort – consumed in pilgrimage could be better expended on other objects also persists, to crop up forcefully in late medieval criticism. The true usefulness of pilgrimage could all too easily be misunderstood if it was taken to be an automatic passport to the forgiveness of one's sins, as the fathers of Châlons had realised.

In principle, these cautions were equally relevant to all Christians; in practice, before the later middle ages, the strongest reservations were expressed about the practice of pilgrimage by professed religious, above all by nuns.[4] However, when in 1298 Boniface VIII insisted on the better enclosure of nuns in the bull *Pericoloso*, he made no specific reference to pilgrimage, implying that involvement in conventual business was the chief problem. Some bishops, however, drew the logical conclusion that pilgrimage was implicated. In 1318 Archbishop Melton of York directed any sisters of Nun Appleton who had taken vows of pilgrimage to say instead as many psalters as it would have taken days to complete the pilgrimage. His spirited attempt to enforce the enclosure enjoined by *Pericoloso* on the nuns of Yorkshire met with an equally spirited response, to the apparent approval of the ever-opinionated chronicler of Meaux Abbey, who reported that the nuns refused to accept any constitution made subsequent to their profession, 'as is right'.[5] A little later Hamo de Hethe of Rochester was also trying to discipline the nuns of at least one house in his diocese [7,d]; but for him, too, pilgrimage was only one issue among many.

The emphasis in arguments against pilgrimage by monks was somewhat different. The best minds in twelfth-century monasticism, most famously but by no means solely Bernard of Clairvaux, argued powerfully that the monk had chosen the better part and had set his feet on the sure road to the heavenly Jerusalem: what need had he then of the mere earthly city?[6] An abbot, who had assumed responsibility for the souls of other monks, had an additional reason for not absenting himself from his monastery [7,b]. The argument that responsibility for subjects should outweigh the calls of foreign travel could in fact also be used to dissuade secular rulers from pilgrimage [2]. Whatever distinguished the nun from the monk, and the monk from the abbot, however, one thing was common to them all, that in choosing their way of life they had taken the opportunity to realise in themselves, as ordinary Christians probably could not hope to do, the spiritual potentialities of the faith. Hildebert of Le Mans congratulated 'an illustrious widow' who had previously wanted to go to Jerusalem on making a better choice: she had presumably entered the cloister, or, as Hildebert phrased it, 'left all for Christ', choosing to follow Christ buried rather than Christ's burial-place.[7] How might the evaluation of pilgrimage be affected if elements of monastic spirituality were successfully exported from the cloister, and laymen (and laywomen) living in the world set out in search of inner holiness?

In and after the twelfth century, features of the contemplative life such as the recitation of private prayers, or the private practice of bodily austerities, found their way more frequently into the devotional practice of the upper classes of lay society, including, increasingly, members of the urban patriciate. In 1215, for the first time, the Fourth Lateran Council imposed a minimum requirement of annual confession and reception of communion on all adult Christians, which meant, in principle, that participation in the Eucharist became part of the layman's personal religious experience. At the same time, activist charity made an increasing appeal to high-minded laypeople. The new orders of friars sought as preachers to inculcate an understanding of religious basics in their audiences, and encouraged both the spiritual life of laymen and women and their involvement in charitable activity through the organisation of confraternities and third orders.

Raimondo Palmario of Piacenza died (in 1200) before either St Francis or St Dominic had founded his brotherhood, but in his own career enacted one version of the shift in lay spirituality. In the crises of his life, first as a young man after the death of his father, and later after the death of his wife and all but one of his children, Raimondo dedicated himself to pilgrimage and intended to end his days at Jerusalem. It was Christ Himself who directed him not to take that course, but to return to his native city and do there all the things that needed doing, from peacemaking to the succour of the poor [3]. The story as we have it seems to imply, not so much a criticism of pilgrimage as a statement that for a given individual, enough might be enough, that there were other important and meritorious possibilities. Raimondo was, of course, from this time forth celibate and as a hospital founder became the focal point of a brotherhood (into which his son in due time entered). Instead of becoming a perpetual pilgrim, he adopted another religious 'profession', in an age in which the possibilities were still multiple and fluid. For other philanthropic activists of the thirteenth century, such as Gualtiero of Lodi, who 'studied' at Raimondo's own hospital, or Fazio of Cremona, pilgrimage was perfectly compatible with their charitable vocation, and there continued to be lay saints in Italian urban society (such as Antonio 'the Pilgrim' of Padua and Novellone of Faenza) who were distinguished for their pilgrimages rather than for their charity.[8]

For women, the pressures towards the contemplative life were more insistent, and it may therefore be significant that the theme of interior pilgrimage features so strongly in some thirteenth-century writing by and for religious women. Two examples must suffice. In discussing penance, the author of *Ancrene Wisse* remarks that there are three categories among God's chosen, the good, the better and the best. The first he likens to 'good pilgrims': 'The good pilgrim always keeps to his right way forward. Although he sees or hears idle games and wonders by the way, he does not stop as fools do, but keeps to his route and hurries toward his lodging. He carries no treasure except for his necessary expenses, and no clothes except those he needs.' This picture of the ideal pilgrim is primarily intended as a metaphorical picture of the individual progressing through the world towards God. The goals of the 'real' pilgrim are in fact secondary: 'For other pilgrims go with much toil to seek the bones of a single saint, like St James or St Giles, but these pilgrims who go towards heaven, they go to become saints themselves and to find God himself and all his holy saints living in joy ... '

Furthermore, the mundane pilgrimage (both real and metaphorical) can go wrong: 'For although pilgrims, as I said before, are always going forward, and they never become citizens of the world's city, at times what they see by the way seems good to them and they stop for awhile – though not altogether – and many things happen to them which hinder them, more's the harm. Some come home late, some never again.' The purpose of the whole passage is to recommend the higher steps, becoming 'dead to the world', and being hung of one's own free will on God's cross.[9] A prayer for returning pilgrims indicates that it was thought likely that they had experienced distractions and temptations along the way [6].

In the opening of the fifteenth letter of the Beguine Hadewijch, reality serves only as a source of similitudes:

Nine points are fitting for the pilgrim who has far to travel. The first is that he asks about the way. The second is that he chooses good company.

The third is that he beware of thieves. The fourth is that he beware of gluttony. The fifth is that he don short dress and tight belt. The sixth is that when he climbs a mountain, he bend far forward. The seventh is that when he descends the mountain, he walk erect. The eighth is that he desire the prayers of good people. The ninth is that he gladly speak of God. So it is likewise with our pilgrimage to God ... .[10]

In both these passages, the affinity with the monastic tradition and its emphasis on the interior quest is clear. Already in the thirteenth century, however, criticism of pilgrimage was being addressed to a potentially wider audience. Readers of a vernacular version of a sermon on 'Two and Twenty Virtues' by the Franciscan preacher Berthold of Regensburg (*c.*1210–72) were urged that salvation was more effectively sought at home. Berthold's first reference to pilgrimage is incidental: criticising idle chatter in church, he observes that what people have seen on their sea-voyages or on their journeys to Rome or St James is a favourite topic of conversation. Later in the sermon he addresses more fundamental issues. The context is an exhortation to church attendance and specifically to devout attendance at Mass. The Christian can by this means at any time obtain more pardon, more grace, at home than by going to St James, no matter how many indulgences he brings back. Berthold says this, not because he wants to deprive St James of his pilgrims, but to inculcate a greater truth, and this leads to a semi-humorous denunciation of the evils incidental on these journeys. To go to St James, the pilgrim sells things which would be necessary and valuable to his children, his wife, and still more to the poor, and even to himself. He so gorges himself on the trip that he comes back much fatter than he departed, and he is full of the things he has seen, although it is not clear that these have been at churches or sermons. 'What did you find when you came to Compostela?' 'St James's head.' 'That's really good. That's a dead man's bone, a dead man's skull; the better part is in heaven. What do you find at home, in your own backyard, when the priest sings Mass at church? There you find true God and true Man, with all the power and strength that He has in heaven, whose holiness is above all saints and all angels.' Berthold then forcefully impresses on his audience the great truth that the holiness of God surpasses that of St James, of all the twelve apostles, of all the saints in heaven, of all the Angels, of the Virgin Mary herself. In another sermon, specifically on the subject of the Mass, he makes the same point in some of the same words, including the reference to St James's skull.[11]

We notice in this critique the strong implication that charity begins at home, that pilgrimage should not be undertaken at the expense of wife, children and the poor. This, as we have seen, was not a new idea. A century earlier Bernard of Clairvaux had attacked, not directly the expenditures to which pilgrims themselves were put, but the speculative greed which, he thought, led to excessive expenditure on the decoration of churches:

> Money is sown with such skill that it may be multiplied. It is expended so that it may be increased, and pouring it out produces abundance. The reason is that the very sight of these costly but wonderful illusions inflames men more to give than to pray. In this way wealth is derived from wealth, in this way money attracts money, because by I know not what law, wherever the more riches are seen, there the more willingly are offerings made. Eyes are fixed on relics covered with gold and purses are opened. The thoroughly beautiful image of some male or female saint is exhibited and the saint is believed to be the more holy the more highly coloured the image is. People rush to kiss it, they are invited to donate, and they admire the beautiful more than they venerate the sacred.

Furthermore, 'The Church is radiant in its walls and destitute in its poor. It dresses its stones in gold and it abandons its children naked. It serves the eyes of the rich at the expense of the poor. The curious find that which may delight them, but those in need do not find that which should sustain them.'[12]

In the fifteenth century, *The Imitation of Christ* encapsulated a range of criticisms, all of which by that date had a more or less long history:

> Many make pilgrimages to various places to visit the relics of the Saints, wondering at the story of their lives and the splendour of their shrines; they view and venerate their bones, covered with silks and gold. But here on the Altar are You Yourself, my God, the Holy of Holies, Creator of men and Lord of Angels! When visiting such places, men are often moved by curiosity and the urge for sight-seeing, and one seldom hears that any amendment of life results, especially as their conversation is trivial and lacks true contrition. But here in the Sacrament of the Altar, You are wholly present, my God, the Man Christ Jesus; here we freely partake the fruit of eternal salvation, as often we receive you worthily and devoutly.[13]

A generation or so earlier, William Langland had incorporated a somewhat different range of criticisms of pilgrims and pilgrimage into *The Vision of Piers Plowman*. Sometimes he seems to endorse the royal governmental rhetoric that was bred by the war with France and the social unrest of the late fourteenth century. In the Prologue, the narrator denounces the 'hermits' he sees setting off for Walsingham, with their whores in tow, as workshy 'layabouts' who by adopting a certain dress acquire a privileged identity. Piers himself swears that he will honour Truth and 'be his pilgrim by ploughing the earth, for the benefit of the poor'. In Passus IV, Reason explodes:

'As for pilgrimages to St James's shrine – these will depart in directions I shall determine, and if people do go to Galicia let them go there once and for all and never come back! No one who trudges the path to Rome to line the pockets of foreign profiteers will be permitted to carry cash overseas: no coin of the realm bearing the impress of the King, nor, for that matter, *any* gold or silver, whether stamped or unstamped. Any such persons arrested at Dover will have the currency confiscated, with these exceptions only: merchants or their representatives, messengers carrying letters, clergy seeking ratification of their benefices, or persons performing a prescribed canonical penance.'

The famous passage describing the pilgrim, hung about with souvenirs, who has never heard of a saint called Truth, encapsulates the most fundamental criticism: this individual professes to have performed his journeys 'for the good of my soul', but (like Greed who, with his wife the fraudulent alewife, thinks he will go to Walsingham and also pray before the Cross of Bromholm to obtain forgiveness of his sins) he has no idea what he is saying.[14] Imagination, meanwhile, expresses the views of the conservative devout when he suggests that a member of a religious order should, 'instead of wandering off to Rome or Rocamadour ... stay put in obedience to your Rule; that too is a direct route to Heaven'.

The attack on pilgrimage which according to his own account the Lollard William Thorpe delivered when he was arraigned before archbishop Arundel at Saltwood castle in 1407, serves well to illustrate how themes with a long ancestry were now being combined in a new polemic [8]. The 'true' pilgrim was he (or she) who was engaged on the search for God by keeping His commandments; pilgrims (who were often woefully ignorant of the basics of the faith) commonly spent ill-gotten resources on unworthy objects, from hostesses of doubtful virtue to priests who were already well enough off, and neglected the vital truth that charity began at home. In yet another transformation of this venerable sentiment, Erasmus imagined the *paterfamilias* conducting his 'pilgrimage' from room to room of his own house, seeing to the welfare of all the members of his household.[15]

William Thorpe also primly objected to the singers and pipers
who accompanied pilgrims on the march, and elicited an amusingly
populist response from the archbishop. Critics of Thorpe's stamp
(even if, indeed because, they were sincerely concerned with the well-
being of the poor) could not but believe that they had perceived a
simple truth, which by inference the masses did not perceive. These
were Sir John Oldcastle's sentiments, when he in turn was accused in
1413: he who neither knew nor cared about the 'precepts of God'
would expect salvation in vain, even if he penetrated the corners of
the earth; he who obeyed those precepts could not perish, even if he
had never been to Rome, Canterbury or Compostela, 'or wherever
the common herd (*vulgus*) are accustomed to wander'.[16] Such views,
when expressed loudly by people beyond the confines of intellectual
and monastic elites, had not merely a suspect but a sectarian ring.
There is little reason to suppose that they had a very wide currency,
even among people who were by tradition and education entitled to
uphold puristic views of the essentially spiritual nature of the
Christian faith. As proprietors of shrines, indeed, many monks and
clergy had every material and professional reason not to endorse
them. Archbishop Arundel's 'populism' was one expression of a not
unnatural alliance between the interests of the clergy and the sentiments of the misguided 'masses'. However, the Meaux chronicler
related how both the monks of his own abbey and those of Pontigny
succumbed to the temptation to encourage female pilgrims, not to
their ultimate advantage [4].

A century after William Thorpe, one witness to the heresy of
Edward Walker of Maidstone (who was released to the secular arm),
hinted at the impact that acquaintance with dissenting notions could
have on the common man. William Baker of Cranbrook testified
that he and others had 'had communication against pilgrimages and
worshipping of saints and of offerings' in Walker's house. When they
had unanimously concluded that it was not 'profitable for man's soul',
the deponent, who had in fact intended to go and offer at the Rood
of Grace (at Boxley Abbey near Maidstone) changed his mind and
gave his offering to a poor man instead.[17] Thinking new thoughts
might be difficult for some, and have painful consequences, but for
others it afforded opportunities for broad vernacular humour, such
as that of the Norfolk heretic who thought that no pilgrimage should
be made to 'Our lady of Falsingham, the lady of Foulpit and to Tom
of Canterbury'.[18]

The need to rebut a criticism which had become locally noisy led to a stiffening of official attitudes. Oldcastle was asked to respond to an article which declared that 'Holy Church has determined that it is necessary for every Christian to make pilgrimages to holy places and above all to adore the holy relics of the apostles, martyrs and confessors and of all the saints whom the Roman church has approved'. Bishop Reginald Pecock of St Asaph in the middle of the fifteenth century gave a more nuanced account of the 'official' view. Space does not permit more than the briefest reference to his lengthy and frequently repetitive arguments, but they are of the utmost interest for our subject.

The rebuttal of the Lollard critique which effectively occupies Part Two of Pecock's *Repressor*[19] takes its starting-point from the sceptical question (ch. 3), 'Why should the Christian believe that any one crucifix or image of the Virgin or the Saints, is holier than another (and therefore a fitter object of pilgrimage)?' Pecock considers this issue together with the broader one of the legitimacy of pilgrimage *tout court*, and basically employs two convergent arguments to enable him to arrive at the conclusion (ch. 8) that 'pilgrimages to be done is a point of God's moral law and of his pleasant service [i.e. service that is pleasing to Him]'. These arguments are basically that God Himself sanctifies particular images by working miracles through them, thus Himself indicating that they are to be especially venerated; and that (since what Scripture does not explicitly forbid is licit, and Holy Scripture nowhere forbids pilgrimages), pilgrimage is sanctioned by Scripture. This conclusion is amplified and clarified in ch. 17. Pecock here concedes something to an imaginary critic who, while accepting the lawfulness of images and pilgrimages, draws attention to the existence of abuses, and maintains that 'though it be lawful and expedient to many folk for to use in the said manner images and for to haunt pilgrimages, yet since it is not to all folk [a]like expedient and profitable, and it is not to any person commanded by doom of reason or by Holy Scripture, we will not hold us bound as by any precept of law of [human]kind or of God for to use images and do pilgrimages'. Pecock acknowledges the validity of the point, but demands that the critic refrain from deterring other men from these pious practices.

The references to images are significant, for Pecock's apologia for pilgrimage is in fact inextricably embedded in an apologia for the use of images, and for very good reason. Oldcastle, before his judges, delivered a critical disquisition on images, and the issues of image and pilgrimage were closely bound up in the minds of Lollards who

came to trial, to judge at least by the record we have of their responses to interrogation. The miller John Skylly of Flixton admitted
before the bishop of Norwich in 1429 that: 'I held and affirmed and
taught that no pilgrimage ought to be done, nor no manner of
worship ought to be done unto any images of the crucifix, of Our
Lady or of any other saints.' Numerous other heretics admitted to
the same set of errors. Hawisia Moon of Loddon was a woman of
trenchant views. 'No pilgrimage oweth to be done nor be made, for
all pilgrimage going serveth of nothing but only to give priests good
that be too rich and to make gay tapsters and proud hostelers.' She
enlarged a little on her objections to images, 'for all such images be
but idols and made by working of man's hand, but worship and
reverence should be done to the image of God, which only is man'.[20]

Again, none of these ideas can be said to be new. In the tenth
century Bernard of Angers had had to work out in his own mind,
after initial repugnance, that images of saints such as Gerald of
Aurillac and Foy of Conques in fact performed a legitimate function;
the strictures of Bernard of Clairvaux on excessive expenditure on
shrines made a different but not unrelated point.[21] Pecock reckoned
among the arguments which he had to answer the contention that the
living human being was a better image of Christ and the saints than
any decorated 'stock or stone' (as Hawisia Moon evidently thought)
and therefore better deserving of expenditure on him (ch. 9). The
Norfolk heretics repeatedly admitted to the view that pilgrimage
should be made 'only to poor people'. The fundamental argument,
however, was (as for Bernard of Angers) about idolatry.

The debate between the visual image and the written word as
vehicles of divine truth was ancient. Pecock was confronted by
dissidents who were urging the primacy and unique authenticity of
the written text and therefore disparaging the images which were the
major goal of pilgrims. His reply echoed what again were well-established arguments about the superior efficacy of images in impressing
holy truths upon men's minds. Interestingly, and not unreasonably
given contemporary literacy rates, he classified Scripture itself among
the '*hearable* commemorative signs' which were to be contrasted with
'*seeable* commemorative signs' (ch. 11). Even if a man could read,
powers of concentration were limited, and images (for example a
saint's life painted on a wall) could convey more information, more
memorably, in a much shorter time. Books would never be able to
achieve what one local pilgrimage might [9]. Pilgrimage in this treatment becomes above all a mode of recourse and access to images

and thereby a mode of instruction in religious truth, conveyed by the most effective means available.

Attempts to cast up a balance-sheet of the popularity and un-popularity of pilgrimage on the eve of the Reformation seem misconceived, as well as probably doomed to failure. Shrines waxed and waned in favour throughout the centuries, and new pilgrimages continued to arise, some of purely local scope involving the relics of obscure holy men and women, others, sealed with the approval of the highest authority, to the shrines of newly canonised saints. The most successful and universal in their appeal were, increasingly, those associated with Christ himself and his Mother, from the Holy Blood of Wilsnack to the Holy House of Loreto. English domestic pilgrim-age reflected the trend, and the chronicler Walsingham noted that the Lollards concentrated their fire on pilgrimages 'especially to Walsingham and to the cross at the north door of St Paul's in London, where there was nothing of the spirit, but only putrid stumps crawling with worms; by which the ignorant mob were misled and forced into the most obvious idolatry'.[22] Half a century later, Pecock (ch. 9) imagined his opponents contending that 'it is vain waste and idle for to trot to Walsingham rather than to any other place in which an image of Mary is, and to the Rood of the north door at London rather than to each other rood in whatever place he be'.

If the late medieval critics were ranged on a spectrum which embraced high-minded spirituality at one extreme and cynical ac-cusations of clerical profiteering at the other, the practitioners of pilgrimage were a similarly varied bunch. Significant numbers of Christians continued to be prepared to make both long and short journeys on pilgrimage. Their motives were doubtless as mixed as they had always been, ranging from genuine penitential fervour, and the quest for indulgences, through an authentic curiosity to behold the Holy Places or the Christian antiquities of Rome, to idler forms of curiosity simply to see unfamiliar sights and to experience change and travel. There was voracious and uncritical consumption of relics and indulgences to be found at all levels of society; there were also humanists of the stamp of Erasmus and Thomas More who could shake their heads over the credulity and the abuses but feel a human sympathy with the simple-minded faith that sustained them.[23] The effect of the Reformation here as in other areas was to install as orthodoxy a radical, and often intemperately expressed, view of pilgrimage and the cult of relics that had not been entirely without its supporters in earlier centuries.

DOCUMENTS

1. A general criticism of pilgrimage: Honorius
   Augustodunensis

Disciple 'Is it profitable to go to see Jerusalem, or other holy places?'
Master 'It is better to spend the money with which one is going to
go on the poor. If anyone should go inflamed with the love of Christ,
and having made confession of his sins, and using money acquired
from their own inheritance or with their own sweat, and commend
themselves on the way to the prayers to congregations of holy men,
and give from their resources to them or to other poor people, they
are to be praised as Helena and Eudoxia were praised, who did this.
If however they gad about to holy places out of idle curiosity or a
desire for human praise, let this be their reward, that they have seen
pleasant places and beautiful monuments, and have heard the praise
which they love. If however anyone makes the journey with money
obtained in ill-gotten gain, or by robbery, or by oppression, they will
be received by God and the saints like one who slaughters a son in
the presence of his father and thus comes to him with bloody hands.'
[*Elucidarium*, II.23, in *PL* 172, col. 1152.]

2. Hildebert of Le Mans reminds the Count of Anjou of
   the duties of rulership, *c*.1127

It is said, mighty count, that you have taken the road to the shrine of
St James. I do not deny that this is good, but whoever undertakes
governance is bound to obedience, against which he offends if he
abandons it, unless he is called to higher and more profitable things.
Wherefore an unavoidable blame attaches to you, dearest son, in that
you are putting the unnecessary before the necessary, diversion before
service, non-obligation before obligation. No doctor, no scripture
records that wandering around the globe was among the talents
which the householder distributed to his servants. According to
Jerome, blessed Hilarion, when he was close to the city of Jerusalem,
visited it once, lest he should seem to hold the holy places in contempt. Besides which, the eye of your mind is more than normally
clouded if you do not see that the pilgrimage you have taken on is
full of perilous possibilities. You will pass among the castles of the
duke of Aquitaine, whose hatred you have aroused, having come off
the better in the siege of Thouars. Almost everyone has a longer

memory for injuries than for benefits. Besides, you do not know whether the treachery of his father has been reborn in the son. You are leaving your people a legacy of fear and trembling, if you entrust yourself to a young man with a grievance, from whom you must fear the treachery of his father, the impulsiveness of his years, and the avenging of his injury. We have heard also that what you have announced you are going to do is gravely displeasing to the venerable king of England and to your uncle, that they take it ill and endlessly deplore it. Surely to spurn their advice is an obstinacy close to madness, for they are both prepared to consider your interests out of affection, and able to do so out of knowledge. Perhaps you are saying, 'I have vowed a vow to the Lord, I shall be guilty of transgression if I fail to fulfil it.' Understand, o prince, that you have bound yourself by a vow, but God has bound you by duty. You have bound yourself to a journey, God has bound you to obedience; by performing the journey you would see the shrines of the saints, by obedience you would be considering the memory of the saints.[24] Consider therefore whether the fruits of your journey are such that they can make up for the loss incurred by failed obedience. [*PL* 171, cols. 181–2.]

3. Christ points out to Raimond Palmario the duties of charity, *c*.1180

Blessed Raimondo was at Rome and in the likeness of a poor pilgrim was sleeping under a portico at the basilica of St Peter, when the blessed Jesus Christ appeared to him in the guise of a pilgrim, as once to the two disciples whom he accompanied to Emmaus, and addressed him thus: 'Raimondo my servant, your prayers have been so acceptable to me that up to this moment I have satisfied your pious desires for pilgrimage, and for this reason I have freed you from the servitude of wife and children. You have now seen all the holy places which you most wanted to see; nor is there any vow remaining, but that you should return to my most holy sepulchre. But I do not approve of this plan; I want you to occupy yourself with things more useful, that is works of mercy. Do not think that I will consider chiefly pilgrimage and pious exercises of that kind at the hour of judgement, when I shall say, "Come, blessed of my Father, take possession of the kingdom of Heaven; for I was hungry and you gave me to eat; I was thirsty, and you gave me to drink; I was naked, and you covered me; I was sick, and you visited me; I was imprisoned and you redeeemed me."[25] My son, I do not wish you henceforward to wander around the world, but to return to your own land of Piacenza; where so many poor, so many abandoned widows, so many who are ill and worn down by various calamities, demand my mercy, and there is none to help them. You will go there, and I will be with you, and give you my aid, whereby you will bring the rich to alms-giving, the quarrelsome to peace, and finally the erring, and especially lost women, to a right way of living.' [Raimondo, 'Palmario' p. 650.]

4. Dubious expedients to encourage female pilgrimage

This Edmund became ever more resplendent with the most glorious miracles after his death, and his fame spread everywhere, so that many people vowed pilgrimages to his shrine. Among them there were women, and they were not permitted access to the Saint within the confines of the monastery of Pontigny. The monks, wanting to encourage the women's devotion while still preserving the ancient customs of the order, and perhaps having an eye to their own profit, took an arm of the saint from the shrine, it is said, and bore it to the gates of the monastery, so that the women would at least not be totally disappointed in the intention of their devotion, and the monks themselves obtained no small income from the women's offerings. This division of the arm from the other members displeased God and the saint, so it is believed, and they refused to reveal any more miracles publicly to the people.[26] [Meaux 2, p. 441.]

Hugh the fifteenth abbot [of Meaux 1339–49] had a new crucifix made for the choir of the lay-brothers. Its maker did no work on its beautiful features except on the sixth day, when he fasted on bread and water only. He had a nude man standing before him according to whose beautiful appearance he aptly designed the crucifix. By means of this Crucifix the Almighty performed an incessant stream of miracles. Wherefore it was thought that if women could have access to the crucifix, the general fervour would be increased and our monastery would derive no little benefit from it. The abbot of Cîteaux was petitioned on this matter and granted us licence that men and respectable women might have access to the crucifix, as long as a woman were not permitted to enter the cloister, dormitory or other offices, unless she were a benefactress, or the wife, daughter or wife of the son of a benefactor; neither such women or others could stay overnight within the confines of the monastery, or stay there before prime or after compline. If we did otherwise, he cancelled the permission. On the strength of this permission, to our detriment, women often came to the crucifix, especially when their devotion grew cold and they only wanted to see inside the church; and they increased our expenses in proffering hospitality to them. [Ibid., 3, p. 35.]

5. The perils of youth and beauty, c.1350

O how dangerous it is to lead attractive, nay beautiful young women (in whom levity and lust are inherent) into foreign parts in quest of indulgences, particularly inexperienced wives. In my own days, Bernardino da Polenta, lord of the cities of Ravenna and Cervia in the Romagnol region, debauched many young and noble women from beyond the Alps who were on their way to Rome in the last Jubilee year, 1350; if only they had stayed at home, they would not have been debauched by him! For indulgences and pilgrimages are more suitable to the old than to the young; for a ship standing in the harbour, which has never been to foreign ports, does not sense the danger of shipwreck. [Pietro Azario, *Liber Gestorum in Lombardia*, RIS 16.iv, pp. 93–4.]

6. A prayer for a returning pilgrim

We ask, almighty God, that you will mercifully forgive and acquit these your servants, whom you have made to return safe from their pilgrimage (*de sancto itinere*), for whatever they may have thereon committed against your law, through the fragility of the flesh, by immodest looking or hearing, by idle talk or in any other way, and, o most holy Father, that you will guard them from all diabolical assaults and make them always devoutly keep your commands. [*Le Pontifical Romain au Moyen Age*, ed. M. Andrieu, 3, pp. 545–6.]

7. Pilgrimage by cloistered Religious

(a) Geoffrey abbot of Vendôme to abbot Odo

There is an unpleasant rumour in circulation, which has come to our ears, that you have it in mind to return to Jerusalem. To have seen Jerusalem once should suffice you; and if you had never seen it, no diabolical calumny could have arisen against you on this acount, nor would you require God's forgiveness. The bond of the monastic profession cannot be maintained by going to Jerusalem, only violated.

For to go to Jerusalem, just as it is prescribed for laymen, is forbidden to monks by the apostolic see. This I myself know, as he does whose ears were close to the mouth of the lord pope Urban, when he directed laymen to go to Jerusalem and forbade this pilgrimage to monks. When St Benedict makes mention of 'pilgrim monks', he is speaking of those who at that time renounced the world, professing themselves to the service of the Lord, but not professing stability in any one place. It is however necesssary that those who make profession in a particular place must take up the cross of the Lord, and follow the Lord, in that place, and not seek a foreign burial ground. Let us not therefore deviate from the path of our profession on account of a journey to Jerusalem, lest, while we seek a false beatitude, we discover a genuine wretchedness of body and soul. Do not let love of your brother after the flesh, who is in Jerusalem – or who is perhaps already dead, or may have died in whatever place he reached – divert your mind to what is forbidden, to abandon the care of the brothers whom you have undertaken and faithfully promised to rule, and of whom you will have to render an account even to the Lord. [*PL* 157, col. 162.]

(b) 1195: Attempts to discpline English monks

(i) The chancellor, that is the bishop of Ely, was exercising the office of legate and held a council at London, and issued several decrees against the Black Monks, talking of their wandering about on the pretext of pilgrimage to St Thomas and St Edmund [at Bury], and speaking against the abbots, limiting them to a certain number of horses. Abbot Samson replied, 'We do not accept any decree which is against the Rule of St Benedict, which accords abbots the free disposition of their monks.' [Jocelin of Brakelond, *Cronica de rebus gestis Samsonis Abbatis Monasterii Sanctio Edmundi*, trans. and ed. H.E. Butler (London 1949), p. 54.]

(ii) *1195: Legatine Council at York, c. 12* The profession of religious holiness requires that monks and canons regular and nuns live religiously and according to rule. So therefore as to deprive them of the opportunity of wandering about, we forbid them to hold the revenues which are called 'obediences' at farm, to undertake pilgrimages, to leave the monastery without definite and reasonable cause, or to go out without the company of someone whose character is beyond doubt. With respect to nuns especially, we add that they must not leave the enclosure of the convent except in the company of the abbess or prioress.[27] [*Councils and Synods*, I. ii, p. 1050.]

(c) 1301: Archbishop Winchelsey to the prior and chapter of Canterbury

... The frequent testimony of reliable witnesses compels us to marvel that several of you, although you have among you, by the gift of God, a greater abundance of the relics of the saints than there is elsewhere, feigning devotion under the veil of pilgrimage as a result of vows (which are not binding when they are made without the licence of the superior), seek the shrines of St Edmund Rich [Pontigny] or Thomas of Hereford and others, and throwing aside monastic modesty expose themselves to the perils of temptation, and thus, wandering around the world, embrace impiety, create scandals and make themselves and others, by their pernicious example, less receptive to regular observance. Wishing therefore to remove the cause of vagabondage and the opportunity for greater evil, we propose to apply a salutary remedy, and for the future, by these presents, prohibit these wanderings; forbidding you, o prior and the other guardians of the order, in virtue of obedience and on pain of canonical sanctions, to issue permissions to leave [the convent] by reason of pilgrimage, until we have had a fuller discussion with you; and you are to know that we intend to punish any who contravene this prohibition with appropriate penalties as disobedient and rebels. [*Registrum Roberi Winchelsey Cantuariensis Archiepiscopi AD 1294–1313*, ed. R. Graham (2 vols, CYS 51–2), 1, p. 413.]

(d) 1344, October 2nd: Hamo de Hethe, bishop of Rochester, to the nuns of Malling

... We have been credibly informed that often before now and since the last visitation by our immediate predecessor, you have received secular women other than your essential servants to stay among you within your enclosure, and you have received men, regular and secular, at night and to spend the night, within your enclosure, and that you, lady abbess and other ladies both young and old, both in your company and by themselves, have left your abbey, wandering around the country on the pretext of pilgrimage (*par couleur de pelrimage*) or of visiting your friends, against the tenor of the holy canons and the promises made by you in virtue of obedience in the said visitation ... [Hamo de Hethe, 2, pp. 735–6.]

8. Lollard criticism, 1407: William Thorpe is examined by Archbishop Arundel

And then he said to me, 'What saiest thou to the third point that is certified against thee, preaching openly in Shrewsbury that pilgrimage is not lawful; and over this, thou saidest, that those men and women that go on pilgrimages to Canterbury, to Beverley, to Karlington [?], to Walsingham, and to any such other places, are accursed and made foolish, spending their goods in waste. And I said, Sir, by this certification I am accused to you that I should teach that no pilgrimage is lawful; but I said never thus. For I know that there be true pilgrimages and lawful, and full pleasant to God; and therefore sir, howsoever mine enemies have certified you of me, I told at Shrewsbury of two manner of pilgrimages.'

And the Archbishop said to me, 'Whom callest thou true pilgrims?'

And I said, 'Sir, with my protestation, I call them true pilgrims travelling toward the bliss of heaven which, in the state, degree or order that God calleth them to, do busy them faithfully for to occupy all their wits, bodily and ghostly, and to know truly and keep faithfully, the biddings of God ... .

Of these pilgrims I said, whatsoever good thoughts that they any time think what virtuous word that they speak, and what fruitful work that they work, every such thought, word, and work is a step, numbered of God, toward him in heaven. ... And again I said, as their works show, the most part of men and women that go now on pilgrimages have not these foresaid conditions, nor loveth to busy themselves faithfully for to have. For, as I well know, since I have full oft assayed, examine whosoever will twenty of these pilgrims, and he shall not find three men or women that know surely a commandment of God, nor can they say their Pater Noster and Ave Maria, nor their Creed readily in any manner of language. And so I have learned, and also know somewhat by experience of these same pilgrims, telling the cause why that many men and women go hither and thither now on pilgrimage: It is more for the health of their bodies than of their souls; more for to have riches and prosperity of this world than for to be enriched with virtues in their souls; more to have here worldly and fleshly friendship than for to have friendship of God and his saints in heaven. For whatsoever thing man or woman doth, the friendship of God, nor of any other saint, cannot be had without keeping of God's commandments. Further, with my protestation, I say now as I said in Shrewsbury, though they that have fleshly wills travel for their bodies and spend mickle money to seek and to visit the bones or images (as they say they do) of this saint or of that, such pilgrimage-going be neither praisable nor thankful to God, nor to any saint of God, since, in effect, such pilgrims despise God and all his commandments and saints. For the commandments of God they will neither know nor keep, nor confirm them to live virtuously by example of Christ and his saints. Wherefore, sir, I have preached and taught openly, and so I purpose all my lifetime to do with God's help, saying that such fond people waste blamefully God's goods in their vain pilgrimages, spending their goods upon vicious hostelers, which are oft unclean women of their bodies; and at the least those with which they should do works of mercy, after God's bidding, to poor needy men and women. These poor men's goods and their livelihoods these runners-about offer to rich priests, who have mickle more livelihood than they need; and thus those goods they waste wilfully and spend them unjustly, against God's bidding, upon strangers, with which they should help and relieve, after God's will, their poor needy neighbours at home. Yea, and over this folly, oft times divers men and women of these runners thus madly hither and thither into pilgrimage borrow hereto other men's goods; yea, and sometimes they steal men's goods hereto, and they pay them never again. Also, Sir, I know well that when divers men and women will go thus after their own wills and finding out on pilgrimage, they will ordain with them before to have with them men and women that can well sing wanton songs and some other pilgrimages will have with them some bagpipes; so that every town that they come through, what with the noise of their singing, and with the sound of their piping, and with the jangling of their Canterbury-bells, and with the barking out of dogs after them, that they make more noise than if the King came there away, with all his clarions and many other minstrels. And if these men and women be a month out in their pilgrimage, many of them shall be a half-year after great janglers, tale-tellers and liars.'

And the Archbishop said to me, 'Lewd lousel! thou seest not far enough in this matter, for thou considerest not the great travail of pilgrims; therefore thou blamest that thing that is praisable. I say to thee that it is right well done that pilgrims have with them both singers and also pipers; that when one of them that goeth barefoot striketh his toe upon a stone, and hurtheth him sore, and maketh him bleed, it is well done that he or his fellow begin then a song, or else take out of his bosom a bagpipe, for to drive away with such mirth the hurt of his fellow; for with such solace the travail and weariness of pilgrims is lightly and merrily born out.'

And I said, 'Sir, St Paul teacheth men to weep with them that weep.'

And the Archbishop said, 'What, janglest thou against men's devotion? Whatsoever thou or such other say, I say that the pilgrimage that now is used is to them that do it a praisable and a good mean to come the rather to grace.' [From the Introduction to Erasmus, *Pilgrimages*, pp. xxi–xxvi.]

9. Bishop Pecock argues for the efficacy of pilgrimage

When the day of St Katherine [November 25th] comes, mark, who so will, in his mind, all the books which be in London, written upon St Katherine's life and passion, and I dare well say that though there were ten thousand more books written in London on that day of the same saint's life and passion, they should not so much turn the city into mind of the holy famous life of Saint Katherine and of her dignity in which she now is, as doth in each year the going of people in pilgrimage to the College of Saint Katherine[28] besides London, as I dare put this into judgement of whomever hath seen the pilgrimage done on the vigil of St Katherine by persons of London to the said college. Wherefore right great special commodities and profits into remembrance making images and pilgrimages have and do, which writings do not so have and do. [*The Repressor of Over-Much Blaming of the Clergy*, ed. C. Babington (2 vols, RS 19), 1 p. 215.]

Notes

Introduction

1. The original edition appeared in 17 volumes (London 1704–17). It was republished with corrections and additions later in the century (10 vols, The Hague 1739–45), and a further correction and expansion was undertaken in the nineteenth century by the Record Commission, but only reached 1383 (3 vols in 6, 1816–30; vol. 4, 1869). I cite here (with one exception) the first edition; as all editions are arranged strictly chronologically, entries can easily be found.

2. Investigating the dates of establishment of shrines still extant in the late twentieth century, Sidney and Mary Nolan found that 1,308 of their inventory of shrines were founded between 1530 and 1779, 32 per cent of datable shrines and more than one-fifth of their total. Of these, they regarded many, but by no means all, as classifiable as of only minor significance. These figures of course do not include more ancient shrines that continued to exist. There was a low point in European shrine-formation generally in the 1530s but some revival from the 1540s on. See their *Christian Pilgrimage in Modern Western Europe* (Chapel Hill, NC 1989), pp. 99–100 and thereafter.

3. For different aspects of this over-lapping relationship, see the books by Bull and Riley-Smith and the articles by Brundage, Markowski and Tyerman in the Bibliography; on the impact of the establishment of the Latin Kingdom of Jerusalem on western Christendom, see Hamilton.

1. The Development of Medieval European Pilgrimage

1. The translation quoted here is by Bertram Colgrave, originally published with the Latin text, Oxford 1969, reprinted separately 1994.

2. Described by his kinswoman Hugeberc in the *Vita Willibaldi* (sometimes called *Hodoepericon*) she compiled from his reminiscences (*MGH SS* 15.i, pp. 80–117, with her life of Winnebald); translated by C.H. Talbot, *The Anglo-Saxon Missionaries in Germany* (New York 1954), reprinted in *Medieval Women's Visionary Literature*, ed. E. Petroff (Oxford 1986), pp. 92–106; and in Noble and Head, pp. 141–64.

3. *Codice Diplomatico Langobardo*, 3 vols, ed. L. Schiaparelli (*FSI* 62–4), 1, n. 24, pp. 91–6.

4. *Memorie e documenti per servire all'Istoria del Ducato di Lucca*, 4.i (Lucca 1818), appendix, pp. 136–9.

5. Translated by R. Davis, *The Lives of the Eighth-Century Popes* (Liverpool 1992), pp. 49, 159, 189.

6. Ibid., p. 222; *The Anglo-Saxon Chronicle*, trans. and ed. M. Swanton (London 1966), pp. 60–1.

7. The letters cited in this paragraph and the next are translated by E. Emerton, *The Letters of Saint Boniface* (New York 1940), pp. 39, 56–7, 140, 177–8.

8. See in general Constable (1976) and below pp. 236–7.

9. S. Elm, *'Virgins of God': The Making of Asceticism in Late Antiquity* (Oxford 1994), pp. 272–81.

10. For later examples see below pp. 102, 200, 248–9; on the barring of women from St Cuthbert's shrine at Durham, see Tudor.

11. J. McNeill and H. Gamer, *Medieval Handbooks of Penance* (New York 1938), pp. 141, 252. It is impossible here to do more than mention the momentous developments in the theory and practice of penance that took place in the early medieval centuries. See O. Watkins, *A History of Penance* (2 vols, London 1920), which surveys the subject down to 1215, and the Introduction to McNeill and Gamer, q.v.

12. *PL* 112, col. 1410.

13. For a detailed discussion of 'the oldest indulgences for almsgiving and pilgrimage', with examples, see N. Paulus, *Geschichte des Ablasses im Mittelalter vom Ursprung bis zur Mitte des 14. Jahrhunderts* (2 vols, Paderborn 1922–23), 1 chap. 4. For indulgences after the twelfth century, see below, Chapter 3.

14. *PL* 145, col. 98.

15. Glaber, pp. 60–1, 202–5, 212–15. See also the later *Chronica de Gestis Consulum Andegavorum*, in *Chroniques d'Anjou*, ed. P. Marchegay and A. Salmon, 1 (Paris 1856), pp. 96, 100–3, 117, which supplies picturesque detail about Fulk's second Jerusalem pilgrimage (for example, he bit a piece out of the Holy Sepulchre), but wrongly claims that he encountered Robert of Normandy there.

16. *Bernoldi Chronicon*, MGH SS 5, pp. 429–30. Sigebert of Gembloux says under the year 1068 that the fate of the count and his entourage 'is as yet unknown' (ibid., 6, p. 361).

17. T. Head and R. Landes, eds, *The Peace of God: Social Violence and Religious Response in France around the Year 1000* (Ithaca, NY 1992).

18. Odo of Cluny, *De Vita Geraldi Comitis Auriliacensis*, PL 133, cols 639–703; translation in Noble and Head, pp. 293–362.

19. Tulle and Rocamadour, pp. 170–2.

20. On the beginnings of the Compostela pilgrimage, see *inter alia Peregrinaciones*, 1, pp. 27–46; Fletcher, pp. 53–77.

21. *Peregrinaciones*, 1, p. 42.

22. Golinelli, p. 771.

23. Helgaud of Fleury, *Vie de Robert le Pieux*, ed. R.-H. Bautier and G. Labory (Paris 1965), p. 126.

24. See especially the writings of Renato Stopani in the Bibliography.

25. *Monumenta Novaliciensia Vetustiora*, ed. C. Cipolla (2 vols *FSI*, 31–2). There was special accommodation for women, who were not permitted to enter the monastic precinct: a cross marked the boundary they could not transgress (2, p. 126).

26. *Codice Diplomatico di San Colombano di Bobbio*, ed. C. Cipolla (3 vols, *FSI*, 52–4), 1, n. 44.

27. Golinelli, pp. 764–70. For late medieval Italian itineraries to Compostela, see Damonte, Delfiol, and Stopani (1991), pp. 125–31, 145–68.

28. *Cartulaires de l'Eglise Cathédrale de Grenoble*, ed. M.J. Marion (Paris 1869), p. 95: 'strata publica, que strata pergit versus Romam vel ad Sanctum Jacobum'.

29. Stopani (1991), pp. 61, 69.

30. Bernard is thought to have died c.1080, but his life has been placed in the tenth century. For further references, see the *Oxford Dictionary of Saints*.

31. *AS* June 2, pp. 1071–89.

32. For grants to the hospital of San Martino between c.1065 and c.1085, see *Regesto del Capitolo di Lucca*, ed. P. Guidi and O. Parenti (3 vols + index, Rome 1910–39), 1, nn. 414, 416, 432, 444, 445, 456–8, 473, 477, 478, 491, 492. For grants and references to other hospitals before c.1110, see nn. 465, 576, 624, 647, 674.

33. Ibid., n. 872. For Altopascio, see also below p. 90.

34. *MGH Scriptores Rerum Merovingicarum*, 6, pp. 296–7.

35. Ibid, 5, p. 205.

36. Garrisson, pp. 1174–5.

37. Vendôme 1, n. 80; *PL* 159, col. 1000 (Honorius *Augustodunensis*); ibid., 172, col. 599 (Gilbert of Limerick).

38. *Cartulaire*, ed. Marion, p. 202.

39. C. Vogel and R. Elze, *Le Pontifical Romano-Germanique du dixième siècle* (3 vols, Città del Vaticano 1963–72, *Studi e Testi* 226–7, 269), 2, p. 362; see also A. Franz, *Die kirchlichen Benediktionen im Mittelalter* (2 vols, Freiburg im Breisgau 1909, 1, pp. 275–89, who includes rites for signing Jerusalem-bound pilgrims with the Cross and for those going by sea.

40. *Chronicon*, *MGH SS* 6, p. 214.

41. de Certain, III, 20, pp. 169–70.

42. A. Mercati, 'Miraculi B. Prosperi Episcopi et Confessoris', *AB* 15 (1898), pp. 212–13, 217–18, 225. A later continuation added the more elaborate story of a girl from the neighbourhood of Reims who had gone as far as Leon, where the relics of St Isidore had been translated in the 1060s, before she was notified in a vision that she must come to San Prospero (pp. 228–31).

43. For Lollard criticism of pilgrimage and images, see below pp. 241–4.

44. Sheingorn, I.13, pp. 77–9.

45. Ibid., II.12, pp. 137–9.

46. Life of Gerald, 29, in Noble and Head, p. 317; Golinelli, p. 766.

47. Sheingorn I.24, pp. 91–2; IV.1, pp. 182–3.

48. Ousterhout, pt 2.

49. Eddius Stephanus, *Life of Wilfrid*, trans. J.F. Webb, in *The Age of Bede*, ed. D.H. Farmer (Harmondsworth 1983) caps. 5 (p. 110), 33 (p. 140), 55 (pp. 167–8).

50. Musset, pp. 131–2.

51. *Vita Richardi Abb. S. Vitoni Virdunensis*, MGH SS 11, p. 289; Hugh of Flavigny, ibid., 8, pp. 396, 397–8. The latter is a later and longer account which incorporates accumulated traditions.

52. *PL* 139, col. 398.

53. Sheingorn, II.3, p. 119.

54. Glaber, pp. 96–7, 133–7, 199–205. For Fulk Nerra's pilgrimages, see note 39 above.

55. *The Ecclesiastical History of Orderic Vitalis*, ed. M. Chibnall (6 vols, Oxford 1969–80) 2, pp. 68–73.

56. For this pilgrimage, see Joranson (1928).

57. *Vita Willibaldi* 4, in Noble and Head, p. 152.

58. *PL* 145, col. 814.

59. That is, run by monks or canons. The following reference to Matthew XXV.35 is repeatedly made throughout the medieval period to encourage 'good works'.

60. The churches visited in Rome have normally been given their present Italian names to aid identification. Not all the places mentioned on the list of Sigeric's overnight stops back to the Channel coast are certainly identifiable, although the route is perfectly clear and is substantiated by many later accounts. Where the modern place-name is very different, the name as given in the itinerary follows in square brackets. Identifications are suggested by Stopani (1991), pp. 43–56, and by G. Caselli, *La Via Romea 'Cammino di Dio'* (Florence 1990).

61. For *mansiones* 23 and 24, Caselli suggests respectively either Fucecchio or Ripoli, and Ponte a Cappiano (pp. 23–4).

62. Bishop of London 996–1002 and archbishop of Canterbury 1002–23.

63. That is, the secular clergy.

64. This story is told by Glaber, pp. 200–1.

65. There is a translation of Turgot's life by W. Forbes-Leith (3rd edn, Edinburgh 1896; reprint Dunfermline 1993).

66. The Latin *hos famulos tuos vel famulas illas* makes it clear that male and/or female pilgrims were envisaged.

67. There is another *ordo*, from San Cugat del Vallés, in *Peregrinaciones*, p. 148; for others see above n. 39.

2. Penitential Pilgrimage

1. Bernard Guidonis, *Practica Inquisitionis Hereticae Pravitatis*, ed. M. Douais (Paris–Toulouse 1886). Relevant chapters include II, 3 [cf. document 5], 5, 6, 15, 22, 23, 25, 27–9; III, 13–14.

2. Ibid., III, 15, pp. 100–1.

3. *The Register of Eudes of Rouen*, trans. S. Brown and J. O'Sullivan (New York and London 1964), pp. 179, 413, 543–4, 577, 593, 622–3, 668.

4. Information in Hamo de Hethe, to which the table refers.

5. Ibid., 1, pp. 387–9.

6. Van Cauwenbergh, pp. 223–36; see also his geographically arranged digest of the destinations included in all the lists he examined (pp. 138–46), and extracts (in Dutch) from the fifteenth-century 'book of correction' of the magistrates of Lier, containing a variety of sentences of penitential pilgrimage (pp. 200–14).

7. See below pp. 225–6.

8. Van Cauwenbergh, p. 216.

9. Ibid., pp. 219, 220–1.

3. Indulgences and Jubilees

1. Paulus, 2, pp. 312–22. For late-thirteenth-century pilgrimage from neighbouring Perugia, see below p. 122.

2. *Les Registres de Nicholas IV*, ed. E. Langlois (2 vols, Paris 1905), 2, n. 653. Nicholas's numerous indulgences to churches elsewhere in Christendom also manifested a tendency to greater generosity, e.g. a year and forty days was common and by 1291 it was the minimum available on any day at St John Lateran [doc. 4].

3. Faillon, 2, cols 829–30.

4. See the chronicle accounts of eye-witnesses below, pp. 117–19.

5. See below p. 93.

6. Albericus de Rosate, *Lexicon sive Dictionarium utriusque iuris* (Pavia 1498) (no pagination) s.v. 'Jubileus'.

7. On the Veronica, see E. Kuryluk, *Veronica and her Cloth* (Oxford 1991) and E. von Dobschütz, *Christusbilder. Untersuchungen zur Christlichenlegende* (Leipzig 1899) which contains much of the relevant source material.

8. For 1300, see the chroniclers' accounts below pp. 117–19, and for Clement VI, *France*, 3, nn. 4569, 4709, 4718, 4734, etc.

9. Ibid., n. 4426. Similar demurrals were addressed to other princes, including the duke of Austria (Clement VI, *Lettres* 1, n. 2045).

10. For example, *CEPR* 3, pp. 338, 382–6, 388, 394–7, 429.

11. *Stacions*, p. 4 and *passim*.

12. *CEPR* 10, pp. 57–8.

13. Clement VI, *Lettres* nn. 2373, 2685; *CEPR* 3, p. 49.

14. See below, Chapter 6.

15. *Historia Anglicana* (2 vols, RS 28), 2, p. 187.

16. For example, *CEPR* 4, pp. 323–6. For examples of commutations of vows, see below pp. 174–5, 190–1.

17. For such grants to English churches see *CEPR* 4, 349, 350; 5, 489, 510, 548–9, 590, etc.

18. *Quellen zur Geschichte der Stadt Köln*, ed. L. von Ennen (6 vols, Cologne 1860–79), 6, pp 277–82, 312–15.

19. *Stacions*, p. 10.

20. *A Parisian Journal 1405–1449*, trans. J. Shirley (Oxford 1968), pp. 363–4.

21. *LC 3*, pp. 243–8, 252–5. In 1487, Canterbury was successful in obtaining from Innocent VIII a plenary indulgence available on the feast of the translation of St Thomas and the day preceding, for a period of three years commencing in 1489; at the same time, the pope granted in perpetuity an indulgence of a fourth part of the penitent's sins, available on a select number of other days, including the feast of the saint (*CEPR 14*, pp. 27–8).

22. *CEPR* 13, p. 203.

23. Ibid., 10, pp. 169–70, 262; 13, pp. 50, 198.

24. *LC* 3, pp 340–7.

25. For an English example, see below p. 82.

26. Schimmelpfennig, p. 295.

27. *Pellegrini Scrittori*, p. 130.

28. Margery, pp. 79, 245.

29. *Pellegrini Scrittori*, pp. 169–70.

30. See below, Chapter 12.

31. H. Wharton, *Anglia Sacra* (2 vols, London 1691), 1, pp. 49–50.

32. Woodruff, pp.18–20.

33. See below pp. 148–9.

34. An icon of Christ 'not made with hands', referred to also by Clement VI, below p. 77 and Urban V, below p. 107.

35. A 'quarantine' was a period of forty days, the standard unit of indulgence.

36. All these saints, the chief patrons of the city, are depicted on Stefan Lochner's great altarpiece, still in Cologne Cathedral. The 11,000 virgins were the companions of St Ursula. For the legend of the translation of the Three Magi from Milan to Cologne, see P. Geary, 'The Magi and Milan', in *Living with the Dead in the Middle Ages* (Ithaca, NY 1994), pp. 243–56, reprinted from *Il millennio ambrosiano: La città del vescovo dei carolingi al Barbarossa*, ed. C. Bertelli (Milan 1988), pp. 274–87.

37. Edmund de Lacy granted numerous other such indulgences: 1, pp. 300, 306, 315; 2, pp. 25, 45, 314, 387, 403; 3, pp. 38, 136, 210.

4. Help and Hazard: The Pilgrim's Experience

1. Part of Book I of the *Liber Sancti Jacobi*, translated in *The Miracles of St James* [hereafter *Miracles*], pp. 8–56.

2. Adhemar of Chabannes, *Chronique*, ed. J. Chavanon (Paris 1897), p. 173.

3. *Statuti di Perugia dell'Anno MCCCXLIII*, ed. G. degli Azzi (2 vols, Rome 1913–16), 2, pp. 120–1.

4. See above pp. 21, 46–7.

5. Respectively *Jugements de l'Echiquier de Normandie au XIIIe siècle*, ed. L. Delisle (Paris 1864) n. 796, p. 183 and *Summa de legibus*, ed. G. Tardif (Rome–Paris 1896), p. 215.

6. *Summa de legibus*, p. 246.

7. For an example of the latter, see above p. 56.

8. See the remarks below p. ooo about Malatesta 'Ungaro'.

9. Urban V, *Communes*, n. 20181.

10. Ibid., nn. 6359, 6360.

11. See above pp. 68–70.

12. Alberigo, pp. 267–71, 311–12. The Lyons decree is translated in N. Housley, *Documents in the Later Crusades, 1274–1580* (London 1996) pp. 16–20. For a selection of Christian and Muslim views of the state of Jerusalem and pilgrimage in the thirteenth century, see Peters, esp. pp. 360–78.

13. See above p. 43.

14. *Les Registres d'Urbain IV (1261–1264)*, ed. J. Guiraud (4 vols + index, Paris 1899–1958), 2, pp. 226–9, nn. 467, 468; *Les Registres de Clément IV*, ed. E. Jordan (Paris 1893–1945), n. 1609, pp. 478–9.

15. Quoted in Peters, p. 612.

16. For some very accessible accounts of fifteenth-century Holy Land pilgrimage, based on pilgrim diaries, see Prescott and Mitchell, as well as much in Peters. For an analysis of surviving guide-books, see Brefeld.

17. *Peregrinaciones*, 3, pp. 111–12.

18. *Statuto del Comune di Lucca dell'anno MCCCVIII* (Lucca 1867), I, xv, pp. 17–18.

19. Ibid., p. 56; Innocent IV, 3, p. 57.

20. *AS* April 2, pp. 449–51. On the pilgrimage 'infrastructure' in this region see Settia.

21. *AS* October 10, p. 235. There are numerous references to the ferry over the Po at Piacenza, for example in a Becket miracle (*Materials*, p. 322), and see above pp. 18, 25.

22. *Materials*, p. 530. This site has been tentatively identified as Shooters Hill, a well-known nest of robbers at a much later date.

23. *Statuta Civitatis Mutine (Monumenti di Storia Patria delle Province Moden-esi, Serie degli Statuti* 1 (2 vols, Parma 1864), 2, p. 268.

24. C. Ghirardacci, *Della Historia di Bologna* 1 (Bologna 1605), p. 421; 2 (Bologna 1657) p. 388.

25. Ibid., 2, pp. 5, 10–11, 53.

26. Ibid., pp. 370, 573. For the provision made for Compostela pilgrims in another Italian city, see below, Chapter 7.

27. Shaver-Crandell and Gerson (p. 266) note that the order was established at Paris by *c*.1180, but built its 'major hospices for pilgrims' there in 1260 and 1314. Philip II's itinerary is in *RS* 49, 2, pp. 229–30; also *MGH SS* 28, p. 131, and is reprinted by Stopani (1991), pp. 86–8. See also above p. 21.

28. For royal letters of Henry III in favour of the brethren of Altopascio see e.g., *CPR H III*, 3, p. 26 (1234), 220 (1238), 6, p. 116 (1267); for St Antony, ibid., 4, p. 12 (1248), p. 624 (1258), 6, p. 171 (1267, order for the arrest of fraudulent collectors).

29. *Peregrinaciones*, 3, p. 67. 'Jubilee' here means the Day of Judgement and has nothing to do with the Jubilees as celebrated from 1300 onwards. For the reference to Matthew 25, see above p. 258 n. 59, for the deed of foundation of Roncesvalles by Sancho bishop of Pamplona, between 1127 and 1132, and his subsequent benefactions, see *Peregrinaciones*, 3, pp. 56–8.

30. *CPR Ed II*, 4, p. 15. For the Hospital of St Mary 'Rounceval' at Charing Cross, and an indulgence for it printed by Caxton *c*.1482, see P. Needham, *The Printer and the Pardoner* (Washington, DC 1986).

31. Cenci, 2, pp. 376, 396, 399, 436, 443, 460, 478, 490, 546. The *capella picta* of the hospital is referred to in 1487 (3, p. 826). For Assisi wills reflecting devotion to James and Antony, see below p. 136.

32. Raimondo, p. 651. For this life, and an extensive treatment of Raimondo, see L. Canetti, *Gloriosa Civitas: Culto dei santi e società cittadini a Piacenza nel Medioevo* (Bologna 1993), pp. 169–285.

33. *Urkundenbuch der Stadt Hildesheim*, ed. R. Doebner (8 vols, Hildesheim 1901, reprinted 1980), 4, pp. 375–6 (revised statutes of 1440). A Spaniard who was lying sick in the hospital of St James and St Antony at Assisi in 1437, allowed his companion, from Zamora, to go home; it is not clear whether they were pilgrims (Cenci, 2, p. 534).

34. For information about Netherlandish brotherhoods, see P. Trio, *Volksreligie als spiegel van een stedelijke samenleving: De broederschappen te Gent in de late middeleuwen* (Leuven 1993).

35. Rupin, pp. 135–6.

36. See above p. 25. For pilgrim souvenirs, see above pp. 25–6 and below, Chapter 5.

37. L.A. Muratori, *Antiquitates Italici Medii Aevi* (6 vols, Milan 1738–42), 3, cols 8821–2.

38. *Miracles*, p. 44.

39. *Urkundenbuch ser Stadt Hildesheim*, 8, nn. 560, 709.

40. M. Tulliani, *Osti, Avventori e Malandrini: Alberghi, Locande e Taverne a Siena e nel suo contado tra Trecento e Quattrocento* (Siena 1994).

41. *ASI* 16.i, pp. 242, 624. *Maestà* presumably means an image of the Virgin and Child enthroned in majesty.

42. This decree implicitly distinguishes pilgrims from 'crusaders': c. 11 takes under protection those 'who undertake an expedition (*iter*) to Jerusalem or Spain' (col. 288).

43. For analogous English practices, see below pp. 163–4.

44. Similar permissions were granted to Compostela by Innocent III in 1207 (*PL* 215, col. 1175) and to Rocamadour by Clement V in 1306 (Rupin, p. 358). The connection here between *contentiones et rixas* and the 'spilling of

seed' is not very clear, but the abbot had presumably claimed that outrages were committed against women pilgrims.

45. Benedict had issued a similar instruction to the bishop of Famagusta in January 1337 (Benedict XII, *Lettres Communes*, ed. J.-M. Vidal (3 vols, Paris 1903–11), 1, p. 449, n. 4803)

46. On February 15th this petition was rejected and the plaintiffs instructed solemnly to request satisfaction from the commune of Rome. Only if within six months they had not received satisfaction, would they have licence to take reprisals (ibid., fol. 34).

47. For Simone Sigoli's account of the pilgrimage, and also that written by Giorgio Gucci, one of Frescobaldi's original companions from Florence, see *Pellegrini Scrittori*, pp. 219–55, 259–312. Gucci kept detailed accounts of expenditures.

48. *Sic*; but this would have been a tiny ship. A cog rated at 1200 *botti* (by Lane's estimation, 720 tons) was built at Venice in 1422–25: F. Lane, *Venice: A Maritime Republic* (Baltimore, MD 1973), p. 123 (for the *botte*, see pp. 478–9).

49. The statutes of the Lincoln Guilds of St Benedict and of the Fullers make very similar stipulations, pp. 177, 180.

50. 'Nor shall it be permitted to married people to undertake a long-distance pilgrimage, unless by their mutual and published consent.' (Council of Westminster, 1200, c. 11: *Councils & Synods*, I.ii, p. 1088).

51. The saga did not end here: soon Margery left her new companions in another attempt to rejoin the 'worshipful woman' of London, only to be cruelly repulsed; by good fortune she was then rejoined by the poor friar and they proceeded together to Calais.

52. A Hildesheim benefactor in 1487 provided coals for the warming of pilgrims in the Holy Ghost Hospital (*Urkundenbuch der Stadt Hildesheim*, 8, p. 147).

53. In the *Ordonnances anciennes* collected in 1351 it is apparent that the twelve 'masters' must have made the pilgrimage personally, 'à piet ou à cheval', but not that all the confraternity members are obliged to have done so (p. 308). Another fifteenth-century brotherhood required that its members had been 'a ung des trois lieux del pelherinaigeis dessoubz nomméz, asscavoir de Saint-Jacques de Compostelle, de Jherusalem ou de Rome': P. de Spiegeler, 'Les Statuts de la confrérie Saint-Jacques de Liège (23 mai 1479)', *Academie Royale de Belgique, Bulletin de la Commission Royale d'Histoire* 147 (1981), p. 209.

54. A 'soul-bath' (mod. Seelbad) was 'a free bath provided for poor people according to the terms of a bequest made for the benefit of the testator's soul'.

55. The identity of this diocese is uncertain.

56. For a comment on the financial motive in 1350, see below p. 121.

57. For Clement's exhortations to Edward III, see below pp. 165, 181.

58. One pilgrim who took advantage of this offer was Albericus de Rosate (see above p. 66) who stayed only six days and with his companions obtained

the indulgence from cardinal Annibaldo. Also on 20th February Clement issued a general request that no exaction of tax be made from pilgrims to the *limina* (n. 2143).

59. For the impact of the 1450 Jubilee on the cost of money, see *ASI* 16.1 (1850), p. 624.

60. At Perugia as elsewhere there were laws restricting the movements of officials during their term of office.

61. Another safe-conduct, with exemption from tolls, issued in 1435 by Niccolò Fortebraccio, captain-general of the church and governor of Assisi, for those coming to the Indulgence specifically excluded 'rebels, traitors and exiles of the said city of Assisi' from its scope (Fantozzi, p. 259).

5. Remembering Pilgrimage: Souvenirs

1. J. Shirley, *Garnier's Becket: translated from the 12th-century Vie Saint Thomas le Martyr de Cantorbire of Garnier of Pont-Saint-Maxence* (London 1975), p. 157.

2. See above p. 25.

3. Vielliard, p. 96; Shaver-Crandell and Gerson, p. 89. For the Santiago souvenir trade, see Lopez Ferreiro, 5, pp. 3809, 125–6 and appendices V and XVII; *Peregrinaciones*, 1, pp. 129–35.

4. *AS* May 7, p. 158.

5. Giraldus Cambrensis, *Opera*, ed. J. S. Brewer, 8 vols, *RS* 21, 1, p. 53.

6. *Materials*, p. 478.

7. *Les Miracles de Notre Dame de Rocamadour* p. 148.

8. B-Text, Passus V, trans. A.V. Schmidt (Oxford 1992), pp. 59–60. 'Vernicle' was a common English corruption of 'Veronica', for which see above p. 66.

9. Description in illustrations in Lubin.

10. Spencer (1968), pp. 138–9.

11. Cohen (1976) with several of the relevant documents.

12. Rupin, pp. 115–16, 233–6, 355–8, 363–4, 377–81. All Rocamadour medals bore the image of the Virgin on one side; some – the more sought-after – had St Amadour on the reverse, others St Veronica, supposedly St Amadour's wife.

13. *The Tale of Beryn*, ed. F. Furnivall and W. Stone, *EETS extra series*, 105, 1887, p. 7.

14. Krötzl, pp. 386–7 (the figures), 134–5. A similar map has been drawn on the basis of finds of pilgrim tokens in Zeeland: see Van Heeringen.

15. Spencer (1968), p. 144.

16. Ibid., p. 142; *Journal of the British Archaeological Association* 19 (1863), pl. 8; 23 (1867), pp. 256–68, 331–2, 370–8.

17. H. Appuhn, 'Der Fund kleiner Andachtsbilder des 13. bis 17. Jahrhunderts in Kloster Wienhausen', *Niederdeutsche Beiträge zur Kunstgewschichte* 4 (1965) p. 199.

18. A rather similar story was told *c*.1475 about a badge of the Virgin of Amersfoort, which kept its shape after it was put in a melting vat: Spencer (1968), p. 144.

19. This text is also in A. Forgeais, *Collection des plombs historiés trouvés dans la Seine* (5 vols, Paris 1862–66), 2, pp. 77. For the Mont St Michel trade, see Lamy-Lasalle. 'Quincaillerie' is 'hardware' or 'ironmongery' in modern French, but here seems rather to mean 'trinkets' or *bijouterie*. Like Compostela, the shrine used the emblem of the shell (*coquille*); what the 'horns' (*cornez*) are is unclear.

6. Pilgrimage Post Mortem: Wills

1. For an Italian record of the fulfilment of this requirement, see below p. 160.

2. For Margaret, see I. Skovgaard-Petersen, 'Queenship in Medieval Denmark' in J. Parsons, ed., *Medieval Queenship* (Stroud 1994), pp. 25–42; S. Imsen, 'Late Medieval Scandinavian Queenship', in A. Duggan, ed., *Queens and Queenship in Medieval Europe* (Woodbridge 1997) pp. 53–73.

3. *Regesten der Lübecker Burgertestamente des Mittelalters*, ed. A. von Brandt (2 vols, Lübeck 1964–73) [modern German summaries of Latin and German originals], 1, n. 873; 2, n. 642.

4. Ibid., 2, n. 660.

5. *Hamburger Testamente 1351 bis 1400*, ed. H.-D. Loose (Hamburg 1970), n. 96.

6. *The Register of Henry Chichele, archbishop of Canterbury 1414–1443*, 2, *Wills proved before the Archbishop or his Commissaries*, ed. E.F. Jacob (*CYS* 42) (Oxford 1937), pp. 280–1.

7. *Magna Vita Sancti Hugonis*, ed. D. Douie and H. Farmer (London 1962) pp. 159–63. For the Order, see above pp. 88, 90.

8. A fine specimen of a Wilsnack pilgrim badge was found King's Lynn: Spencer (1968) p. 145 and Plate IV, 6. For Scottish pilgrims, see below pp. 215, 221–2.

9. For the testamentary evidence for Umbrian pilgrimage, see Melloni.

10. Cenci, 1, pp. 187–8, 232–3, 455; 2, p. 769.

11. Ibid., 2, pp. 38, 42–3, 327.

12. Ibid., 1, pp. 187, 279, 319, 353, 374, 398, 415, 416, 418, 478, 495.

13. Ibid., 1, p. 428. This was the period of the foundation of the joint hospital of St James and St Antony (above p. 90). Later bequests for St Antony alone are on pp. 509; 2, p. 683. In 1471 a testator left money to pave the 'roads of Santa Maria of the Angels', in place of a vow made to go to Vienne (p. 717)

14. Ibid., 2, p. 709, 810, 887, 1090.

15. I am indebted to my colleague Dr Robert Frost for help with the Danish text, and also to Krötzl, pp. 127–9. I have ventured to disagree with Krötzl on some identifications of shrines: for example, would not a pilgrim

to the Magdalen in the early fifteenth century have gone to Provence rather than to Vezelay?

16. The Scala Coeli was just outside Rome, named for a legend that St Bernard, praying there, saw the soul of a departed friend released from Purgatory and ascending a stairway to Paradise. An English guide-book explains that 'he that saythe a mase there witt good devossyon may brynge a soule out of purcatorry to hevyn & gretly helpe his frende that is alyve' (*Stacions of Rome*, p. 31).

17. For Master John Schorne, see above p. 128.

18. There were 'Roods of Rest' at West Malling near Maidstone and also at Schorne. Boxley is also near Maidstone. In St Mary's, Newington, near Sittingbourne, there are remains of the shrine, dated *c.*1350, of 'St Robert le Bouser' (J. Newman, *The Buildings of England: North East and East Kent*, 3rd edn (Harmondsworth 1983), p. 402).

19. A gold coin bearing the image of the Virgin 'saluted' by the Angel.

20. For this crucifix as an object of Lollard criticism see p. 245.

21. The editor, James Raine, commented of this will: 'I am not aware of the existence of any other document from which we can ascertain that some of these shrines were places of fame. This passage, therefore, is of singular interest.'

7. Pilgrimage in One City: Pistoia

1. The legend is in *Acta Sanctorum* July 6, pp. 59–68.

2. For the *Opera* and the cult, see *L'Opera di S. Jacopo in Pistoia e il suo primo statuto in volgare (1313)*, ed. L. Gai and G. Savino (Pistoia 1994).

3. For this subject in general, see Webb (1986).

4. Ibid., p. 214.

5. Pistoia, Archivio di Stato, Archivio di San Jacopo, 759, fols 285, 336v, 368; 756, fols 169, 296v.

6. For a fuller account of these records, see Webb (forthcoming).

7. For English pilgrims to Santiago or elsewhere who departed at the Purification, see below pp. 171, 175, 176, 183.

8. D. Bornstein, *The Bianchi of 1399: Popular Devotion in Late Medieval Italy* (Ithaca, NY 1993).

9. Especially as the numbers of pilgrims receiving alms grew, the clerks used the repeated formula *per la soprascritta* [or, *detta*] *cagione* reserving *ando a San Jacopo* for the beginning of the list or the top of a new page.

10. Cinto Benti's will is extant, in Archivio di San Jacopo, 33, fol. 109.

11. Piero di Bene is recorded as going to St James at least ten times, in 1380, 1384, 1385, 1386, 1388, 1389, 1393, 1399, 1400 and 1403.

12. The manuscript reading 'della Magna' is probable but not quite certain.

13. The famous Volto Santo, housed in the cathedral of San Martino.

14. The 'servant saint' (d. 1278) who was venerated in the church of San Frediano at Lucca.

15. Lucha di Quartino da Casore received £3, clearly for himself and his two companions although no companions are mentioned, on 8th September, two days after he was released from his debt and six days before, apparently, he set out: Archivio di San Jacopo, 756, fol. 51v.

16. Vanni di Vita received alms from the *Opera* before departing for St James: Archivio di San Jacopo, 753, fol. 225v.

8. Englishmen Abroad

1. *The Treatise on the Laws and Customs of the Realm of England commonly called Glanvill*, ed. G. Hall (Oxford 1993), pp. 17–18, 150–1.

2. *Bracton on the Laws and Customs of England*, ed. G. Woodbine and trans. S. Thorne (4 vols, Cambridge, MA 1968–77), 4, pp. 72–7; also *RS* 70, 5, pp. 158–69.

3. *Accounts and Surveys of the Wiltshire Lands of Adam de Stratton*, ed. M. Farr (*Wilts Archaeological and Natural History Society, Records*, Branch 4, 1959), p. 71; *John of Gaunt's Register 1379–1383*, ed. E. Lodge and R. Somerville (2 vols, Camden Third Series 56–7, 1937), 1, n. 381.

4. *CPR Ed II*, 2, pp. 380, 381; 3, p. 261.

5. *CCR H III*, 7, p. 433.

6. *Foedera* (Record Commission edition), 3.i, pp. 4, 5 (not in Rymer's original edition).

7. *CEPR, Petitions*, p. 50.

8. For the Jubilees, see above pp. 65–70, 117–22.

9. See Schimmelpfennig. For the fullest treatment see Storrs, esp. pp. 64–6, 111–27, 185–9.

10. *The Stacions of Rome*, p. 37; *Paston Letters* 5, p. 190.

11. *Foedera*, 8, p. 775; 9, p. 8.

12. *CPR H VI*, 4, p. 234.

13. This early licence remains unparalleled before the later fourteenth century.

14. For measures taken to ensure access for women to St Edmund's shrine, see above p. 102 and below p. 248.

15. There are numerous other references to departure on or around the Feast of the Purification; see nos. 21, 36, 40, 44, 61. Cf. above p. 149.

16. The king had just, after initial reluctance, implemented the pope's decision, under pressure from Philip IV of France, to disband the Order of Templars.

17. Edmund Woodstock was executed in March 1330 on charges of treason. His mother, the second wife of Edward I, had died in 1317.

18. Bartholomew Burghersh was appointed Warden of the Cinque Ports on 11th August of this same year (*Foedera*, 4, p. 792). In June 1350, when he still held that office, he was indulted to visit the Lord's Sepulchre with two knights and thirty squires (*CEPR* 3, p. 353); in 1353 he was permitted to defer it for three years (pp. 394–5) and in 1353, he, Roger Mortimer earl of March,

John Beauchamp and Edward himself were permitted to prorogue Compostela vows for three years (ibid., p. 560).

19. On the same day Edward also wrote to the pope, the cardinals and the king of Sicily on Kildesby's behalf. On the 14th he had granted him safe-conduct and appointment of attorneys (ibid., p. 358). On 1st May, called 'king's clerk', he and his prebend of Wetwang received protection for one year (CCR Ed III, 7, p. 107).

20. On 13th August the king directed letters to several Pisan and Lucchese notables, and also to Luchino Visconti of Milan, detailing the circumstances of the case and requesting their intervention. It was alleged that the pilgrims had been unjustly arrested 'under colour of the plunder of a ship of the city pretended to have been made at sea by certain of the king's subjects, although it was not, but by certain banished men of the realm' (ibid., pp. 646–7). From later entries it transpires that Genoese, Florentine and English merchants intervened to bail the Lucchese merchants and to secure the release of the supposed pilgrims, but the case dragged on well into 1347 (CCR Ed III, 8, pp. 81, 136–7, 175, 235–6, 253, 292, 294).

21. On 13th September, at the petition of John de la Ryvere, the pope granted John Noble, 'accompanying him to the Holy Sepulchre', a benefice in the gift of the abbot and convent of Tewkesbury (CEPR, Petitions 1, p. 119).

22. The presumable significance of this condition is that had John appointed a deputy in the 'cause of blood', he might have been regarded as trying to evade moral responsibility for any death sentences that might have been imposed.

23. On March 3rd 1350 the pope wrote to Philip VI and reported on further diplomatic exchanges which had extended the truce until 2nd April. For this letter and its content so far as it concerns the Jubilee, see above pp. 78–9.

24. A lengthy list of similar mandates is given with some detail of numbers of servants and horses, Foedera, 5, pp. 681–3. This list is supplemented in CCR Ed III, 9, pp. 267–8, 271–2, although not all the supposed additions are in fact missing from Foedera.

25. Andrew Luttrell was granted power to appoint attorneys on departure for the Holy Land on 25th July 1360 (CPR Ed III, 11, p. 446).

26. This was a popular destination for Scottish pilgrims (below p. 215) but the only other English pilgrims I have noted who were specifically going there were Ellen de Risceby and her daughter Maud, licensed to cross from Dover in 1368 (CPR Ed III, 14, p. 129).

27. Several clerks were licensed to proceed to Rome in late 1389/early 1390, presumably for the Jubilee.

28. On 30th November 1413 William de Botreaux [the younger] was granted two years' leave of absence to go to the Holy Land (Foedera, 9, p. 77).

29. Thomas Lord Scales, Lancastrian partisan, murdered after the battle of Barnet in 1460.

30. Executed in 1483.

31. On 8th November 1479 the pope rescinded this monition. Edward IV had protested against the infringment on his jurisdiction and also reported 'that it was believed that Richard's proposed pilgrimage to the said city was feigned' (*CEPR* 14, pp. 252–3).

9. Pilgrimage in England

1. *CCR H III*, 2, p. 382; see also p. 413. Henry was expected to visit Bromholm in June 1232 (ibid., 1, p. 70). For the Rood of Bromholm, see Wormald.

2. *The Will of King Henry the Seventh* (London 1775), p. 37. For English wills relating to pilgrimage and shrines, see Chapter 6.

3. In apparent exception to this rule, royal protection was granted to pilgrims to 'St Theobald' (*CPR H III*, 5, p. 239; 6, p. 650) in 1263 and again in 1272. The editor of the Patent Roll assumed that this was the shrine of this saint which existed at Colaton Ralegh in Devon; the rector complained of threats to pilgrims there in 1347 (see below p. 205). There is no other apparent case, in the thirteenth century, of a grant of royal protection to an English subject going on pilgrimage within England; and the duration of the grant (seven months) exceeded what was allowed to many pilgrims to Santiago. Is it possible that the shrine of St Theobald intended here was the one at Thann, in Alsace, which was flourishing in the later middle ages?

4. See Maddicott ; Valente; J. McKenna, 'Popular Canonization as Political Propaganda: The Cult of Archbishop Scrope', *Speculum* 45 (1970) pp. 608–23.

5. On 2nd October 1323 Edward II complained that seditious persons were faking miracles to the credit of Henry de Montfort and Henry Willington, who had been hanged at Bristol and their bodies left on the gallows as a public example (*Foedera*, 4, pp. 20–1).

6. *RS* 28, 1, pp. 189, 288; 2, p. 195. Edward III's three petitions, in 1327, 1330 and 1331, are in *Foedera*, 4, pp. 268–9, 421–2, 478–80. See also Tait.

7. For Lollard criticism, see Chapter 12.

8. Margery, p. 200.

9. For episcopal sentences of penitential pilgrimage, see above pp. 52–4.

10. *Calendar of Inquisitions Miscellaneous*, 2, pp. 459–60.

11. *CPR R II*, 5, pp. 712–13.

12. *Paston Letters* 4, p. 256, n. 650 (abstract only). Some references other than those given among the Documents here are in 3, p. 40; 5, pp. 31, 144; 6, pp. 1, 57, 59, 119.

13. For a permission to women to enter another Cistercian monastery for the purpose of pilgrimage, see above p. 102.

14. On this cult and shrine see Finucane (1977), chap. 10; Vauchez (1981)

annexes I and II; M. Jancey, ed., *St Thomas Cantilupe, Bishop of Hereford: Essays in his Honour* (Hereford 1982).

15. Almost certainly Blean Forest, still a wooded tract of country on the approach to Canterbury from the London direction.

16. On the following January 19th, this was repeated (ibid, p. 343), again with effect until Michaelmas.

17. For the 1342 statutes of the Eastbridge Hospital see above pp. 106–7.

18. On 8th May in this same year of 1347, agreement was reached between the Dean and Robert, vicar of Colaton, in respect of the revenues of the church. The 'offerings at the chapel of St Theobald' were allotted to the Dean (Grandisson pt 2, p. 1021).

19. This may well just mean 'pilgrim'.

20. Henry VII referred to this statute in a proclamation dated 8th February 1493 (*CPR H VII*, 1, pp. 434–7), declaring that he wished to modify the severity of its provisions; he made no reference to Edward IV's related proclamation of May 1473 (see below p. 211).

21. The exposure of the English coast to French piracy is underlined by the letter written on the following day by Margery Paston to John: 'enemies … came up to the land and played them on Castor Sands, as homely as they were Englishmen' (p. 136, n. 106).

10. Pilgrimage to and from Scotland

1. Their expenditures on these purposes are recorded in the published volumes of the *Accounts of the Lord High Treasurers of Scotland*. The best sense of the sources for Scottish medieval pilgrimage is given by McRoberts. See also Henderson.

2. Thomas Macolagh first received a safe-conduct for Canterbury in March 1358; another was issued for both Thomas and Gilbert Macolagh in May. In April 1361 Thomas was again proposing to visit Canterbury, with his wife; in November 1363 he and his brother were permitted to come to England on business (*Rot. Scot.*, 1, pp. 820, 824, 856, 875).

3. *Foedera*, 4, p. 400; *CPR Ed III*, 1, p. 436; McRoberts, pp. 87–8.

4. *Foedera*, 10, p. 690.

5. *LC* 2, n. 851, pp. 373–5.

6. *Rot. Scot.*, 1, pp. 881, 884, 887, 892, 899, 900, 917.

7. *CPR H III*, 2, pp. 80–1. It is curious that the editor of the Patent Roll interpreted *iter peregrinationis versus Sanctum Andream* to mean a pilgrimage to Santander in Spain.

8. *Calendar of Documents Relating to Scotland*, ed. J. Bain (4 vols, Edinburgh 1884), 2, n. 1225.

9. In 1496 Dame Margery Salvin, late of York, bequeathed a relic of St Ninian to the Greyfriars there. The Christian name 'Ninian' occurs from time to time in Yorkshire wills of this period, for example, a son of Sir

Thomas Markenfield, mentioned in 1497 (*Testamenta Eboracensia* 4, nn. 57, 63, Surtees Society 53, 1868, pp. 116, 125).

10. Van Cauwenbergh, p. 144. Pilgrim-badges from St. Andrew's have been found at Middleburg and at Sluis on the coast of Zeeland, which was the likely embarkation point for pilgrims to this destination from the southern Netherlands: see Van Heeringen, pp. 100–1; Van Beuningen, p. 122.

11. McRoberts, p. 90, points out that some of the members of the original party may have stayed for a while in the east.

12. This safe-conduct, which was for Edward's own sister, the widow of Alexander III of Scotland, was renewed on 13th September and again on 26th December, when it was made valid for one year; she was now declared to be 'passing through the realm on her pilgrimage' (ibid., pp. 160, 186).

13. The countess received a safe-conduct for St Thomas again in 1373: *Rot. Scot.*, 1, p. 963.

14. Roger Hog appears again in 1363 as 'burgeys de Edynburgh en Escoce', receiving licence to do business in England (ibid., pp. 863–4, 872.)

15. This seems most likely to be the church of Seton in East Lothian, which was dedicated to the Virgin. Dean Stanley gives a shorter and in other respects different text of this declaration, although the basic story is the same, in his *Historical Memorials of Canterbury*, 11th edn, (London 1912), pp. 280–1.

16. Master John Legat received another safe-conduct for Rome in 1448 (ibid., p. 332).

17. Of this party, Abbot Andrew of Melrose, Andrew lord Gray and Master John Methven had received safe-conduct for Canterbury also in September 1451, with William Edmonstone and Alexander Napier, knights (ibid., p. 349). A William Edmonstone had been a pilgrim in England in 1428 (p. 263) and Andrew of Melrose came to Canterbury again in 1456 (p. 376).

18. This safe-conduct was issued again, to the same people and for the same destinations, on 14th March 1466 (p. 419).

11. European Visitors

1. *LC* 3, pp. 26–9.

2. *CCR H III*, 3, p. 345.

3. See above pp. 51, 59.

4. Information from Van Cauwenbergh, pp. 9–10.

5. For Malatesta and his pilgrimage, see P. Jones, *The Malatesta of Rimini and the Papal State* (Cambridge 1974), esp. pp. 79–90; Haren and Pontfarcy, pp. 174–6; F. Cardini, 'L'avventura cavalleresca nel Italia tardomedievale', in *L' acciar de' cavalieri* (Florence 1997), esp. pp. 41–5. In 1364 Urban V permitted him to postpone for two years his vow to visit the Holy Land (Urban V, *Secrètes*, n. 1113).

6. Haren and Pontfarcy, ch. 6. On 2nd April 1412 Laurence was licensed by Henry IV to leave the country for parts overseas (*CCR H IV*, 4, p. 274).

7. Ramón's account of his pilgrimage is translated by Dorothy Carpenter in Haren and Pontfarcy, pp. 99–119.

12. Criticism and Evaluation of Pilgrimage

1. *Materials*, p. 107. Cf. the Italian word *gallioffi* (good-for-nothings): above p. 155.

2. For a succinct account of the the beginnings of Christian pilgrimage to the Holy Land, and of early criticism, see R. Wilken, *The Land Called Holy* (New Haven, CT 1992), esp. ch. 6.

3. Formulary of Marculf, II, c. 49, *MGH Legum*, 5, p. 104. The reading *vacandi* seems better supported than *vagandi* ('wandering about') which might seem an equally plausible accusation.

4. For earlier such criticism, see above pp. 13–14.

5. Meaux 2, p. 243; *A History of the County of York [Victoria County History]*, ed. W. Page (3 vols, London 1907–13), 3, pp. 171–2. In 1489 Archbishop Thomas Rotherham made a similar injunction, but in less stringent terms, insisting on 'grete cause' and the need for a suitable companion. On *Pericoloso*, see J. Brundage and E. Markowski, 'Enclosure of nuns: the decretal *pericoloso* and its commentators', *JMH* 20 (1994) pp. 143–55; also K. Gill, '*Scandala*: controversies concerning *clausura* and women's religious communities in late medieval Italy', in S. Waugh and P. Diehl, eds, *Christendom and its Discontents* (Cambridge 1996), pp. 177–203.

6. In general on this theme, see Constable, with abundant references.

7. *PL* 171, cols 148–9.

8. On these saints and on the importance of pilgrimage in concepts of lay sanctity, see Vauchez (1981), esp. pp. 232–4; (1997), pp. 197–9.

9. *Ancrene Wisse*, 6, in *Anchoritic Spirituality*, trans. A. Savage and N. Watson (New York 1991), pp. 176–7.

10. Hadewijch, *The Complete Works*, trans. C. Hart OSB (New York 1980), p. 77.

11. Berthold von Regensburg, *Vollständige Ausgabe seiner Predigten*, ed. F. Pfeiffer (2 vols, Vienna 1862), 2, pp. 448, 459–60, 493.

12. C. Rudolph, *The 'Things of Greater Importance': Bernard of Clairvaux's Apologia and the Medieval Attitude Toward Art* (Philadelphia 1990), pp. 281–3.

13. *The Imitation of Christ*, trans. L. Sherley-Price (Harmondsworth, 1952) p. 186.

14. *The Vision of Piers Plowman*, trans. A.V. Schmidt (Oxford 1992), pp. 2, 39, 49, 59–60, 67, 127. For royal proclamations on the export of money and on vagabondage under cover of pilgrimage, see above e.g. pp. 171, 181–2, 207–8, 211–12.

15. Erasmus, pp. 58–9.

16. *Foedera*, 9, p. 63.

17. *Kentish Heresy Proceedings, 1511–12*, ed. N. Tanner (*Kent Records* 26, 1997), p. 53.

18. *Heresy Trials in the Diocese of Norwich, 1428–31*, ed. N. Tanner (*Camden Fourth Series* 20, 1977), p. 148. 'Foulpit' is a pun on 'Woolpit'.

19. *The Repressor of Over-Much Blaming of the Clergy*, ed. C. Babington (2 vols, RS 19), 1, pp. 131–274.

20. *Heresy Trials*, pp. 57, 142. See *Kent Heresy Proceedings, passim*.

21. See above, pp. 23–4. The literature on this issue is vast. For one stimulating treatment over a wide chronological range, see D. Freedberg, *The Power of Images* (Chicago 1980).

22. *Historia*, RS 28, 2, p. 189. Walsingham laid notable emphasis on miracles which occurred contemporaneously in the part of England most familiar to him, at Ely, Cambridge, St Albans itself and also, 'as we think, to confirm pious believers and confute heretics', at Wymondham Abbey, 'at a certain cross erected on the public road' (pp. 183–4, 188–9).

23. See Erasmus, *passim*; for More, *A Dialogue Concerning Heresies*, in *Complete Works*, ed. T. Lawler, G. Marc'hadour and R. Marius (New Haven, CT 1981), 6.i., pp. 226–34, modernised by J. Shinners in *Medieval Popular Religion, 1000–1500: A Reader* (Peterborough, Ontario 1997), pp. 201–10.

24. 'Agnosce o princeps quia tu quidem te alligasti voto, sed te Deus officio: tu viae, sed Deus obedientiae; viae, qua sanctorum memoriam videres; obedientiae, qua sanctorum memoriis providires.' There is a pun here on two possible meanings of the phrase *sanctorum memoria*, respectively 'shrine' and 'memory' of the saints. The addressee of this letter was Fulk the Younger, count from 1123; William VIII became duke of Aquitaine in 1127.

25. See above pp. 30, 90, 258 n. 59.

26. For another version of the solution to the monks' problem, see above p. 102.

27. This prohibition was in essentials reiterated at the Council of Oxford, c. 52, in 1222 (*Councils & Synods*, II.ii, p. 123). As these texts show, the thrust was initially and in theory towards the restraint of religious of both sexes, but the concentration on nuns later became more and more pronounced (see, for example, the legatine council of Ottobuon Fieschi in 1268, ibid., pp. 789–91).

28. This was situated east of the Tower, in the area that was flooded early in the nineteenth century to form St Katharine's Dock.

Select Bibliography

Sources and Collections of Sources

Bernard of Ascoli, *Descriptio Terrae Sanctae* in S. Sandoli ed., *Itinera Hierosolymitana Crucesignatorum*, 2 (Jerusalem 1980)

The Book of Margery Kempe, ed. S.B. Meech and H.E. Allen (Early English Text Society 112, 1940)

The Book of Margery Kempe, trans. B. Windeatt (Harmondsworth, 1985)

Brewyn, William, *A XVth Century Guide-Book to the Principal Churches of Rome*, trans. C. E. Woodruff (London 1933)

Burchard of Mount Sion, *The Holy Places*, Palestine Pilgrims Text Society 12 (1896)

Capgrave, J., *Ye Solace of Pilgrimes: A Description of Rome circa A.D. 1450*, ed. C. Mills (London 1911)

Casola, Pietro, *Canon Pietro Casola's Pilgrimage to Jerusalem in the Year 1494*, trans. and ed. M. Newett (Manchester 1907)

Certain, E. de, *Les Miracles de Saint Benoit* (Paris 1858)

The City of Jerusalem, 1220 A.D., Palestine Pilgrims Text Society 6 (1896)

Damonti, M., 'Da Firenze a Santiago di Compostella: l'itinerario di un anonimo pellegrino nell'anno 1477', *Studi Medievali* 13 (1972) pp. 1043–71

Dardano, M., 'Un itinerario dugentesco per la Terra Santa', *Studi Medievali*, 3rd ser., 7 (1966) pp. 154–96

Delehaye, H., 'Le pèlerinage de Laurent de Pasztho au Purgatoire de S. Patrice', *AB* 27 (1908) pp. 35–60

Delfiol, R., 'Un altro "itinerario" tardo-quattrocentesco da Firenze a Santiago di Compostella', *ASI* 137 (1979) pp. 599–613

Erasmus, D., *Pilgrimages to Saint Mary of Walsingham and Saint Thomas of Canterbury*, trans. J. Nichols (London 1875)

Fabri, Felix, *The Wanderings*, Palestine Pilgrims Text Society 7–9 (1892); reprint (2 vols, New York 1971)

Faillon, E., *Monuments inédits sur l'Apostolat de Sainte Marie-Madeleine en Provence* (2 vols, Paris 1848)

Fantozzi, A., 'Documenti perusina ad indulgentiam Portiunculae spectantia', *Archivum Franciscanm Historicum* 9 (1916), pp. 237–93

Fazio of Cremona, *see* Vauchez 'Sainteté Laïque'

Gerson, P., Shaver-Crandell, A., Stones, A. and Krochalis, J., *The Pilgrim's Guide to Santiago de Compostela: Critical Edition* (2 vols, London 1998)

Golinelli, P., 'La "Vita" di s. Simeone monaco', *Studi Medievali*, 3rd ser., 20 (1979) pp. 709–88

Gregory, Master, *see* Nardella, C.

Herbers, K. and Plötz, E., *Nach Santiago zogen sie: Berichte von Pilgerfahrten ans 'Ede der Welt'* (Munich 1996)

The Holy Jerusalem Voyage of Ogier VIII, Seigneur d'Anglure [1395–96], trans. R.A. Browne (Gainesville, 1975)

Kemp, B., 'The Miracles of the Hand of St James', *Berkshire Archaeological Journal* 65

Künig von Vach, H., *The Pilgrimage and Path to Saint James*, trans. J. Durant (Confraternity of St James Occasional Paper 3, London 1993)

Lehrand, L., 'Relations du pèlerinage à Jérusalem de Nicolas de Martoni, notaire Italien (1394–95)', *Revue de l'Orient Latin* 3 (1895) pp. 566–9

Ludolph von Suchem, *Description of the Holy Land and of the Way Thither*, Palestine Pilgrims Text Society 12 (1895)

The Marvels of Rome (Mirabilia Urbis Romae), trans. F. Morgan (New York 1986; first published in London 1889)

Melczer, W., *The Pilgrim's Guide to Santiago de Compostela* (New York 1993)

Les Miracles de Notre-Dame de Rocamadour au XIIe siècle, ed. E. Albe, new ed. by J. Rocacher (Toulouse 1996)

The Miracles of St James, ed. T.E. Coffey, L.K. Davidson and M. Dunn (New York 1996) [a translation of parts of Book I of the *Liber Sancti Jacobi*]

Miracula Beati Egidii, auctore Petro Guillelmo, in MGH SS, pp. 312–23 [incomplete; supplemented by] *Liber miraculorum Sancti Egidii*, AB 9 (1890) pp. 393–422

Mitchell, R., *The Spring Voyage* (London 1965) [a Holy Land pilgrimage of 1458, based on contemporary accounts]

Nardella, C., *Il fascino di Rome nel Medioevo. Le 'Meravaglie di Roma' di maestro Gregorio. Con il testo latino e traduzione italiana della Narracio de mirabilibus urbis Romae* (Rome 1997)

Noble, T. and Head, T., *Soldiers of Christ: Saints and Saints' Lives from Late Antiquity and the Early Middle Ages* (London 1995)

Omont, H., 'Journal d'un pèlerin français en Terre Sainte (1383)', *Revue de l'Orient Latin* 3 (1895) pp. 457–9

Pellegrini Scrittori: Viaggiatori toscani del Trecento in Terrasante, ed. A. Lanza and M. Troncarelli (Florence 1990)

Raimondo 'Palmario', *Vita*, in AS July 7, pp. 638–63

Roberto da Sanseverino, *Viaggio in Terra Santa (1458)* (Bologna 1888)

Saint Patrick's Purgatory: A Twelfth-century Tale of a Journey to the Other World, trans. J.-M. Picard (Dublin 1985)

Shaver-Crandell, A. and Gerson, P., *The Pilgrim's Guide to Santiago de Compostela: A Gazetteer with 580 Illustrations* (London 1995)

Sheingorn, P., trans, *The Book of Sainte Foy* (Philadelphia 1995)

The Stacions of Rome and the Pilgrims Sea-Voyage, ed. F. Furnivall (Early English Text Society 25, 1867)

Stopani, R., *Le vie di pellegrinaggio del Medioevo* (Florence 1991)

Stopani, R., *Il pellegrinaggio a Santiago de Compostela di fra Giacomo Antonio Naia (1717–1718)* (Florence 1997)

Tate, R. and Turville-Petre, T., *Two Pilgrim Itineraries of the Later Middle Ages* (Santiago de Compostela 1995) [Purchas's Pilgrim and Master Robert Langton]

Theoderich, *Guide to the Holy Land*, trans. A. Stewart, new ed. by R.G. Musto (New York 1986)

'Viazio al Sancto Sepolcro per lo Marchese Nicolò da Este' and 'Viaggio de S. Antonio de Viena in Franza', in *Johannes Ferrariensis Ex Annalium Libris Marchionum Estensium excerpta*, ed. L. Simeoni, *RIS* 20. ii, pp. 51–7

Vielliard, J., ed., *Le Guide du Pèlerin au Saint-Jacques de Compostelle* (5th edn, Paris 1990)

Vita et Miracula S. Leonardi Nobiliacensia, in *AS* November 3, pp. 148–73

Wey, William, *The Itineraries of William Wey* (London, Roxburghe Club 1857)

Wilkinson, J., *Egeria's Travels* (London 1971)

Wilkinson, J., *Jerusalem Pilgrims before the Crusades* (London 1977)

Wilkinson, J., *Jerusalem Pilgrimage 1099–1185* (Hakluyt Society, 2nd ser., 167, London 1988)

Secondary Works

Abou-El-Haj, B., *The Medieval Cult of Saints: Formations and Transformations* (Cambridge 1994)

Adair, J., *The Pilgrims' Way: Shrines and Saints in Britain and Ireland* (London 1978)

Alexander, J. and Binski, P., *Age of Chivalry: Art in Plantagenet England 1200–1400* (catalogue of an exhibition at the Royal Academy, London, 1987), pp. 205–25, 'Pilgrimage: devotion to the saints'

Barber, R., *Pilgrimages* (Woodbridge, 1991)

Barreiros Rivas, J.L., *La función politica de los caminos de peregrinación. Estudio del Camino de Santiago* (1997)

Becker, M., *Rochester Bridge 1387–1856: A History of its Early Years, compiled from the Wardens' Accounts* (London 1930)

Birch, D., *Pilgrimage to Rome in the Middle Ages* (Woodbridge, 1998)

Bonner, G., Rollason, D. and Stancliffe C., *St Cuthbert: His Cult and His Community to AD 1200* (Woodbridge 1989)

Borenius, T., *Medieval Pilgrims' Badges* (London 1930)

Brefeld, J., *A Guidebook for the Jerusalem Pilgrimage in the Late Middle Ages: A Case for Computer-aided Textual Criticism* (Hilversum 1994)

Brundage, J., '"Cruce Signari": The Rite for Taking the Cross in England', *Traditio* 22 (1966) pp. 289–310

Brundage, J., *Medieval Canon Law and the Crusader* (Madison 1969), ch. 1, 'The Pilgrimage Tradition and the Holy War before the First Crusade'

Bull, M., *Knightly Piety and the Lay Response to the First Crusade: The Limousin and Gascony c. 970–c. 1130* (Oxford 1993)

Bulles, B., 'Saint Amadour: Formation et Evolution de sa Légende (XIIe-XXe siècle)', *Annales du Midi* 107 (1995) pp. 437–55

Cardini, F., ed., *Toscana e Terrasanta nel Medioevo* (Florence 1982)

Cardini, F., *Il Pellegrinaggio: una dimensione della vita medievale* (Rome 1996)

Cheirézy, C., 'Hagiographie et Société: l'Exemple de Saint Léonard de Noblat', *Annales du Midi* 107 (1995) pp. 417–35

Cohen, E., '*In haec signa*: Pilgrim-badge Trade in Southern France', *Journal of Medieval History* 2 (1976) pp. 193–214

Cohen, E., 'Roads and Pilgrimage: A Study in Economic Interaction', *Studi Medievali* 2 (1980) pp. 321–41

Coleman, S. and Elsner, J., *Pilgrimage Past and Present in the World Religions* (London 1995)

Constable, G., 'Opposition to Pilgrimage in the Middle Ages', *Studia Gratiana* 19 (1976) pp. 125–46

Davies, J.G., *Pilgrimage Yesterday and Today: Why? Where? How?* (London 1988) [with good bibliography of sources]

Dickinson, J., *The Shrine of Our Lady of Walsingham* (Cambridge 1956)

Duffy, E., *The Stripping of the Altars* (London 1992)

Dupront, A., 'Pèlerinage et lieux sacrés', in *Mélanges en 'Honneur de Fernand Braudel* 1 (Toulouse 1973), pp. 189–206

Farmer, S., *Communities of Saint Martin: Legend and Ritual in Medieval Tours* (Ithaca, NY 1991)

Favreau-Lilie, M.-L., 'The German Empire and Palestine: German Pilgrimages to Jerusalem between the 12th and 16th Century', *JMH* 21 (1995) pp. 321–34

Finucane, R., *Miracles and Pilgrims: Popular Beliefs in Medieval England* (London 1977)

Finucane, R., *The Rescue of the Innocents: Endangered Children in Medieval Miracles* (London 1997)

Fletcher, R., *St James's Catapult: The Life and Times of Diego Gelmírez of Santiago de Compostela* (Oxford 1984)

Gai, L., ed., *Pistoia e il Cammino di Santiago: una dimensione europea nella Toscana medioevale: Atti del Convengno Internazionale di Studi, Pistoia 28–29–30 settembre 1984* (Perugia 1987)

Garrisson, F., 'A propos des pèlerins et de leur condition juridique', *Etudes Historiques du Droit Canonique*, ed. G. Le Bras (Paris 1965) 2, pp. 1165–89

Gauthier, M., *Highways of the Faith: Relics and Reliquaries from Jerusalem to Compostela*, trans. J. Underwood (London 1983)

Geary, P., *Furta Sacra: Thefts of Relics in the Central Middle Ages* (Princeton, NJ 1978)

Goodich, M., *Violence and Miracle in the Fourteenth Century: Private Grief and Public Salvation* (Chicago 1995)

Hamilton, B., 'The Impact of Crusader Jerusalem on Western Christendom', *Catholic Historical Review* 80 (1994) pp. 695–713

Haren, M. and de Pontfarcy, Y., *The Medieval Pilgrimage to St Patrick's Purgatory* (Clogher 1988)

Head, T., *Hagiography and the Cult of Saints: The Diocese of Orleans, 800–1200* (Cambridge 1990)

Heath, S., *In the Steps of the Pilgrims* (London 1950; revised edition of *Pilgrim Life in the Middle Ages*, originally published in 1911)

Henderson, P., *Pre-Reformation Pilgrims from Scotland to Santiago de Compostela* (The Confraternity of St James, Occasional Paper 4, London 1997)

Hohler, C., 'The Badge of St James', in I. Cox, ed., *The Scallop: Studies of a Shell and its Influences on Humankind* (London 1957), pp. 49–70

Howard, D., *Writers and Pilgrims: Medieval Pilgrimage Narratives and their Posterity* (Berkeley, CA 1980)

Hyde, J.K., 'Italian Pilgrim Literature in the Late Middle Ages', in D. Waley, ed., *Literacy and its Uses: Studies on Late Medieval Italy* (Manchester 1993), pp. 136–61

Jancey, M., ed., *St Thomas Cantilupe Bishop of Hereford: Essays in his Honour*, (Hereford 1982)

Joranson, E., 'The Great German Pilgrimage of 1064–1065', in L. Paetow, ed., *The Crusades and Other Historical Essays presented to Dana C. Munro* (New York 1928), pp. 3–43

Joranson, E., 'The Palestine Pilgrimages of Henry the Lion', in *Medieval and Historiographical Essays in Honor of James Westfall Thompson* (Chicago 1938), pp. 146–225

Jusserand, J., *English Wayfaring Life in the Middle Ages* (London 1889)

Köster, K., 'Pilgerzeichen Studien: neue Beitrage zur Kenntnis eines mittelalterilichen Massenartikels und seiner Überlieferungsformen', in *Bibliotheca Docet: Festgabe für Carl Wehmer* (Amsterdam 1963), pp. 77–100

Krötzl, C., *Pilger, Mirakel und Alltag: Formen des Verhaltens in skandinavischen Mittelalter* (Helsinki 1994)

Labande, E.-R., '*Ad limina*: Le pèlerin médiéval au terme de sa démarche', in P. Gallais and J.-Y. Riou, eds, *Mélanges offerts à René Crozet* (Poitiers 1966), pp. 283–91

Labande, E.-R., 'Recherches sur les pèlerins dans l'Europe des XIe et XIIe siècles', *Cahiers de civilisation médiévale* 1 (1966) pp. 159–69, 339–47

Labande, E.-R., 'Les pèlerinages au Mont Saint-Michel pendant le Moyen Age', in *Millénaire Montastique du Mont Saint-Michel*, vol. 3, *Culte de Saint Michel et Pèlerinages au Mont*, ed. M. Baudot (Paris 1971), pp. 237–50

Lamy-Lasalle, C. 'Les Enseignes de Pèlerinage du Mont Saint-Michel', in *Millénaire Monastique du Mont Saint-Michel*, vol. 3, *Culte de Saint Michel et Pèlerinages au Mont*, ed. M. Baudot (Paris 1971), pp. 271–86,

Lomax, D., 'The First English Pilgrims to Compostela', in H. Mayr-Harting and R.I. Moore, eds, *Studies in Medieval History presented to R.H.C. Davis* (London 1985), pp. 165–75,

Lopez Ferreiro, A., *Historia de la S.A.M. Iglesia de Santiago de Santiago de Compostela* (11 vols, Santiago de Compostela 1873–75)

Lubin, H., *The Worcester Pilgrim* (*Worcester Cathedral Publications* 1, 1990)

Maddicott, J., 'Follower, Leader, Pilgrim, Saint: Robert de Vere, Earl of Oxford, at the Shrine of Simon de Montfort, 1273', *English Historical Review* (1994) pp. 641–53

Magoun, F.P., 'The Rome of Two Northern Pilgrims: Archbishop Sigeric of Canterbury and Abbot Nikolas of Munkathvera', *Harvard Theological Review* 33 (1942) pp. 267–89

Markowski, M., '*Crucesignatus*: Its Origins and Early Usage', *JMH* 10 (1984) pp. 157–65

Mayr-Harting, H., 'Functions of a Twelfth-century Shrine: The Miracles of St Frideswide', in H. Mayr-Harting and R.I. Moore, eds, *Studies in Medieval History presented to R.H.C. Davis* (London 1985), pp. 193–206

McRoberts, D., 'Scottish Pilgrims to the Holy Land', *Innes Review* 20 (1969) pp. 80–106

Melloni, P.L., 'Mobiltà di devozione nell'Umbria medievale: due liste di pellegrini', in *Chiesa e Società dal secolo IV ai nostri giorni: Studi storici in Onore del P. Ilarino di Milano* 1 (*Italia Sacra* 30, Rome 1979), pp. 327–59

Millénaire Monastique du Mont Saint-Michel, vol. 3, *Culte de Saint Michel et Pèlerinages au Mont*, ed. M. Baudot (Paris 1971)

Mullins, E., *The Pilgrimage to Santiago* (London 1974)

Musset, L., 'Recherches sur les pèlerins et les pèlerinages en Normandie justqu'à la Première Croisade', *Annales de Normandie* 12 (1962) pp. 127–50

Nilson, B., *Cathedral Shrines of Medieval England* (Woodbridge 1998).

Nolan, M. and Nolan, S., *Christian Pilgrimage in Modern Western Europe* (Chapel Hill, NC 1989)

Ohler, N., *The Medieval Traveller*, trans. C. Hillier (Woodbridge 1989)

Ortenberg, V., 'Archbishop Sigeric's Journey to Rome in 990', *Anglo-Saxon England* 19 (1990) pp. 197–246

Ousterhout, R., ed., *The Blessings of Pilgrimage* (Illinois Byzantine Studies 1, Urbana 1990)

Paulus, N., *Geschichte des Ablasses im Mittelalter vom Ursprunge bis zur Mitte des 14. Jahrhunderts*, 2 vols (Paderborn 1922)

Pellegrinaggi e culto dei santi in Europa fine alla 1e crociata, Convegni di Centro di Studi sulla Spiritualità Medievale, 4 (Todi 1963)

Pennington, K., 'The Rite for Taking the Cross in the Twelfth Century', *Traditio* 30 (1974) pp. 429–35

Peters, F., *Jerusalem: The Holy City in the Eyes of Chroniclers, Visitors, Pilgrims and Prophets from the Days of Abraham to the Beginnings of Modern Times* (Princeton, NJ 1985)

Plötz, R., ed., *Europäische Wege der Santiago-Pilgerfahrt* (Tübingen 1990)

Prescott, H., *Jerusalem Journey: Pilgrimage to the Holy Land in the Fifteenth Century* (London 1954) [based on the journals of Felix Fabri]

Prescott, H., *Once to Sinai: The Further Pilgimage of Friar Felix Fabri* (London 1957)

Quintavalle, A.C., *La strada Romea* (Milan 1976)

Quintavalle, A.C., *Vie dei Pellegrini nell'Emilia Medievale* (Milan 1977)

Rapp, F., 'Les pèlerinages dans la vie religieuse de l'occident médiéval aux XIVe et XVe siècles', in M. Philoneenko and M. Simon, eds, *Les Pèlerinages* (Paris 1973), pp. 140–3.

Ravensdale, J., *In the Steps of Chaucer's Pilgrims: From Southwark to Canterbury from the Air and on Foot* (London 1989)

Riley-Smith, J., *The First Crusaders 1095–1131* (Cambridge 1997)

Rollason, D., 'The Miracles of St Benedict: A Window on Early Medieval France', in H. Mayr-Harting and R.I. Moore, eds, *Studies in Medieval History presented to R.H.C. Davis* (London 1985), pp. 73–90

Rollason, D., *Saints and Relics in Anglo-Saxon England* (Oxford 1989)

Ruggieri, J.S., 'Il pellegrinagio compostellana e l'Italia', *Cultura Neolatina* 30 (1970) pp. 185–98

Rupin, E., *Roc Amadour: Etude Historioque et Archéologique* (Paris 1904)

Santiago de Compostela: 1000 Ans de Pèlerinage Européen (Ghent 1985) [catalogue of an extensive and important exhibition]

Schimmelpfennig, B., 'Die Anfange des Heiligen Jahres in Santiago de Compostela im Mittelalter', *JMH* 4 (1978) pp. 285–303

Schmitt, J.-C., *The Holy Greyhound: Guinefort, Healer of Children since the Thirteenth Century* (Cambridge 1979)

Settia, A., 'Strade e Pellegrini nell'Oltrepò pavese', in his *Chiese, strade e fortezze nell'Italia medievale* (*Italia Sacra* 46) (Rome 1991), pp. 303–31

Sigal, P.-A., 'Maladie, pèlerinage et guérison au XIIe siècle. Les miracles de saint Gibrien à Reims', *Annales* 24 (1969) pp. 1522–39

Sigal, P.-A., *Les marcheurs de Dieu* (Paris 1974)

Sigal, P.-A., *L'homme et le miracle dans la France médiévale (XIe–XIIe siècle)* (Paris 1985)

Spencer, Brian, 'Medieval Pilgrim Badges: Some General Observations Illustrated Mainly from English Sources', *Rotterdam Papers: A Contribution to Medieval Archaeology* 1, ed. J. Renaud (Rotterdam 1968), pp. 137–53

Spencer, Brian, 'A Scallop-Shell Ampulla from Caistor and Comparable Pilgrim Souvenirs', *Lincolnshire History and Archaeology* 6 (1971) pp. 59–66

Spencer, Brian, 'King Henry of Windsor and the London Pilgrim', in J. Bird, H. Chapman and J. Clark, *Collectanea Londoniensia: Studies Presented to Ralph Merrifield, London and Middlesex Archaeological Society, Special Paper* 2 (1978), pp. 235–64

Spencer, Brian, 'Pilgrim Souvenirs from the Medieval Waterfront Excavations at Trig Lane, London 1974–76', *Transactions of the London and Middlesex Archaeological Society* 33 (1982) pp. 304–23

Spencer, Brian, 'A Thirteenth-century Pilgrim's Ampulla from Worcester', *Worcestershire Archaeological Society Transactions*, 3rd ser., 9 (1984) pp. 7–11

Springer, O., 'Medieval Pilgrim Routes from Scandinavia to Rome', *Medieval Studies* 12 (1950) pp. 92–122

Stancliffe, C. and Cambridge, E., *Oswald, Northumbrian King to European Saint* (Stamford 1995)

Stanley, H., *Historical Memorials of Canterbury* (London 1854; many subsequent editions)

Stopani, R., *La Via Francigena in Toscana: Storia di una Strada Medievale* (Florence 1984)

Stopani, R., *La Via Francigena: Una strada europea nell'Italia del Medioevo* (Florence 1988)

Stopani, R., *La Via Francigena del Sud: L'Appia Traiana nel Medioevo* (Florence 1992)

Storrs, C., *Jacobean Pilgrims from England to St James of Compostella from the Early Twelfth to the Late Fifteenth Century* (Santiago de Compostela 1994)

Sumption, J., *Pilgrimage: An Image of Mediaeval Religion* (London 1975)

Tait, H., 'Pilgrim-Signs and Thomas, Earl of Lancaster', *British Museum Quarterly* 20 (1955) pp. 39–47

Tate, B. and Tate, M., *The Pilgrim Route to Santiago* (Oxford 1987)

Tate, R.B., *Pilgrimages to St James of Compostela from the British Isles during the Middle Ages* (Liverpool 1990)

Tate, R.B., 'Robert Langton, Pilgrim (1470–1524)', *Nottingham Medieval Studies* 39 (1995) pp. 182–91

Thiers, O., *Bedevaart en kerkeraad: De Amerfoortse vrouwevaart van 1444 tot 1720* (Hilversum 1994)

Tudor, V., 'The Misogyny of Saint Cuthbert', *Archaeologia Aeliana*, 5th ser., 12 (1984) pp. 157–67

Turner, V. and Turner, E., *Image and Pilgrimage in Christian Culture* (Oxford 1978)

Tyerman, C., 'Were There any Crusades in the Twelfth Century?', *English Historical Review* 110 (1995) pp. 553–77

Valente, C., 'Simon de Montfort, Earl of Leicester, and the Utility of Sanctity in Thirteenth-century England', *JMH* 21 (1995) pp. 27–48

Van Beuningen, H. and A. Koldeweij, *Heilig en Profaan: 1000 Laat-Middeleeuwse Insignes uit de Collectie H.J.E. Van Beuningen* (Rotterdam Papers 8) 1993.

Van Cauwenbergh, E., *Les Pèlerinages expiatoires et judiciaires* (Louvain 1922)

Van Heeringen, R., Koldeweij, A. and Gaalman, A., *Heiligen uit de Modder: In Zeeland gevonden Pelgrimstekens* (Utrecht 1988).

Van Herwarden, J., ed., *Santiago de Compostela in woord en beeld* (Utrecht 1985)

Vanhemelryck, F., *Kruis en Wassende Maan: Pelgrimstochten naar het Heilig Land* (Leuven 1994)

Vasqué z de Parga, L., Lacarra, J.M. and Riu, J.U., *Las Peregrinaciones a Santiago de Compostela* (3 vols, Madrid 1948–49)

Vauchez, A., 'Sainteté Laïque au XIIIe siècle: la Vie du Bienhereux Facio de Crémone (v. 1196–1272)', *Mélanges de l'Ecole Française de Rome* 84 (1972) pp. 13–53

Vauchez, A., *La Sainteté en Occident aux derniers siècles du moyen age* (Rome 1981); *Sainthood in the Later Middle Ages*, trans. J. Birrell (Cambridge 1997)

Vogel, C., 'Le pèlerinage penitentielle', in *Pellegrinaggi e culto dei sancti in Europa fine alla le crociata, Convegni di Centro di Studi sulla Spiritualità Medievale*, 4 (Todi 1963)

Wall, J.C., *Shrines of British Saints* (London 1905)

Ward, B., *Miracles and the Medieval Mind: Theory, Record and Event 1000–1215* (2nd edn, Aldershot 1987)

Wasser, B., *Pelgrimages: Bedevaartsplaatsen van de westerse christenheid* (Nijmegen 1993)

Webb, D., 'The Holy Face of Lucca', in *Anglo-Norman Studies, IX: Proceedings of the Battle Conference 1986*, ed. R.A. Brown (Woodbridge 1987) pp. 227–37

Webb, D., 'Saints and Pilgrims in Dante's Italy', in J. Barnes and C. Ó'Cuilleanáin, eds, *Dante and the Middle Ages* (Dublin 1995), pp. 33–55

Webb, D., *Patrons and Defenders: The Saints in the Italian City-States* (London 1996)

Webb, D., 'Women Pilgrims of the Middle Ages', *History Today* 48 (7) (July 1998) pp. 20–6

Webb, D., 'St James in Tuscany: The *Opera di San Jacopo* of Pistoia and Pilgrimage to Compostela', *Journal of Ecclesiastical History* (forthcoming)

Woodruff, C., 'The Financial Aspect of the Cult of St Thomas of Canterbury as Revealed by a Study of the Monastic Records', *Archaeologia Cantiana* 44 (1932) pp. 13–32

Wormald, F., 'The Rood of Bromholm', *Journal of the Warburg Institute* 1 (1937–38) pp. 31–45

Wunderli, R., *Peasant Fires: The Drummer of Niklashausen* (Bloomington, IN 1992)

Yates, N. and Gibson, J.M., *Traffic and Politics: The Construction and Management of Rochester Bridge AD 43–1993* (Woodbridge 1994)

Index

It has not been possible to index every reference to individuals, to place-names mentioned incidentally, or to pilgrimage to Rome, the Holy Land or Compostela.